The Accessorized Bible

The Accessorized Bible

DAVID DAULT

Yale UNIVERSITY PRESS

New Haven and London

Yale University Press books may be purchased in quantity for educational, business, or promotional use. For information, please e-mail sales.press@yale.edu (U.S. office) or sales@yaleup.co.uk (U.K. office).

Set in Minion Pro type by IDS Infotech Ltd.
Printed in the United States of America.

Library of Congress Control Number: 2025935449
ISBN 978-0-300-15312-5 (hardcover)

A catalogue record for this book is available from the British Library.

Authorized Representative in the EU: Easy Access System Europe, Mustamäe tee 50, 10621 Tallinn, Estonia, gpsr.requests@easproject.com

10 9 8 7 6 5 4 3 2 1

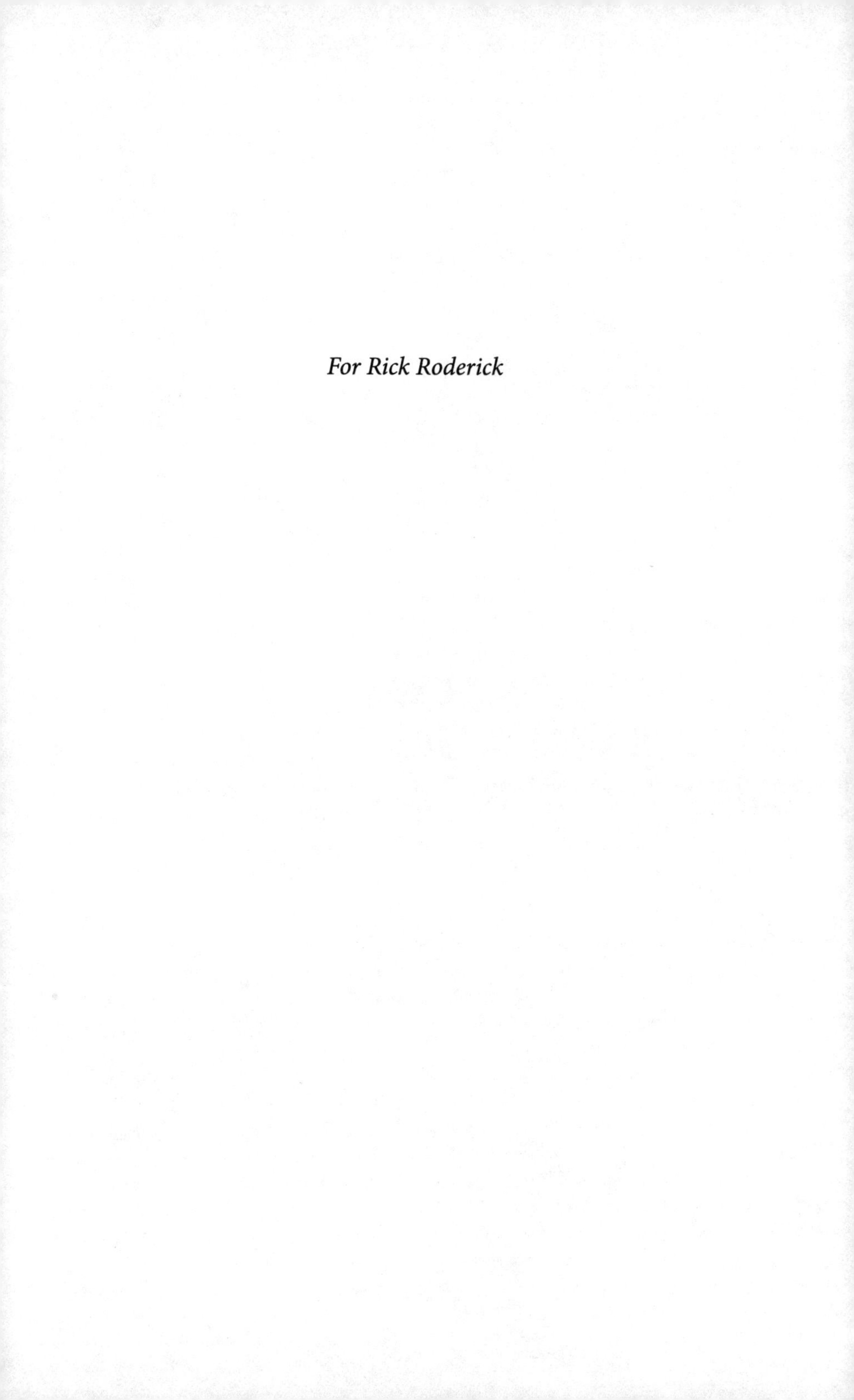

For Rick Roderick

Contents

The Accessorized Bible

Introduction

A couple of years before he passed away, the biblical scholar James Barr gave an informal talk at Vanderbilt Divinity School in Nashville, Tennessee. At the time, I was midway through my doctoral studies in theology at Vanderbilt, and I went with my friend and colleague James "Jimmy" Barker, who was studying New Testament. We had discovered a shared set of passions at the intersection of philosophy, ancient languages, and the history of biblical interpretation. Jimmy and I had spent the previous summer reading through a number of the classic theologians of the Old Testament—Walter Eichrodt, Edmond Jacob, and Gerhard von Rad—and emerged with a set of questions about the entire school of thought behind such works.

So as Professor Barr was speaking after his talk with various students, Jimmy and I got in line. When it was our turn, we asked whether, in Barr's opinion, the discipline of "Old Testament theology" should be considered a branch of *theology* or a branch of *biblical studies.* Without hesitation, Barr answered that it was a subdiscipline of biblical studies.

Some may find this answer surprising, and to others it will seem perfectly sound. It certainly gave Jimmy and me a lot to talk about, and I have continued those conversations with him and other colleagues in the many years since. In professional religious circles, we may use terms like "bible" and "theology" with ease, but their simple use can lead to complex entanglements: Should our reading of the biblical text be normed to church doctrine—that is to say, to theology—or should theology submit itself to the biblical text? Or do both find themselves in thrall to some other authority, greater still than either or both combined? I imagine each of my readers will plant their flag in a different spot in answering these questions.

As I shared early drafts of this book with readers, some came away convinced that it was a work of biblical theology, perhaps in the spirit of James Barr's unhesitating classification above. Other readers received the project as something more akin to cultural history or even anthropology. As each reader suggested a different disciplinary place for it, there followed as well a set of suggestions about how the arrangement of the material and chapters might better fit that genre.

In light of these myriad (and perhaps conflicting) expectations, I must confess clearly that I do not think that what you are about to read is a good example of biblical theology, or cultural history, or anthropology. To be sure, this book borrows from and blends aspects of these disciplines, as well as a number of others. However, the intention here is to attempt something different from the work these fields do, and to look at the objects we call bibles in a way that differs from the approaches offered by these fine and well-established traditions. For now, it is enough to say that *The Accessorized Bible* is animated by the same spirit of study and boundary-crossing that led to the question Jimmy and I asked Professor Barr that afternoon at Vanderbilt.

I undertake this present project with none of the self-confidence shown by Professor Barr when Jimmy and I asked him about Old Testament theology. He spoke with assurance about the essence and definition of his subject matter, and about how it as a *Wissenschaft* (a fancy term for an "ordered body of inquiry") might fit in relation and deference to other *Wissenschaften.* My approach and intent here in *The Accessorized Bible* are markedly different. As I describe in the coming chapters, my aim is more toward a kind of epistemic humility, one might even say a modesty. I am not seeking to offer readers a definitive claim about what "The Bible" is, or to hunt after some timeless essence of "bibleness." Following the lead of my colleague and friend Nicholas Adams, I am not trying to ground these terms; rather, my hope is to give an ordered account of a set of eclectic practices that over time I have found to be useful for thinking about the objects we call bibles. It is an attempt to step back for a moment and theorize *from* these practices, rather than offer a theory that could be *put into* practice.[1]

Let me say again, and as plainly as I can: This is not a book about "The Bible." It is not a book about what "The Bible" is, or how we might achieve its common and universal meaning. It is not an attempt to define or locate "The [Real] Bible" against rivals, counterfeits, or pretenders. This is a book about *us*—you and me, in our extraordinary variety—and how we treat each other.

In his *Philosophical Investigations,* Ludwig Wittgenstein says, "The aspects of things that are most important for us are hidden because of their simplicity and familiarity."[2] I think this assertion describes very well the way we encounter the objects we call bibles. If we think of this object as something we *already know,* it can become difficult to engage in a close examination of it. What we know—about both the objects we call bibles and our idea of "The Bible"—is often structured by the aspects we are *not* observing. As writer and religion scholar David Dark once put it, "good analysis shows relationship, and bad analysis obscures relationship."[3] I am aiming, as much as possible, for the former.

My desire to interrupt this familiarity and simplicity is part of an attempt to lift up certain *ethical* relationships we have with—and as a result of interactions with—these objects we call bibles, relationships that have become (perhaps usefully) obscured. The essayist Rebecca Solnit has suggested that "there is an art of making things unfamiliar again."[4] So my aim here is to artfully defamiliarize our ideas of "The Bible" in order to bring into better view the extraordinary variety of the objects we call bibles. The ultimate aim of this work is to turn the analysis back on ourselves, to name and examine—*in a manner that is morally serious*—the ways in which our relationships to these objects lead us to do things like bind up the broken (or not), welcome the stranger (or not), or kill the infidel (or not).

This project does not attempt to offer a history or an ontology of "The Bible." In fact, I work throughout the book to refer to "The Bible" as little as possible. In most cases, I have made the decision to leave the word "bible" uncapitalized, except in the cases where we are discussing a specific object referenced by an identifiable community. I make this stylistic choice to resist assigning an undue amount of power to the general reference term. It is my task here to talk about *the objects we call* bibles, not *The* Bible.

Thus the most useful description of this project might be a genealogy of dissimilar objects that have been predicated through time in a similar way using a similar name. "Genealogy" here is just a fancy way of saying I attempt to preserve the messiness and the contradictions that go into our looking at a given object in a certain context at a certain point in time and saying, "Yes, that's a Bible."

To get there, I need to tell a bit about the journey that has brought me to this way of thinking, and some of the folks I have met along the way. This book is the result of more than ten years of talking, thinking, writing, and sketching diagrams in notebooks. It has been rewritten at least twice, as the conversations deepened and the ideas changed. My intention in Part One is to give the reader a coherent glimpse into that process of vision and revision, and to name a few of the key strands that have been woven into the argument.

Two questions often get collapsed into each other, but for the purposes of this project, I want to keep them separate. Those questions are "What is a bible?" and "What is scripture?" These two questions actually address different and distinct states of affairs, and it is of value to analyze them each in their own turn. I have already addressed the question of scripture in *The Covert Magisterium.* And while *The Accessorized Bible* touches at certain points on this question, the book remains focused on the question of bibles. To state the distinction more clearly, *The Covert Magisterium* explores the material conditions that allow an individual or a community to look at an object and declare, "This is scripture." In contrast, the present volume analyzes the material conditions that allow an individual or a community to look at an object and declare, "This is a bible."

I recognize that this analytic distinction will be frustrating for some readers. However, I would like to make the case for why I think it is of paramount importance. Not every object that is called a bible functions as scripture. For example, in *The Covert Magisterium,* I examine an object called *The Golfer's Bible,* which has nothing whatsoever to do with Christian practices and everything to do with improving the reader's performance in the game of golf. It is an instruction manual for a sport. Now, it is clearly called a "bible" (it says so on the cover), and yet I know of no community that treats this object as *scripture.*

Conversely, we can also understand that various communities treat objects as scripture, even when they do not consider the objects to be bibles. For example, the engagement of Jewish communities with the Talmud is arguably a *scriptural* engagement, but no Jewish community I am aware of conflates the Talmud with the Tanakh. Similarly, many regard the *Tao Te Ching* or the Upanishads as scriptural texts; nevertheless, no one I am aware of refers to such texts as bibles.

We often enter into these tensions of bibles and scripture at a point in the process where key decisions have already been made. Often, our community has already articulated for us which objects are considered bibles, as a fait accompli, and any engagement with one of those objects is then undertaken as if the object's existence were the result of a simple and natural occurrence. In such contexts, the object called "The Bible" has always been there, unchanged and unchanging, beyond the reach of questions regarding its complex origins. Yet it is demonstrable that various objects that bear the name "Bible" differ one from another, and it is demonstrable as well that different individuals and communities profoundly disagree about which objects are permitted to be called bibles, and about the meanings and interpretations that arise from interactions with these objects.

These actualities argue against the assumption that a bible is a simple object, an object that might present itself as simply recognizable to all. Instead, these realities suggest that there are antecedent conditions (ideological, political, but above all *material*) that have influenced the production and the predication of these objects *as* bibles. *The Accessorized Bible* is one attempt to understand the mechanics of these preexisting conditions, these social relations, and these intra-actions.

I hope it will be clear to readers that if we come to the question "What is a bible?" with a response like "The Bible is the church's holy book," we have raised as many questions as we have answered, and probably more. It follows that we might ask, "What is a book?" That is, does an object we call a bible always have to look like the other books on our bookshelf? Further, we might rightly ask, "Which church?" That is, are we restricted only to the variety of Christian communities that describe themselves with the label "church"—even when it is often the case that one community refuses to recognize the legitimacy of other similar communities? Finally, we might ask, "What are the criteria by which a given community declares an object to be 'holy'?" That is, we are asking a question that involves matters of inclusion and exclusion, or more deeply, matters of politics, violence, and power.

Look around, through history and in our present circumstance, and we see everywhere that a bible can be used to create communities of exclusion, of exploitation, and of violence. I know this is true of my own history. I was raised in an atheist family, living in the Deep South, and my encounters with bibles in my early years were all moments of shock and fear. More than once, I was cornered by an elementary school classmate to demand an account of why I dared not to believe the things their parents had taught them. I had no answer then, but I knew this book they cited, whatever it was, was a manual that must have instructed them to treat me this way.

It was only when I was much older, and in college, that my dear friend Julia Sibley Jones opened a bible in my presence and chose not to attack me with it, but instead to invite me into its story. I mentioned David Dark a moment ago. He talks about those in our lives who hold a door open for us, and this was one of those moments for me. Julia held a door open for me. She invited me into her community, which that day was only as large as the two of us and our conversation together around that book. It was enough. Because of that welcome, I came back for more conversations, and eventually invited folks to my own.

Many excellent histories have been written about the objects we call bibles. Even as I read them, I resist their assumption that it is possible to offer a history of "The Bible," as if this term referred to a set of agreed-upon actualities that exist in a simple and uncontested way. Any object we call a bible not only has a history, but a prehistory (or, as suggested above, a genealogy): a set of material conditions and antecedent decisions that have caused this object to be present(ed) to us in this moment with such a peculiar and even singular pedigree. These conditions and decisions are not "The Bible," and in practice the conditions often become unrecognizable and even invisible once the object we call a bible is itself in play. Yet as is true of the relationship of scaffolding and foundation to a wall, the construction of the finished object could not have happened without their presence.

Of course, another way of saying that we never encounter "The Bible" in a simple way is to say that each bible we encounter is always and already *accessorized.* Any object we call a bible will come to us adorned with these material conditions and antecedent decisions, but like any effective accessory, those conditions and decisions will blend into the whole and reinforce an illusion of coherence. This is one reason why it is apt to name this present project *The* Accessorized *Bible,* though as I discuss in due course, there are other reasons as well.

Throughout this volume, I resist presenting myself as "the expert." I want to undermine that position of authority as much as I can—in part because we have had entirely too many examples of white men like me assuming a position of mastery where the objects we call bibles (and their interpretations) are concerned. This book you hold in your hands may frustrate you at times; it has certainly frustrated me. What I have learned from the process of writing *The Accessorized Bible* is that it is not my book to own, and it is not my place to tell you what it means. I want to abandon the idea that it is possible for me to get this right. My aim instead is to get things wrong in interesting and useful ways.[5] In the process I hope to create for you some clarity and unfamiliarity that you might find interesting and useful.

The book is divided into two parts and a conclusion. Part One begins with "Provenance and Terroir," a chapter designed to introduce you to the many colleagues, theories, and schools of thought that have shaped my admittedly eclectic approach to looking at the objects we call bibles. The musician Julien Baker once said, "Punk teaches the same inversion of power as the Gospel. You learn that the coolest thing about having a microphone is turning it away from your own mouth," and it is my intention at the outset to turn the mic around.[6] This first chapter articulates connections between two scholarly methods that have arisen in the past two decades, the first associated with the Iconic Books Project and the second with Scriptural Reasoning. Iconic Books provides a set of methods to explore the varieties of material culture around the objects we call bibles, while Scriptural Reasoning, a method for reading texts across the Abrahamic traditions, is centered upon the Jewish concept of *tikkun olam*, or the healing of the world, as the ethical goal of interpretation.

The second chapter consists of an extended meditation on moral seriousness, an idea first introduced to me by my friend David Dark. The chapter finds its center of gravity in a key moment in the life of American author James Baldwin, when he decided to leave a life of safety in Paris and return to the Jim Crow South to bear witness to the events unfolding there. In this chapter I try to imagine what tikkun olam looks like in daily practice.

Part One concludes with a chapter on "material scripture," my version of a set of methods that has arisen from conversations with my Iconic Books colleagues, combined with the ethical focus that arises from practices of Scriptural Reasoning. These three chapters provide a high-altitude view of the landscapes I explore in the second part of the book.

Part Two is an exploration of four distinct but overlapping theses. The reader is invited to look at the objects we call bibles from various predications: A bible is a book, a bible is a platform, a bible is a community, and a bible is an accessory. These predications are not presented as definitions. It is not my intention to present them as final statements on the matter; rather, each is offered as a way of beginning conversations that I hope will travel far beyond the limits of my imagination and beyond this book. As I have arranged them, the predications build on each other, but each also stands independent of the others. Many other theses might be offered, and again, I hope others will find better ways to engage these predications than I have here.

The Conclusion, "On Catastrophic Love," brings together threads from both parts of the book, offering a step toward a material-ethical hermeneutic of self-decentering radical inclusion. James Baldwin reenters the frame, inviting us to tear down every structure until only the solidity of love remains. Writing that chapter scared me, and I hope reading it does you too, a little.

In a recent lecture at the Massachusetts Institute of Technology, Lupe Fiasco invited his audience to "relax yourselves," and that is my invitation to you as well.[7] It might get a little weird before it gets a little clear, and I am grateful for your staying awake with me as long as you can.

I

Contexts and Methods

1
Provenance and Terroir

It can be hard to know where to begin.[1] There is always something tangible that exists before the starting point: an object, a context, a decision. We never begin *alone,* so a starting point is never a simple decision; calling something "a starting point" is itself a matter of ethics. That is to say, as I begin this endeavor, what will I name and recognize as the ground of this *production?* Where will I claim to have lodged my initial push and momentum? Further, in this claim, what will remain *unnamed?*

What follows is not a book about "The Bible." Rather, it is a book about the objects we *call* bibles, and what goes into the process of giving these objects that *particular* name. Moreover, this is a book about the very edge of this predication, the territory where we map out what is "bible" from "not-bible." Rather than a clear distinction, we find that this territory at the edge is a fuzzy space, a marshy space. Concepts blur, and straight lines curve. At the edge of the field are gleanings that are not for us but are for the life and livelihood of someone strange to us.[2]

When we look closely at this in-between space, between "bible" and "not-bible," we have entered a realm of weirdness, of *accessorization.* To use the term "accessory," or to deploy the verb "accessorize," is to admit we have already entered the middle of a conversation, the edge-space of the field, the area of the gleanings. We have not said the first word or the last, but we are part of an ongoing and dynamic exchange between *self* and *stranger.* I set out to begin, only to find (again) that things have already begun.

This book is not representative of the origin point of my thinking about what an object we call a bible is and might be. Neither does it represent a culmination of that thought. Rather, even as I have structured and restructured this project, I have constantly discovered there is more to say, and that there might be better and better arguments to make against what I have just said. Contemplating the accessory, thinking about accessorization, reminds me (again) that an item that one person considers essential might, to another, be simply a matter of taste. I suppose these realizations are there for any writer in the midst of a project, but they have been especially acute for me.

What follows, then, is neither systematic nor exhaustive, but rather is a set of overlapping materials with many of the edges still showing. As I discuss more in Chapter 3, this is a matter of natality, not finality. When looking at accessories, we are aware that something might always be added. The project is ever unfinished—a future that always remains open.

The idea of an accessory, of accessorization, inhabits a peculiar edge-space. It functions as a both/and, rather than an either/or. It pulls in resonances from fashion and philosophy, as well as from the law. So when we look at an object that someone (self or stranger) has called a bible, we might rightly wonder: Are we adding something to it, or is it adding something to us, when we give it this name? Is this object already complete, or does it need to be completed by this naming? And what does this (in)completeness say about us, as well as our relationship to this object?

In this first chapter I look at some of the lines of thought that brought me here. As an organizational metaphor, I am borrowing the image of a wild forest landscape, or an overlapping root system, from thinkers such as James C. Scott, Giles Deleuze, and Felix Guattari.[3] I wish to give the reader a bit of the earthy flavor of my ideas, their terroir and provenance, if you will, to help ground what is to come.

The sources and various projects I mention are each worth deep exploration. I say this as both invitation and caveat: My approach to ideas is more eclectic than systematic. What I mine here from these projects for my own work may introduce unfair limitations and characterizations that these thinkers did not intend. It is therefore important to emphasize that such limits and limitations are likely mine, and not theirs. It is my hope that you, after encountering the thinkers and projects I mention here, will engage them on their own terms, and benefit from them in their native states, as I have.

To return to the entwined roots I mentioned a moment ago, they include several recent schools of thought in religious scholarship, literary criticism, and other social sciences, which I deal with each in their turn. In the next few pages, I look particularly at the Iconic Books Project, Scriptural Reasoning, and the work of Franz Rosenzweig. After these individual discussions, I mention a few other connections that add nutrients to the soil, and then we'll move into the next chapter. The journey begins with what I call my suspicion of hermeneutics.

In seminary I focused on theology but was drawn as well to biblical languages, and to the history of Old Testament interpretation in particular. I was not on the ordination track. Instead, I was pursuing a master of arts in theological studies, for which I was expected to write a thesis. So, as I spent my time thinking about possible topics, I became fascinated—distracted, even—by the idea of lexicons, the various kinds of "translation dictionaries" used for ancient texts.

Students and preachers alike use lexicons to help them discover possible meanings and ideas from ancient Greek and Hebrew texts, and to translate these texts into English or other contemporary target languages. Translation is a complex dance, not a one-to-one correspondence of meaning, and the purpose of a lexicon is not to "solve" translational and interpretational problems. You cannot just plug in a set of ancient words on one end of the translational puzzle and have the lexicon produce a modern-language result on the other end.

As I looked around, however, I saw that some were using lexicons in exactly this sort of manner. This was even more apparent when the lexicon was combined with an apparatus like the Strong numbers, a system first introduced by James Strong in his *Exhaustive Concordance of the Bible* in 1890, where each individuated word in the Old and New Testaments is indexed and cross-referenced with a lexical equivalent. In such arrangements, the complexity of translation risks becoming flattened and simplified into a bland mechanical exercise.

More than these mechanical interactions, however, I also noticed a sort of feedback loop. A lexicon is often received (in its visual rhetoric and academic usage, at least for beginning students) as an objective apparatus. This is a naive position, but one we have all observed and can easily imagine. We've all had moments in our studies when we grab a dictionary and treat it like a machine you open to get an answer about what a word means.

Granted, when a reader is fluent in the language, comfortable with idiomatic structures, and the dictionary is relatively current, this interaction between reader and dictionary has one sort of dynamic force. But a lexicon is not actually a dictionary, at least not in this responsive and dynamic sense. A dictionary is produced and revised in close contemporary relationship to a large sample of fluent speakers, whereas a lexicon reflects the developing consensus of a relatively small and highly specialized set of scholars. In broad strokes, a dictionary is an apparatus for speakers of a living language, whereas a lexicon is an apparatus for scholars of a dead one.

The lexicons used for New Testament Greek and Old Testament Hebrew in my seminary studies did not arise ex nihilo. In the process of their assemblage, some aspects of scholarly conjecture about ancient cultures had been emphasized, and other aspects had been diminished. How do the presuppositions of these scholars toward certain narratives of ancient cultures, and therefore certain readings of texts, create biases in the translational tools they create for students? Not only intentional biases, but also those assumptions that enter despite our best intentions to remain neutral. In simple terms, I became suspicious of how biblical grammar instruction and the use of lexicons might be deployed to create or maintain certain states of interpretive affairs, rather than merely or innocently describing those states of affairs.

Probably the most illustrative example of what I mean would be the case of Gerhard Kittel. He was the German Lutheran theologian who helped found and coedit the monumental *Theologisches Wörterbuch zum Neuen Testament* (*Theological Dictionary of the New Testament*). Now published as a ten-volume unabridged set, the *Theologisches Wörterbuch* is in many regards *the* reference lexicon for New Testament scholarship. The publisher markets it with promotional materials that claim that it is "known commonly as 'Kittel' and considered by many scholars to be the best New Testament Dictionary ever compiled."[4] So here we have what is in many respects the standard New Testament lexicon, against which others are judged. Moreover, the lexicon is wholly identified with Kittel himself; the publishers invite us to think of it not as the *Theologisches Wörterbuch* but as "the Kittel."

So who was Gerhard Kittel? Alongside his towering achievement of inaugurating the standard lexicon of the New Testament, we also note that in 1933 Kittel became a member of the Nazi Party in Germany. Around that same year he presented a series of lectures, which later were printed and widely distributed, in which he engaged with "the Jewish Question" (this being a euphemism for any number of anti-Semitic tropes). Kittel advocated for the total divestment of Jewish people from German civic life, and he became increasingly supportive of National Socialist race policies.[5]

In her book *The Aryan Jesus,* Susannah Heschel noted that for Kittel, "Jews possessed an immutable moral and spiritual degeneracy reflected in their religion, which in turn made Jesus's antagonism to Judaism not merely religious but also racial."[6] Heschel observes, specifically regarding Kittel's lexicon, that "no Jewish scholars contributed to the Dictionary, nor were [German Christian] contributors warned against injecting political views into their articles."[7] She goes on to show how the majority of scholars involved in the first edition of the lexicon, under Kittel's editorial guidance, were publicly advocating for the total "overthrow" of Judaism, both as a religion and as a race.[8] Writing soon after the conclusion of the Second World War, American scholar William F. Albright offered a summary of this side of Kittel's legacy, noting that "in view of the terrible viciousness of his attacks on Judaism and the Jews, which continues at least until 1943, Gerhard Kittel must bear the guilt of having contributed more, perhaps, than any other Christian theologian to the mass murder of Jews by Nazis."[9]

This is one clear example of what I started calling my suspicion of hermeneutics. In this case, Gerhard Kittel was both an incredibly influential lexicographer and an influential and unrepentant Nazi.[10] He was fully invested in asserting the racialized superiority of Christianity over Judaism, based in views that were fully compatible with the genocidal policies of National Socialism. My suspicion goes like this: It is possible that Kittel's views on Judaism could negatively influence the translation and interpretation of biblical texts in ways that will support the historically demonstrable tendency of Christians to do violence to Jewish people.

The people who work to create a lexicon, or the editors who craft insertions in the bodies and marginalia of the objects we call bibles, or those who stand in pulpits to proclaim interpretations based on the readings of these bibles and lexicons, all wield not only theological but coercive influence. Thus, I am suspicious of any hermeneutics that positions itself as banal or neutral. Every interpretation is fundamentally about exclusion or inclusion; every interpretation contains the possibility of underwriting violence, and that possibility must be met with a hermeneutic that not only names this danger, but actively resists it at every turn. This book is an attempt to develop one such hermeneutic, and to offer support to others engaged in the development of other such inclusive, liberatory hermeneutics.

When it came time to write my thesis in seminary, a note, on a half-folded sheet of paper, appeared in my campus mailbox. It was from my advisor, Walter Brueggemann. Students who have worked with him through the years will confirm that Brueggemann is well known—infamous, really—for his sprawling, barely legible cursive handwriting. It took me a few moments to decipher what he had written, except for the portion that was in all caps. The message read, in full, "David: It occurs to me that your proper work is ROSENZWEIG. We can talk about it.—WB."

It turns out the "ROSENZWEIG" he meant was the early twentieth-century German-Jewish philosopher Franz Rosenzweig, author of *The Star of Redemption.* He fought in the First World War and passed away before the second one, succumbing to the slow paralysis of Lou Gehrig's disease. I had never heard of him, but I quickly discovered that a number of thinkers I admired did know him and saw him as a guiding light. To begin with, he and Martin Buber wrote an amazing set of essays on their differing theories of translation and were close collaborators who translated the Hebrew Bible into German. Also, in the introduction to his book *Totality and Infinity,* Emmanuel Levinas said he did not footnote Rosenzweig, because if he had, Rosenzweig would be noted on every single page. I mention this somewhat involved backstory to say, in a spirit similar to that of Levinas, that there will be an awful lot of Rosenzweig in the connective tissues of *The Accessorized Bible,* and not always in ways that I will be able easily to cite. There are, however, two that I can name and talk about very clearly here at the outset: Rosenzweig's concept of *Schriftsprache,* and the role of modesty (*tzniut*) in his ideas about translation.

The term Schriftsprache comes from an essay by Rosenzweig titled "Scripture and Luther."[11] One might render it in English as "the written language," but this does not communicate the full scope of Rosenzweig's meaning, which denotes a kind of unavoidable influence within a given language. Rosenzweig's thesis is that, at a key point in a given language's development, the Schriftsprache serves to anchor the fluidity of spoken language into a stable written form; it "reigns over" the language, even as that language continues to develop.[12] Rosenzweig offers three examples of this phenomenon: first, in Italian, Dante's *La Divina Commedia;* next, in Arabic, the Qur'an; and finally, in German, the *Lutherbibel.* Rosenzweig suggests that each is pivotal in creating the stability of its respective language, where markers like grammar, spelling, and usage all crystallize in each book's wake.

However, Rosenzweig notes that construction of the *Lutherbibel* was unlike that of the Qur'an, which was originally written in Arabic, or *La Divina Commedia,* which was originally written in Italian. Although written in (and hence "original" in) German, the *Lutherbibel* was both central to standardizing the German language and dependent upon a translation that "borrows" from a number of other languages: not only Koine Greek and Hebrew, but also and especially Latin, as found in particular in Jerome's Vulgate. Rosenzweig observes that these linguistic interactions within the *Lutherbibel* have the curious result of subjecting Hebrew to a kind of double erasure. As he puts it in the essay, "When Luther investigated the meaning of the Hebrew text, he was not thinking Hebraically; nor was he, as he later did in rendering the investigated meaning into German, thinking Germanically; he was thinking Latinately."[13]

Rosenzweig thus shows how Luther's choices as a translator create spaces of anti-Judaism within the German language itself. In particular, Rosenzweig argues, Luther's translational choices create a German version of the Hebrew text that undermines and even erases its Jewish character.[14] In making such observations Rosenzweig suggests that, for German, the Schriftsprache of the *Lutherbibel* is creating a foundation for the German language that operates simultaneously as an assertion of Christian characteristics and an erasure of Jewish characteristics. Expanding on this point in her essay "Making Room for the Hebrew: Luther, Dialectics, and the Shoah," Oona Eisenstadt observes that "Rosenzweig leaves us with the strong impression that [German and Latin] are the two languages whose genii are wedded in [Luther's] translation . . . Hebrew is not company but a crowd."[15]

Rosenzweig did not live long enough to see its ominous outcomes, but Eisenstadt's essay draws our attention to the deadly material consequences to be found in the wake of this double erasure of Hebrew from the German Schriftsprache. As those who live in its aftermath, we can understand the potential connection to be drawn between this first erasure of the text's Hebrew character and later attempts to erase Jewishness itself from German culture, up to the full blossoming of such textual seeds in the material realities of the 1935 Nuremberg race laws, the pogroms that resulted, and the Shoah.

Given what I said above about lexicons, I hope it becomes clear why encountering both Rosenzweig's thought and the essay "Scripture and Luther" was foundational for me. Here was an example of a scholar doing a genealogical exploration of how a particular bible came to be, as well as the ethical and cultural consequences we might extrapolate from such a genealogy. Moreover, Rosenzweig's work demonstrated methods capable of exploring how a book like the *Lutherbibel* mattered in the past and continues to matter in the present. Whatever else it may be, Rosenzweig's concept of the Schriftsprache helps us see that an object we agree to call a bible is never neutral. It is an object whose existence has material consequences, perhaps even mortal ones.

In English, of course, our Schriftsprache is not so much a solitary work as it is an entire persona, and an entire industry surrounding a persona—namely that of William Shakespeare. Though literary critic Harold Bloom does not specifically use Rosenzweig's language, his assertion about Shakespeare gives us a clear example of Rosenzweig's idea when he says, "Our true relation to Shakespeare is that it is vain to historicize or politicize him. No strong writer since Shakespeare can avoid his influence."[16] To think *outside* the influence of Shakespeare,

Bloom argues, one would have to make the effort to *think outside one's very language itself,* in an entirely *different* language. However, Bloom suggests that this move to the outside is impossible in practice if the gravity of the Schriftsprache is strong enough. "Real multiculturalists, all over the globe," Bloom insists, "accept Shakespeare as the one indispensable author . . . [He] quite simply not only is the Western canon; he is also the world canon."[17] Whichever way we might wish to turn, Bloom contends, Shakespeare has already anticipated us.

For Rosenzweig, the goal is never to have our moves and desires anticipated fully in advance, to be restricted by a text or a person—even a person as august as Shakespeare himself. This raises a second dynamic for us, one that I think is equally important to the Schriftsprache: Rosenzweig's theory of translation, and in particular the role of modesty (tzniut) in that theory.[18]

When we hear this word "modesty" in English, it conjures for us images of a plain or reserved style of dress, and a general manner of speech and action intended to draw attention away from oneself. Similarly, in Orthodox and Conservative Jewish traditions, the idea of tzniut evokes these same registers.[19] Certainly Rosenzweig has these meanings in mind as he engages in his reflections, but he also raises the idea of tzniut to a more active philosophical (and even theological) construct, one that points in fact to an entire theological ethics. He understood the concept as a form of intellectual humility, one that should caution us from attempting to fully know a text, a person, or God. Not that we *cannot* fully know—this is not a matter of a present limit to our knowing that we might overcome with tactics or technology—but that we must commit to reserving for the other and for ourselves a space of *mystery.* The other (text, person, and God) must always be able to *surprise* us, and we must be able to preserve a space from which we can surprise them.

For Rosenzweig it is this commitment to modesty that creates the possibility for moral relationships and is at the heart of what we might call *moral seriousness* vis-à-vis the other. Rosenzweig suggests that following the command "Love your neighbor as yourself" cannot mean simply loving the parts of our neighbor that are identical to us, or the parts that we already know and can anticipate. To love in this way—whether in relation to a text, a person, or the divine—is for Rosenzweig the definition of idolatry.[20] This is to say we create an idol when we look into the other (even the divine other) and see only ourselves reflected back to us. In this manner, "knowing" the other cannot be simple reflection, but rather suggests the idea of diffraction.[21]

It is precisely the *otherness* of the other that we are called to love: that which is beyond our control, beyond our narration, and beyond our ability even to anticipate. To love the other is to remain open to the possibility of surprise. That otherness could consist of those parts of the other's self that the other chooses (in their modesty) to refrain from showing us and showing the world. Therefore, we must not claim or aspire to possess the beloved in totality, to know them without reserve. To do so makes us idolaters, and the other becomes merely an idol of ourselves and our colonizing vanity. As the other properly holds back from us a part of the other's self in tzniut, they create a reserve of unexpected capacity. This reserve is a wellspring for us of delight, of frustration, and of new growth in the relationship. To be ethical, to proceed with moral seriousness, our relation to all others must remain open to an unexpected future, a future outside of our control, a future of surprise.

Thus the scholar, the theologian, and any person who aspires to moral seriousness does well to practice their own form of tzniut in their relations with others. We must not only assume but actively support the modest reserve of the other.

Again, this is not simply to assume a modesty regarding our own epistemic capacity. We must be willing, in conversation, in analysis, in all our relationships, to *avert our eyes.* We must allow some aspects of the other to remain hidden, even as other aspects are revealed and gifted to us. Even if our catechesis, and even our logic, were to assure us that the future is closed and all ends properly known, we would be obliged by the ethic of tzniut to avert our eyes and allow ourselves to remain in a state of being surprised by the hiddenness of the other. We must above all never presume to know the other with more fullness and surety than they know themselves—and again, for Rosenzweig, this injunction applies to *all* our interactions, whether with a text, with another human being, or with the divine other. The moral seriousness of the scholar proceeding with tzniut will manifest in an insistence that parts of the other must remain forever illegible to us, and thus beyond our urge to subject the other to our idolatry.

Scriptural Reasoning

I think Professor Brueggemann suggested Franz Rosenzweig to me in part because Rosenzweig's thought was a starting point for a set of academic conversations, known at first as postmodern Jewish philosophy and then as Textual Reasoning (TR). These efforts eventually came to be known as Scriptural Reasoning (SR). The conversations developed among scholars at Drew University and then at the University of Virginia, with a cognate group based at Cambridge University in England. Rosenzweig was a touchstone for this group, and for many of its participants, an inspirational figure.

The development from Textual Reasoning to Scriptural Reasoning is worth taking a moment to review. The conversations began among Steven Kepnes, Robert Gibbs, and Peter

Ochs and were collected (along with several commentaries by other scholars) in a volume called *Reasoning After Revelation.* This work offered a number of thoughtful approaches to what was then called dialogic practice but soon became more formalized as Textual Reasoning, with its own collected volume.[22] The foundational TR groups were focused on Jewish texts and developed a distinct style of reading that sought to keep one foot in the academy and one foot in both liturgically and prayerfully informed traditions of Jewish reading. It was a style of interpretation that they referred to as a "fourth paradigm" of Jewish reading traditions (the previous paradigms being the Neo-Platonic paradigm of Saadya Gaon, the scholastic paradigm of Maimonides, and the Kantian/modern paradigm of Hermann Cohen). This fourth paradigm claimed direct lineage to the work and thought of Martin Buber, Emmanuel Levinas, and, as noted above, Franz Rosenzweig.[23] These experiments in "traditioned reading" culminated in a large-scale public gathering at Drew University in 1997 under the title "Textualities: An International Conference on Postmodern Jewish Reasoning." Coming out of this conference, the groups' reading practices began to be referred to with the common title of Textual Reasoning.[24]

A key focal point for the textual reasoners was *dialogue.* Ochs explained that TR did not use this term to mean simple agreement, but rather to indicate "a relationship that persists despite difference: one that honors difference, argument and even verbal struggle as instruments of *tikkun olam,* rather than as obstacles."[25] Reading together forms bonds among the readers. The community created by the shared reading praxis of Textual Reasoning, however, "is not merely an end in itself, but also a means of working for a much wider world."[26]

This concept of tikkun olam—a Hebrew phrase for the repair or healing of the world—is the vital, beating heart of these evolving textual practices. Where we might classify many academic reading strategies as *reading to understand,* or perhaps even as *reading to master,* the textual reasoners explicitly rejected these motivations and instead pursued a practice of *reading to heal*—to heal the brokenness of communities, to heal the ruptures caused by inequity and violence, and to heal the divisions that had become part of the DNA of religious identity.[27] As the work of Peter Ochs and his colleagues has matured through the subsequent decades, this goal of healing remains, such that Ochs's most recent book bears the aspirational title *Religion Without Violence.*

This fourth paradigm of reading, aimed toward healing rather than mastery, does not simply turn inward to work for a more healed Judaism. Rather, it turns outward to attend to the suffering of the wider world. As they continued to explore and refine their explorations of Jewish texts, these practitioners of TR soon realized that this "working for a much wider world" led some of them increasingly to engage with voices outside the Jewish tradition. They began to experiment with reading sessions with Christian academics, specifically those who shared commitments to the postliberal and postcritical goals embraced by the textual reasoners. This new practice expanded the texts being considered from solely Jewish writings to include Christian writings as well. In these shared textual practices, the aim often was to start with a common character or set of narratives that were shared across the two traditions.[28]

With this shift in focus, the textual reasoners saw the need for a different description for what they were doing. One of the earliest dialogue partners in this "wider world" of reading was Cambridge University professor of divinity David Ford. In his recounting of the development of Textual Reasoning into *Scriptural* Reasoning, Ford notes that the move beyond purely Jewish communities of reading necessitated moving beyond engagement with only Jewish texts. Groups began to explore characters and narratives that existed in the wider Abrahamic tradition as a point of common ground. So, for example, a character like Noah, who shows up in both the Tanakh and the New Testament (as well as in the Qur'an, though this connection would arise somewhat later), could become a bridge for readings that spanned across both Judaism and Christianity. As Ford recalls, this led to a growth of the practice from a specifically *textual* reasoning, which was focused on Jewish writings, "into 'scriptural reasoning,' which was first Jewish-Christian, and then in the late 1990s became Jewish-Christian-Muslim."[29]

I should note that I refer to this version of events as "Ford's recounting" because—by intention and design—there is never one official description of Scriptural Reasoning. Those who have written about the development of SR over the years have emphasized that the practice is experimental and pragmatic rather than structural and dogmatic. Thus, rather than beginning with a well-structured theory or a well-outlined plan, SR begins with action and only later proceeds to reflection.

That being said, some consistent features of SR can be noted.

First is the observation made by Nicholas Adams that SR is "a practice of 'publicizing' deep reasonings, so that others may learn to understand them and discover why particular trains of reasoning, and not just particular assumptions, are attractive or problematic."[30] Practitioners of SR commit to sustained, often intense dialogue, but also commit to make available the "deep reasonings" that result from these dialogues being open to a wider public. This idea of openness has become a central tenet for many SR groups, though these different groups have latitude to interpret what this "making public" might mean.

A second feature of SR is its frequent use of a set of metaphoric structures to differentiate focal points within the practice. These metaphors, which are also used to introduce some of the basics of SR to new practitioners, are the House, the Campus, and the Tent of Meeting.[31] In SR parlance, the House is read as the house of worship, the community where the practitioner engages in liturgical life and catechesis. It follows that the Campus is the academy, where some go to study the faith more deeply. Both are considered to be spaces of *preparation* for venturing into the depths of specific faith traditions, but these preparatory practices are distinct from one another. If we had to choose one as primary, it would be the House.

In contrast to both the House and the Academy, which are both structures of tradition and relative permanence, the Tent arises in SR practice as the portable space of hospitality. It is intentionally a temporary and liminal space where experimental interactions can occur between and among these traditioned ways of reading and being. In this third space, those who come together are exploring what happens when "iron sharpens iron," when one well-formed faith identity encounters another (distinct and different) well-formed faith identity in committed dialogue. As David Ford explains it, SR participants are "simultaneously members of a synagogue, church, or mosque ('houses'), of a university ('campus'), and of a scriptural reasoning group ('tent')."[32]

House, Campus, and Tent are distinct but interrelated. In the permanent structures, practitioners undertake what might be called "preparatory reasoning." Those who would participate in SR must first be formed by communities where they are taught to think like Christians, Jews, or Muslims. From the standpoint of SR, these styles of thinking are distinct; moreover, there is no assumption that some generic "religious identity" lingers behind them. Preparatory reasoning involves the commitment to certain traditions and the eclipse of others. In practice, these preparations might include catechesis, doctrinal training, and traditioned study of scripture. SR understands that it will be these more permanent communities that form the identities of those who come to engage in SR. Thus, a good deal of the work that *results* in Scriptural Reasoning occurs in the more permanent "houses" of our various faith communities.

As these identities are formed and reinforced by repetitive practices of preparatory reasoning, participants are made ready for brief forays into the unique space that has itself been constructed out of the zones found between the three Houses of Judaism, Islam, and Christianity. It is in this "middle space" that the metaphorical Tent of Meeting is erected. In this space, a group chooses to gather, scriptures are selected, and SR can occur.[33] The metaphor of the Tent foregrounds the role of hospitality, as it is assumed that those who gather in the Tent will do so in a spirit of *reading with* and *reading to heal,* rather than *reading to master* (understood here in both senses of to "master the text" and to "master the other"). In other words, a Tent is a space of shared experience, not evangelization. Not only is the Tent a space of tikkun olam, but this healing is undergirded by a commitment to something like Rosenzweig's notion of tzniut. In modesty, we refrain from mastery of the other.

Soon after I began work on my master's thesis with Walter Brueggemann, I had the opportunity to meet with Peter Ochs at an academic conference. I became involved with the North American community of SR practitioners, who shaped the way I think about the study of scripture. In particular, SR has given me a well-defined ethic of hospitality that now limits and governs my practices of reading holy texts. Thus, rather than understanding SR primarily as a practice of hermeneutics, I have learned over time to think of it instead, most fundamentally, as a practice of intrarelational ethics. When I participate in SR as a Christian reader, I keep in mind that my role in the Tent is not to convert my Muslim and Jewish partners to my reading of the texts, and especially to my Christian faith. Instead, I enter the Tent with modesty, regarding it as a place where all readers are invited to dwell together for a brief time in a space where "the text is our only host."[34] Thus, we return to the central focus of SR, as a practice that seeks tikkun olam, the healing of broken relationships. As Steven Kepnes has noted, "SR begins with the scriptural sense that the human world is broken, in exile, off the straight path, filled with corruption, sickness, war and genocide. SR practitioners come together out of a sense of impoverishment, suffering, and conflict to seek resources for healing."[35]

Iconic Books

In 2010 I was fresh out of graduate school and was trying to figure out my place in and relationship to academic life. Through a happy set of circumstances I became involved in a series of conversations with a diverse group of scholars who were looking at the function of "scriptures"—a term that here is not limited to mean only Christian scriptures, but rather includes a wide cross section of books from various world religious traditions—not only as liturgical or homiletic resources, but as material objects and especially as *iconic* presences.

I was invited to attend a multiday symposium at Syracuse University on iconic books, hosted by Old Testament scholar James W. Watts, which featured presentations from Dorina Miller Parmenter, S. Brent Rodriguez-Plate, Timothy Beal, Vincent Wimbush, Deirdre Stam, and Karl Solibakke, among numerous others. The participants at the symposium constituted a group that included bibliographers, Old and New Testament scholars, librarians, philosophers, theologians, and historians. This particular meeting in 2010 was the third of three. The first was at Syracuse in 2007, along with another at Hamilton College in 2009. The proceedings of these meetings and further conversations have been collected into a growing number of edited volumes and have formed the backbone of what has come to be known as the Iconic Books Project.[36]

This phrase, "Iconic Books," comes from the investigations that Watts and Parmenter began in the early 2000s, when Parmenter was a graduate student. Parmenter came to her doctoral work with an MFA that focused on book arts. Drawing on this training, she started asking questions in the doctoral seminar, "The Idea of Scripture," that Watts was teaching. Parmenter suggested that "half the subjects" that they should be considering had been left out of the syllabus, and that they should be thinking about the *material* side of holy texts as well as the literary side. Watts, whose primary work up to that point had been in the Hebrew Bible, was intrigued by Parmenter's enthusiasm for these sorts of questions and was surprised to discover that very little scholarship existed on the subject. Soon they were thinking together about how this might become an ongoing project for themselves and other scholars. As Watts put it later, "After considering and rejecting possibilities such as 'idol,' 'fetish,' and 'talisman,' we settled on the adjective 'iconic' to describe the form and social function of these objects . . . even if the term itself is ultimately inadequate to cover the range of phenomena under discussion."[37]

We could say then that the Iconic Books Project begins its method by asking a simple question: *Why do books matter?* Here we might mean "matter" in a multivalent sense—why do books take the *forms* they do; how do these forms *affect* our social interactions around these books and the *care* we put into our interactions with these books? Form, affect, care: Each of these *ways of mattering*, and more still, were taken up by the various conversations of Iconic Books. This attention goes beyond traditional hermeneutics. As Watts reminds us, we cannot simply look at the words on the page, but rather we might imaginatively expand the scope of our idea of *hermeneutic* itself, to a point where we "look closely at the social functions and significance of written texts," considering the *sociality of their materiality* as part of our interpretive action. This closer look causes us then to arrive at a more technical form of the core question: not simply why books matter, but *how* books matter.[38]

Having chosen the adjective "iconic," Parmenter and Watts then began conversations and examinations with other scholars, based on the hunch that we could begin to discover *how* and *why* books matter by focusing on "the books that matter the most."[39] That is, through close analysis of the central texts that the religions of the world, large and small, have classified in one way or another as *holy* or as *scripture*, these texts could become a model for understanding the manner in which books become iconic more generally. It soon became clear to Watts, Parmenter, and their conversation partners that the inquiry into iconic texts should not be limited solely to the *religious* functions of these books. Thus, the Iconic Books Project expanded to inquire into the broad array of ways in which holy books can occupy and anchor not only liturgical, but also cultural (and even secular) activities. As Watts has noted, "recognizing the iconic dimension of written texts and how it gets ritualized should play an essential part in describing the motives and methods for writing, publishing, marketing, buying, handling, displaying and storing books in any literate culture in the world."[40]

As a result of this wide-ranging inquiry, an ongoing goal of the Iconic Books Project has been to create methodologies for understanding the function of scriptures, where the term "function" denotes a broad landscape of possible predicates. For example, dancing around a sanctuary with a Torah scroll, or placing a hand on a Protestant Holy Bible during an inauguration for political office, or substituting calligraphic passages of the Qur'an for representational art, or placing an oblation of fresh fruit and mint in front of the Guru Granth Sahib—each is available to us as an example of iconic data, as we examine how these books *matter* to these various groups and communities.

An ambitious research field with a wide scope of inquiry necessitates the assemblage of a wide array of tools and techniques of analysis. The Iconic Books Project accomplished this in part by welcoming several other disciplines and their various analytic traditions into conversation. As a result, over the years Iconic Books discussions have experimented with and incorporated the methodologies of media studies, book history, bibliographic analysis, anthropology, economics, and library science, among others. Their reflections have also drawn from the critical theorists, particularly Walter Benjamin (especially from his "The Work of Art in the Age of Mechanical Reproduction") and poststructuralists like Jacques Derrida (especially from his later works such as *Archive Fever*).[41]

My intent here in *The Accessorized Bible* is to analyze and describe the objects we call bibles in a manner that is both materially grounded and culturally attentive. In doing so, I am drawing on the spirit that animated those Iconic Books symposia more than a decade ago. In *The Accessorized Bible* I cross disciplinary boundaries to find methods that work, navigating as best I can (and ignoring wherever possible) those traditional disciplinary antagonisms that often divide scholars from each other. My attempts here are eclectic and draw upon a variety of techniques and discourses. Thus, if we are looking for a root system running beneath this wild forest, the natural grounding point for this book you have in your hands, it would be the Iconic Books Project.

To stay with this tactical approach, I now begin to gather some tools developed within the Iconic Books Project to assist us as we proceed in thinking together.

The first comes from the early work done by James Watts as he tried to map an understanding of iconic books and texts and is found in his foundational essay "The Three Dimensions of Scriptures." Watts's essay builds on the prior work of thinkers such as Wilfred Cantwell Smith and Martin Marty and seeks to address the growing necessity in the twenty-first century to understand the role of holy books as objects of popular as well as liturgical and scholarly cultures. Watts demonstrates this necessity by giving a brief review of news reports of events such as Qur'an burnings, battles over monuments with religious character, inscriptions of the Ten Commandments on public buildings, and other examples of scriptures rushing into the headlines and the battle fronts of the culture wars.

As the title of the essay implies, Watts suggests there are three analytic dimensions that can be utilized to explore these deployments of holy books in their various iterations. These are the *semantic* dimension, the *expressive* dimension, and the *iconic* dimension.[42] The semantic dimension deals with the interpretation of what is written, such as when someone preaches from a holy book. The expressive dimension (sometimes referred to in early Iconic Books writings as the *performative* dimension) includes those occasions when a holy book is read aloud or its words or ideas transposed into song, visual art, theater, or film. In these cases, it is an expression or performance of what is written in the holy book.

As Watts notes, these first two dimensions are rather well understood. In contrast, the iconic dimension "finds expression in the physical form, ritual manipulation, and artistic representation of scriptures."[43] These highly visible (and often visual) ornamentations and manipulations can help to establish the legitimacy and importance of the book itself. In turn, possession of or proximity to such a book helps to establish the legitimacy and importance of the person holding it. Interestingly, however, the iconic dimension can often impede the function of the holy book *as a book*. For example, "Iconic ritualization frequently *interferes with reading* by making the text inaccessible to most people," as Watts points out, "or by making its proper use so encumbered with rituals as to be impractical."[44]

What I find useful about this three-dimensional approach is that it provokes us into a reconsideration of these objects we call books. Confronting especially the *iconic* dimension of scripture demands that we abandon the notion that a book is (or could ever be) *just* its stories or *only* its written text (those aspects that Watts classifies in the semantic dimension), or that a *holy* book might be limited *only* to the preaching and public explication of its text authorized in liturgies by religious authorities (what Watts calls the expressive dimension). An object that a given community calls a holy book is always so much more than its mere semantic or performative presentation. It is always semantic *plus* . . . , expressive *plus* . . . , with each of these overflowing into the iconic dimension.

Thanks to the insights developed in the dialogues of the Iconic Books Project, we now have a robust set of analytic tools to help us understand that an object we call a bible is always a presentation of materiality and ideologies—unfolding in at least three dimensions—in addition to being a site of interpretive and liturgical opportunity.

Dialectic: Scriptural Reasoning and Iconic Books

Thanks in part to the foresight of Walter Brueggemann and the hospitality of Peter Ochs, his colleagues, and their students, I have now been involved with Scriptural Reasoning for close to two decades. In a similar fashion, thanks to the welcome of James Watts, Dorina Miller Parmenter, and their colleagues, I have been part of the conversations regarding Iconic Books for more than ten years. These two sets of conversations are of similar influence and importance to the development of my own thinking that has become part of *The Accessorized Bible.* Though Scriptural Reasoning and Iconic Books have developed largely independently of each other (I cannot be sure, but my involvement may be one of their only points of overlap), in this final section of the chapter, I suggest some points of affinity, and even synthetic intersection, that I have observed between these two schools of thought. As they interact dialectically, I also explore how some natural gaps arise from this overlap between Iconic Books and Scriptural Reasoning that open up possibilities for new thinking that builds bridges between them and draws on the strengths of both projects.

On one side of the dialectic, Iconic Books has put a key focus on *material* aspects of scripture, while largely suspending considerations of the ethical dimensions of reading.[45] On the other side, Scriptural Reasoning has made a point of foregrounding the *ethical* reading of scripture (particularly with its aspirational goal of tikkun olam), although the practice has remained (for the most part) aloof from, and even allergic to, the material analysis of texts.[46] In my view, this complementary set of lacunae offers an opportunity for fruitful intersection.

As noted above, Watts's "Three Dimensions of Scripture" are the *iconic,* the *expressive,* and the *semantic.* The semantic dimension is the one concerned with acts such as interpretation, preaching, commentary, and *ritualized study.* As such, I think the semantic dimension is the one most apt to locate our understanding of the practice of Scriptural Reasoning, as ritualized study is very much at the heart of (perhaps even the whole of) what SR intends to be. If we apply Watts's three dimensions to our understanding of SR, we could venture the hypothesis that Scriptural Reasoning is preoccupied with the semantic dimension to such an extent that it actively ignores, or even suppresses, the expressive and iconic dimensions of scripture in its communal study practices. The themes and characters shared by the three Abrahamic traditions become the focus, such that the aesthetic and performative aspects of the texts are stripped away. In a similar fashion, the power and potential violence of the texts that arise from their iconic dimension are also suppressed for the sake of hospitality.

Of course, SR practitioners who have reflected on this emphasis within the practice have surmised that they have good reasons for making this move. Because of the explicit focus of SR on building and healing relationships (again, with its ethic of tikkun olam), it makes sense that SR would bracket out many aspects of scripture studies that have proved historically divisive. That is to say, SR has explicitly avoided the expressive dimension, which would mean avoiding disagreements over liturgical practices. SR has avoided as well engagement with the iconic dimension, which helps practitioners avoid disagreements over the political use of scripture.

Though they do not use Watts's language to describe the space they hold, I suggest that practitioners of SR have chosen to stay in the semantic dimension, to maintain a space where "the *text* [as invitation to interpretation] is our only host."[47] To preserve the fragile possibility of truly *ethical* and healing-centered relationships in the Tent of Meeting, SR has chosen to bracket out those aspects of scripture that form the explicit points of demarcation (and disagreement, and violence) among the various *Houses,* as understood by their practice.

In a similar fashion, on the other side of the dialectic, it is understandable that Iconic Books has chosen to bracket out ethical questions as it has sought to define and solidify its language of analysis. In the earliest conversations, those scholars who eventually coalesced around Iconic Books were coming from very disparate methodological backgrounds. In that space, the task was simply to explore whether there could be a common practice or language among them. With such methodological complexity already in the mix, adding in a layer of ethical analysis might have seemed to be a distraction, or superfluous to the establishment of the discourse. With that said, a decade on from the initial Syracuse symposium, I am happy to note that Iconic Books practitioners are beginning to find ways to incorporate ethical questions into their praxis.[48]

Moving Forward from Here

I think this open space between the ethical concerns of Scriptural Reasoning and the material concerns of Iconic Books offers an interesting opportunity. It allows us to ask some questions about method, as well as about the hermeneutic and cultural power of the objects we call bibles. My hope in *The Accessorized Bible* is to offer some possibilities for what might usefully fit into this open space. My offering here is not the only possibility, and it is likely not the best one. Nevertheless, it is the best I have been able to propose up to this point.

In this chapter I have tried to explore and explain some of the major ideas from which I have constructed this project. There are others. Careful readers will find the nominalism and parsimony of William of Ockham, the reader-response ideas of Stanley Fish, and the methodological anarchism of Paul K. Feyerabend in the mix of what follows, as well as the influence of the bibliographic explorations of Thomas Tanselle and the exemplary historical works of Richard Rhodes. I am inspired by the urgency of thinkers and theologians like James Cone, Myles Horton, Miguel De La Torre, Patrick Califia, and Kelly

Brown Douglas. My thinking is often rearranged as well by my engagements with the scientific community, particularly with physicists who continue to be generous with their time and expertise. I do my best to credit all these influences where I can, but some will escape me. All of these swirling influences (and many others) have helped to shape a project that entwines its root system with both Iconic Books and Scriptural Reasoning.

With that said, once again, we begin.

2
On Moral Seriousness

It is 1956, and James Baldwin has been in Paris for eight years.[1] He fled New York at the age of twenty-four, with forty dollars to his name. He bid goodbye to his mother, his family, and what he had hoped would be the last indignities of racism he would have to endure.[2] In Paris he found himself in conversation with Simone de Beauvoir and Jean-Paul Sartre, Max Ernst, Norman Mailer, and Maya Angelou, among many other literary luminaries. Biographers have suggested that it was during his time in Paris that Baldwin found his literary voice, and even perhaps a few fleeting moments of true love. He had every reason to stay.

It is a photograph that arrests him, that wrenches his vision homeward, back to America. It is a photograph that draws his gaze back to the cauldron boiling over from centuries of the violence of white racism, and back to the questions of nonviolence bracketed by Baldwin's first glimpses in 1955 of the Reverend Doctor Martin Luther King Jr. It is this photograph that tells him, in no uncertain terms, that he now must return to America.

The photo that grabs him that afternoon in Paris is of a young Black woman, Dorothy Counts. She is fifteen years old, and she was photographed on her first day trying to attend Harry Harding High School in Charlotte, North Carolina. It is a white school, and that September morning Dorothy Counts and several others are the first Black students to make the attempt to attend there. Over the next few days, as she moves about the school grounds, she will be hit by rocks and blackboard erasers. She will be jeered and shouted at by crowds and ignored by school authorities, whose nominal job it was to be there to protect her and to help. Her food will be spat upon in the lunchroom. The windshield of her father's car will be smashed.

It is the face of Dorothy Counts that greets James Baldwin on the Paris streets that fall. Later Baldwin will suggest the image was inescapable, as he said it was on every front page of every paper in every news kiosk in his corner of the city. "There was unutterable pride, tension, and anguish in that girl's face as she approached the halls of learning, with history jeering at her back . . . Some one of us should have been there with her!" Baldwin would later write. "It was on that bright afternoon that I knew I was leaving France. I could simply no longer sit around Paris discussing the Algerian and the Black American problem. Everybody else was paying their dues, and it was time I went home and paid mine."[3]

In this chapter I explore what took hold of Baldwin that autumn day, and what, on our better days, might take hold of us. Reflecting on that Paris moment, Baldwin reported that seeing the proud face of Dorothy Counts amid that violent mob filled him with a mixture of rage, shame, and above all, responsibility: *Some one of us should have been there with her!* This sense of responsibility took hold of Baldwin, even as the events unfolding were more than a thousand miles away and involved a place he had never been, with people he had never met. We could give this sudden flood of feelings a number of different names. It is empathy, yes, and it is solidarity. For the purposes of this chapter, however, I would like to gather all these various responses—shame, rage, responsibility, empathy, and solidarity—under a phrase that I first heard used by author and educator David Dark: *baseline moral seriousness.*

Dark has described this moral seriousness as a form of slowing down, with an aim of encouraging himself and others to notice details about people and situations that are often missed in our haste to win a point in a debate. "My job, as I understand it, is to help people pay deep attention to their deepest selves in relationship with other selves," Dark says. "I'm trying to conjure a sacred space of responsiveness in a sea of reactivity."[4] I believe it is this *responsiveness* that James Baldwin means. It would have been so easy to rush past it, to distract himself with any triviality or shiny thing there on the boulevard. It was Paris, after all. Yet it was instead Baldwin's instinct to *slow down,* and to gather himself in all the swarming feelings of that moment—rage, shame, and responsibility—those feelings we have been trained so well to run from and ignore. As W. H. Auden once put it, "We look round for something, no matter what, to inhibit our self-reflection," but this was not the path Baldwin chose.[5] There, with an entire ocean between him and the trouble descending on Dorothy Counts, he had every reason to keep his distance and mind his business. Instead, he knew—he *knew—Some one of us should have been there with her!* Was it a call that came from deep within Baldwin, or from beyond him? We will never know. We can only know the effect: Drop everything—drop safety, and distance, and the steady momentum of your daily life—and run toward the danger, run toward the suffering, that you may stand shoulder to shoulder with the vulnerable. That you may bear witness.

Whatever else this call may be, it is moral, and it is serious.

I find a resonance here between the experience of James Baldwin on that Paris boulevard and what David Dark says about this process of being called and claimed. "The courage and loneliness of another person's face draws on me and claims me," Dark says, "because *I cannot help but understand* their singular relation to my own [face]. I'm called to see myself within their vision."[6] What Dark and Baldwin are telling us is that there is nothing particularly special or singular about a moment like this; the call is awaiting us at every possible moment, if only we have eyes to see and ears to hear. That afternoon on the boulevard, James Baldwin was available for the gaze of Dorothy Counts, and that gaze changed the trajectory of his whole life. What Dark is suggesting, and he is not alone in this suggestion, is that we might find little ways, each day of our lives, to practice this sort of availability. We might practice, as one practices scales and arpeggios, to be limber and ready for the performance that is to come, when the eyes of the audience are finally upon us, and the moment truly counts. James Baldwin, David Dark, and the cloud of witnesses that surround them—they are all suggesting that we might make a daily practice of moral seriousness.

I have since come to understand that this idea—practicing so we might be prepared to be publicly and morally serious—is quite an ancient concept. It did not begin with Dark or Baldwin, but it stretches far back through our shared intellectual history, to thinkers like Aristotle. In Book I of his *Nicomachean Ethics,* Aristotle notes that, while many may study the harp or the violin, we have a particular meaning when we suggest that someone is *serious* about their study of that instrument. In such a case, we use the word "serious" to mean that this person is not simply studying the technique or the performance of the instrument, but also the history, the beauty, and the lore at the heart of the instrument. In other words, when we say someone is *serious* about the violin, we mean, in a very real sense, that the instrument has found a connection to, and perhaps even become an extension of, that performer's soul.[7]

To give an example of what I mean, I turn to a 2013 lecture from world-renowned cellist Yo-Yo Ma. He titled the talk "Art for Life's Sake," and midway through his remarks, Ma took a moment to explore what he called a "seemingly contradictory thing": Musicians, he said, spend years learning and practicing their technique, "but the point of art is always to transcend technique. That's when we get to *meaning*." In other words, we do not practice so that we can become perfect. Rather, we practice so that we may be prepared for this moment of transcendence, when we move toward something greater, something more noble, something *serious*. "We transcend technique in order to seek out the truths in our world in a way that gives meaning and sustenance to individuals and communities," Yo-Yo Ma told his audience. "That's art for life's sake."[8] If we extend this line of reasoning—the practice of moral seriousness is akin to the practice of an instrument, where each individual can transcend technique into *meaning*, into the moment-by-moment living of our lives with others—then we are imagining a possibility where we might live our lives with a kind of *sincerity*. In each moment, we might aspire to interact with others with a seriousness that takes them seriously. We might even call this baseline moral seriousness a continued recognition of the *dignity* of others.

In that moment he recalls back in 1956, then, I sincerely believe James Baldwin did not think of his decision to depart from Paris in terms of leaving a *place of safety* for a *place of danger*. Rather, I think that Baldwin knew that staying in Paris would mean a different sort of threat. Not to his body, perhaps, but a threat to the state of his *soul*.[9] To stay in Paris was the most rational course of action; from this position, he could have written eloquently on behalf of the suffering of Dorothy Counts and moved many hearts with his words. In that moment, however, he knew that this path of self-preservation was ultimately a lie. *Some one of us should have been there with her!* In other words, it was not enough to possess a theoretical solidarity with Dorothy, across an ocean, in the Paris cafés. Baldwin knew that he would need to go to the heart of the suffering, and to experience this solidarity with his body.

In his life and in his art, Baldwin was a person preoccupied with the question of what it might mean to truly *love* another person. The possibility of love, or the lack of it, was the subject of his 1956 novel *Giovanni's Room* as much as it was the subject of *Remember This House,* the manuscript he left unfinished at the time of his death. It was this latter work in which he recalled seeing the arresting face of Dorothy Counts, and his certainty that *Some one of us should have been there with her!* This idea—needing to be present, with and for the other, so that love might be *embodied*—forms a through line in Baldwin's fiction and nonfiction writings. This love he was constantly pondering was not merely affection, but an ever-deepening possibility of *response* to the (sometimes verbal, often unspoken) call of another. In this sense, the question of love is also the preoccupation of every incendiary page of a work like *The Fire Next Time.*

If we *wish* to love, we must move in the world with the *intention* to love. To meet that intention, we must practice this love, not in our minds, but in the presence of others. We must repeat the scales and arpeggios of love, until the techniques of loving become part of our nature. We must practice, not so that we may become perfect, but so that we might become available. When the call comes, we must be ready, and to be ready, we must be serious.

What, then, might we mean when we say that we seek here a *moral* seriousness? David Dark suggests that we may find one key in an article from philosopher Hannah Arendt, called "The Crisis in Education." Here Arendt states that "education is the point at which we decide whether we love the world enough to assume responsibility for it."[10] Moral seriousness begins in a taking of responsibility within the world(s) we know. So when Baldwin looked at the photo of Dorothy Counts and his thought was that *Some one of us should have been there with her,* he was assuming responsibility for Dorothy and the world she lived in—even though that world was an ocean away from the world Baldwin knew at that time. Here again, in Arendt's assertion, we see the parallel of *love* and *response.* Moral seriousness is that practice of love that prepares us to respond when called, to stand with and to bear witness to the struggle and the suffering of our beloved. Again, not simply to respond in theory, or with mental affection, but rather to respond with our whole selves, in an embodied solidarity. It is as if when we hear the call—*Some one of us should have been there with her!*—we respond with the words of the prophet Isaiah: "Here I am . . . send me!" (Isa 6:8 NAB). We practice the scales and arpeggios of response, with seriousness, not so that we might be perfect, but rather so that when we are called, we might be *able* to respond: *responsible* and *response-able, for life's sake.*

We might then ask, what *manner* of responsibility is being referenced when Arendt says the goal of our education (or our practice) is to love the world enough to take responsibility for it? I suspect the responsibility Arendt is talking about is akin to what Emmanuel Levinas means when he declares that we are "responsible for a total responsibility, which answers for all the others and for all in the others, even for their responsibility."[11] This may seem an overwhelming expectation, but in a Christian context, it echoes the Gospel of John, where in chapter 15 we are told,

"No one has greater love than this, [than] to lay down one's life for one's friends" (John 15:13 NAB). Sometimes this does indeed mean a physical death. At other times, however, this means allowing ourselves to undergo a kind of death-to-self, that we might experience a resurrection into a new life, a life-with-others. That afternoon in Paris in 1956, James Baldwin felt an overwhelming responsibility—*Some one of us should have been there with her!*—and he laid down the life he knew, taking responsibility even for this friend, Dorothy Counts, whom he had not yet met. Fundamentally, however, we must remember that the focus of Jesus's invitation to lay down one's life is not *death.* Jesus is not glorifying death. This is an invitation into life itself: a life of abundance—*with others*—that we might not yet be able to imagine.

I have some examples in mind to illustrate what I mean. A bit of a controversy erupted when Derek Webb, the lead singer of the Christian band Caedmon's Call, attended the 2023 Dove Awards in a dress. On social media, Webb explained this choice by saying, "As a cis, straight, white man, I walk into a room like that (and any room) with a tremendous amount of privilege. If I'm attending as an ally of friends and colleagues, I should do everything possible to surrender that privilege at the door. If the way you're looking at my loved ones isn't the way you're looking at me, I'm not truly standing *with* them." Webb then added a quote attributed to the pastor Stan Mitchell: "If you claim to be someone's ally, but aren't getting hit by the stones thrown at them, you aren't standing close enough."[12] In this message, we can clearly hear the echo of Baldwin's *Some one of us should have been there with her!* Indeed, Webb has faced a backlash from a variety of conservative Christian organizations and news outlets. Making yourself available to participate in the suffering of those who have been told by institutions that they do not belong is one form, I think, of moral seriousness.

A second example is that of Larycia Hawkins. Hawkins was the first African American woman to be given tenure as a professor at Wheaton College, a conservative Christian college west of Chicago and the alma mater of evangelist Billy Graham. Graham's son, Franklin Graham, had publicly positioned himself as opposing public displays of the Muslim faith, calling Islam "wicked" and "evil."[13] In the summer of 2015 the younger Graham went so far as to call for a halt to "all immigration of Muslims to the U.S."[14] Graham was just one of a number of evangelical Christian leaders who took similar hardline positions at that time.

In the fall of 2015, Hawkins, a political scientist, had discussions with her students about how one might respond when religious leaders use public platforms to create exclusions of vulnerable minorities. In part because of those discussions, Professor Hawkins, herself a Christian, decided that she would spend the Advent season that year wearing a hijab, the traditional headscarf worn by many Muslim women around the world. She also wrote on Facebook, "I stand in religious solidarity with Muslims because they, like me, a Christian, are people of the book. And as Pope Francis stated last week, we worship the same God."[15]

What followed is chronicled in the documentary *Same God*, which tells the story of the Wheaton administration's reaction to Hawkins, and her eventual dismissal from the school. As Hawkins reflected on the events, both philosophically and theologically, she developed an ethical position that she calls *embodied solidarity*. As she puts it, in embodied solidarity, "my body is called to *be* justice, not just to *do* justice," going on to say that it is also "calling the powers-that-be to task for failing to do justice, *because in our bodies we are righteousness and justice*."[16] This transformation of our bodies *into* vessels of righteousness and justice is, I suggest, the fruit of the daily practices and repetitions of moral seriousness I described above. We practice the scales and arpeggios of response, with seriousness, not so that we might be *perfect,* but rather so that when we are called, we might be *prepared* to respond, for life's sake, *with embodied solidarity.*

What needs to be stressed and repeated in these examples, however, is that moral seriousness is not to be reserved for some magical moment or special occasion. There was no audience on that afternoon in 1956, and no bandstand playing a solemn march as Baldwin made the decision to return home. That choice was made in the quiet everydayness of a walk down the street. Moral seriousness is at work in the terrain of our smallest decisions, or it is of no use to us at all. As David Dark has put it, when we talk about baseline moral seriousness, we're "trying to describe the very small but enormously consequential moves with which a person makes their witness in the world, standing in integrity and holding the doors of perception open."[17] Or again, following Emmanuel Levinas, we should assume that becoming morally serious involves no special or extra action, but rather arises from undertaking our pursuits with a certain *intention:* "We breathe for the sake of breathing, eat and drink for the sake of eating and drinking, we take shelter for the sake of taking shelter, we study to satisfy our curiosity, we take a walk for the walk. All that is not for the sake of living; it is living. *Life is a sincerity.*"[18]

So moral seriousness is a practice that we undertake in our everydayness, not so that we can be perfect, but so that we can be prepared to respond to the call that comes to us. Moral seriousness is rooted in an intention that is available to us in our every action and in each moment, because to live seriously is to rehearse in each moment the knowledge that we may be called to respond, for life's sake, *with a sincerity* that leads us past theoretical solidarity into embodied solidarity.

This love to which Baldwin, Dark, Arendt, Levinas, Hawkins, and many others beckon us is not an empty word. It is not something marketed to us from a Hallmark card. It is, again following Levinas, a love that responds *and is responsible* to the other in the sincerity of our everydayness. Following Derek Webb and Larycia Hawkins, it is a love that bids us to join others in the crosshairs of oppression, to witness and even to experience the violence to which they are subject. Moral seriousness hears the call, *Some one of us should have been there with her,* and then responds, *Here I am . . . send me!*

This response is the fruit of the daily practice of the scales and arpeggios of moral seriousness. It echoes the clarity that Saint Paul knew: "And if I have the gift of prophecy and comprehend all mysteries and all knowledge; if I have all faith so as to move mountains *but do not have love,* I am nothing" (1 Cor 13:2 NAB; my emphasis). It echoes the truth that Jesus himself understood: that the love we are talking about here is deeply and inescapably entwined with responsibility. Consider, for example, when Jesus told the story of the Good Samaritan:

> A man fell victim to robbers as he went down from Jerusalem to Jericho. They stripped and beat him and went off leaving him half-dead. A priest happened to be going down that road, but when he saw him, he passed by on the opposite side. Likewise a Levite came to the place, and when he saw him, he passed by on the opposite side. But a Samaritan traveler who came upon him was moved with compassion at the sight. He approached the victim, poured oil and wine over his wounds and bandaged them. Then he lifted him up on his own animal, took him to an inn and cared for him. The next day he took out two silver coins and gave them to the

> innkeeper with the instruction, "Take care of him. If you spend more than what I have given you, I shall repay you on my way back." (Luke 10:30–35 NAB)

In this parable, we are taught that the manner of "taking responsibility for the world" involves transcending the limitations of tribal enmity and the limitations bequeathed upon us by our social status (where, as we see in the case of the priest and the Levite, the rich and respectable are strangely *dissuaded* from acting responsibly). In the fearless acts of neighbor love shown by the Samaritan, more than the body of the victim is healed. The actions of the Samaritan are not transactional but transformational.

In this sense, then, analyses undertaken with moral seriousness are not about the mere acquisition and comprehension of knowledge. That is, they are not transactional actions. Rather, the hope is that our common work of inquiry will aim and aspire to become a praxis animated by responsibility (per Levinas) and love (per Arendt) into an embodied reality we can practice in our very everydayness (per Hawkins). To borrow an idea from Jesuit spirituality, we could understand the actions of the morally serious Samaritan to be an example of *cura personalis,* or "care for the entire person." It is a care that is serious, sincere, and embodied. It is a practice that suggests individualized attention to the specific needs of the other. In this way, moral seriousness is attentive to tikkun olam, to that which needs to be repaired in the world, starting with the person in front of us who is harmed or under the threat of harm. In Jesus's parable, we are shown a pastoral moment that is both loving, responsible, and response-able. The lesson it seeks to teach us is grounded in two core possibilities: First, that we *can* love, and second, that we *will* respond to the need before us with healing actions based in that love.

I suggest, both here and elsewhere, that this responsibility for the repair of the world, which Arendt called love, is not embodied as a denial of the reality of violence, but rather is always embodied as a movement toward healing in the face of violence or the possibility of violence. It means bearing responsibility for the one who does not feel safe, until they are (and feel) safe. Solidarity with the person who has been harmed, or who is under the threat of harm, means that we are available for them to *interrupt* us, to tell us, "I do not feel safe here," so that we might respond, as the Samaritan did, to care for them until they can again say, "I am safe now." Further, solidarity means we grieve the person who has been harmed, or who is under the threat of harm, when they are no longer there to interrupt us. Embodied solidarity, response-able love, means we allow those who have been harmed or who are under the threat of harm to become part of our story, not as side characters, but as protagonists.[19]

Thus, to love seriously, we must take violence seriously. Let us begin with a counterintuitive definition offered by geographer Ruth Wilson Gilmore: *Violence is organized abandonment.* That is to say, we encounter violence in actions or situations that are designed for someone or many someones to experience an *isolation whose ultimate aim is premature death.* Violence is not simply a positive motion of harm, but also can arise from a lack of action: a refusal to provide timely aid, resources, or care. In Gilmore's analysis, we commit violence when we erase others (or allow others to be erased) from our community.[20]

This view is complemented by the work of philosopher Slavoj Žižek, who suggests that violence takes three forms.[21] The first is the visible, often brute force of an individual harming another individual, which he calls *subjective* violence (read as violence from subject to subject). This is the violence that most often distracts us and dominates our field of view. But, Žižek continues, we would do well to reckon with two other forms of violence: the violence of our language and the violence of our institutions. As opposed to the eruption of subjective violence, these *objective* forms of violence (read as violence from an entity external to our shared subjectivities, such as an institution or a "juridical person") might be said to exude, or to emanate, to create a field of background radiation from which it can be difficult to shield oneself or others. In this latter form of violence, we are often caught in a bind where we depend on certain institutions for our livelihood, and these institutions in turn demand that we participate in their exclusionary practices of isolating others toward premature death.[22] This is what Sara Ahmed has called "the violence of everyday life, the violence of having to make do, the violence of having to get by."[23] We catch sight of this violence out of the corners of our eyes, for when we try to look at it head-on, it simply looks like *the way things are.*

Judith Butler engages this field of violence, this force field, with the observation that our task cannot be to simply define some *essence* of violence upon which we all agree and then exclude that essence. If violence has a general nature, Butler suggests, that *natural state* is as a contested field; what looks like violence to some will appear as something else to others. *Violence is always interpreted,* but it is not limited to interpretation.[24] Violence has material effects, even as these effects defy our direct gaze and our attempts to name them *as violence.* Violence, for Butler, is not encountered as an entity, but as a strategy. Combining Butler's position with that of Žižek and Gilmore, we can say that violence is an ongoing strategy of organized exclusions whose aim is premature death and that are deployed both in subjective interactions and in objective institutions—often the very institutions upon which we depend for our livelihood.[25] Violence is the routinization of exclusions into an everydayness of isolations that result in premature death.

Thus, when Butler considers *nonviolence,* Butler considers it also as a *strategic* engagement against material harm: "My inquiry is meant to ask about the possibility of safeguarding life against modes of destruction," Butler writes, "including the kinds of destruction that we ourselves unleash."[26] This is why I insist that the possibility of response-able love begins in a ground state of violence. Moral seriousness is that set of practices—those repeated scales and arpeggios—that increase the probability of *interruption* by another who has been harmed, or who is under the threat of harm. Over time, through this practice, we learn to receive this interruption as a call—*Some one of us should have been there with her!*—to which we might respond—*Here I am . . . send me!*—with a sincerity, *for life's sake.*

For Butler, the background radiation of violence is also a call. Because we are always already situated in a network of preferences and exclusions, it is a call that comes from within our own house. It takes the form of a *short circuit.* A short circuit is the misdirection of *power.* Like a short circuit, violence may manifest effects that have the *appearance* of power reaching an intended conclusion, but this appearance only misleads us. This was Hannah Arendt's revolutionary insight, that violence is the *opposite* of power: "where one [power or violence] rules absolutely, the other is absent."[27] Power, for Arendt, arises from an organized and uncoerced solidarity of *action,* of humans working together to explore and negotiate the meeting of their needs in an open and unpredicted future. Power, in this sense, is not only antiviolence, but *antideath.*[28] Power is action, taken together with others in *embodied solidarity, for life's sake.* For Arendt, this solidarity can be rooted in both our possibility and our *natality,* the shared fact that each of us has been born into *interdependence,* embodied, and striving together, each with the other.[29]

Although in resonance with Arendt, Judith Butler adds nuance to her assertion that power is available in the active (and, following Hawkins, we can add *embodied*) solidarity of uncoerced people. Where power is manifest, we must always proceed in the awareness that we have not *arrived* at any place in particular. This is to say, power is not simply the opposite of violence, as if we could rest at one pole or the other. Rather, where power can be achieved, it is achieved as a continuing *strategy* of nonviolence. This is an ethical strategy (Butler calls it "ethico-political") that comprehends that not every collective action undertaken is equal and that we are constantly at risk of having a solidarity that decays into self-preservation of some remnant: an *exclusion* that has an aim of the preservation of some, and thus the premature death of others. A strategy of nonviolence is always at risk of becoming violence by another name.

Thus, both our nonviolence and our power are always tentative. As we negotiate together, we must listen intently for the call of those who have been harmed, or who are under the threat of harm. In the language of Matthew 9, we must be available for *interruption* by someone who has been excluded from community and from life. In the language of Matthew 25, we must be available for interruption even by the *least of these* among us, for it is most often these people who have been harmed, or are under the threat of harm, from both subjective and objective violence. It is the least of these who are most at risk of becoming victims of the organized exclusions whose aim is premature death. We practice strategies of nonviolence by doing the opposite of violence, as much as we are able—refusing to participate in these lethal exclusions. That practice begins by becoming available for interruption.

As Butler reminds us, we do not *arrive* at nonviolence. Rather, we constantly renegotiate the possibility of nonviolence amid the background radiation of exclusions aimed at premature death. If we wish to *continue* in nonviolence, then, we must constantly ask: What manner of life has been *excluded* from our considerations? Who is the person or group of people—who have been harmed or are under the threat of harm—who are still *forbidden* to interrupt us? For Arendt, we cannot be powerful alone, and for Butler, we cannot be nonviolent alone; for the possibility of both to remain open, we must continually make the *active* choice to turn away from violence and toward life. We must daily undertake tikkun olam, the process of healing the world, as a continual strategy of embodied solidarity with those who have been harmed or are under the threat of harm—the least of these. "It is precisely because we can destroy that we are under an obligation to know why we ought not to do it," Butler writes, "and to summon those countervailing powers that curb our destructive capacity [and that lead] us to reconsider whether self-preservation is not linked to preserving the lives of others."[30]

The continued work to summon the countervailing powers that curb our destructive capacity is, I submit to you, the harvest of the fruit of moral seriousness. In this present project, then, it remains to ask: How might we engage with the objects we call bibles in a spirit of moral seriousness? For me, one example arises from the exciting and provocative work of Botswanan postcolonial feminist theologian Musa W. Dube. In a 2016 essay, "The Subaltern Can Speak: Reading the Mmulte (Hare) Way," Dube employs a "trickster" hermeneutic that invites readers to develop "skills of rewriting and redirecting a story toward new and unexpected ends in the service of resistance, survival, and liberation."[31] Dube begins by examining a series of stories from southern Africa in which the hare, Mmulte, plays a central role as a trickster figure.[32] As Dube notes, characters like Mmulte played not only a powerful social but also a *political* role for those in the African diaspora.[33] Trickster narratives form an ongoing site of both resistance to violence and solidarity with those who have been harmed or are threatened with harm. Considering our above discussions in this chapter, I suggest that Dube's trickster hermeneutic can serve as a good example of a morally serious reading of a text. This becomes especially clear when Dube says:

> To read from the trickster perspective is to first and foremost recognize one's situation of vulnerability but not incapacity. It is to take a position for one's own empowerment and to be in solidarity with many others who find themselves living with and among the powerful, who are potential oppressors and, in many cases, indeed oppressors. A trickster reading perspective insists that, regardless of one's vulnerability, one still has power to resist, survive, and liberate oneself, but one must always take one's own side and the side of others who are oppressed.[34]

To put this in the language we have been using in this chapter, a trickster reading begins with an embodied solidarity that refuses to participate in organized exclusions whose aim is premature death. By inviting us to "recognize one's situation of vulnerability but not incapacity," Dube is opening the space for both call and response. A trickster reader begins in a context that is *already* violent but takes responsibility (and demonstrates response-ability) for themselves and others to engage in continued strategies of nonviolence. Taking the side of others who have been harmed or who are under the threat of harm, a trickster reader both interrupts the everydayness of violence and is available for interruption by the least of these, with whom they practice embodied solidarity.

What is compelling about this sort of reading as a lens through which we engage the objects we call bibles is that it helps us see these objects apart from their supposed neutrality. Following the combination of Gilmore's and Butler's insights suggested above, we are always already beginning in a context of organized exclusions whose aim is premature death. That is to say, the default condition of all our relations (and all the objects that arise from those relations) is one of violence (subjective or objective, interpersonal or institutional, exclusions that are aimed at premature death), and we must deploy active strategies of nonviolence (availability to interruption, response-ability, tikkun olam, and solidarity) if we wish to disengage from this background state of violence.

If we always begin in a context of violence, this means that the objects we call bibles—and our interpretations of the messages we receive from these objects—will begin in this context as well. Dube makes this explicit when she suggests that a trickster hermeneutic will start in a place of suspicion and will treat our relationships (and readings) as if they were "a crime scene"—a place where the eruption of violence has *already* happened, and now (following Arendt) a site where that harm can and must be repaired, if we dare to be serious.[35]

In the conclusion of her essay, Dube puts the question to us squarely, urging us to ask ourselves as readers and interpreters of biblical texts, "how can I apply the trickster strategies of reading a situation to evade their potential or actual oppression toward the vulnerable?"[36] This must be the starting point of all engagements with the objects we call bibles, if we wish to be both moral and serious in that engagement.

We must begin with the assumption that we are *already* participating in a ground state of violence, even as we begin to read. The goal of our hermeneutic, then, must be to read in a manner that renders us more and more available to interruption, more willing to take responsibility for repair.

Musa Dube gives us one example of what this might look like. In the following chapter, I offer my own example, in a method I have come to call *material scripture.*

3
On Material Scripture

We have looked at two established projects, Scriptural Reasoning and Iconic Books. In this chapter we take a look at a third, *cultural materialism*. You'll notice that the first two schools of thought are identified using capital letters, indicating that their participants largely work on a common project, with conversations aimed at mutual concerns and goals. By contrast, in this chapter I present a set of ideas that are not gathered under a capitalized title. This is a concept that I and others have variously referred to as *material scripture.* Unlike an established school of thought or project, however, I would prefer to think of material scripture more like a common tool. So I would say to you, "This is material scripture" in much the way I might say, "This is a hammer." That is, this is a tool I use for certain projects and purposes, realizing that others will use their hammer, or their versions of material scripture, in different configurations and for different projects and purposes. There is nothing particularly special about the fact that the tool is in my hands, but it is useful in confronting the tasks before us.

This chapter outlines and explores material scripture as a strategy for (mis)reading and (mis)interpreting the objects we call bibles. As was mentioned in the first chapter, my particular approach grows just as much out of my "suspicion of hermeneutics" as it does out of any hermeneutics of suspicion. As I went in search of tools to help me study this obscured world of editorial ideologies that work at the edges of our pages and "behind" our books, that journey led me in a number of directions.

In the first part of the chapter I briefly explore how the ideas of "materiality" and "materialism" have been used in the fields of religious studies, theology, and biblical hermeneutics, with a particular focus on the work of several of my colleagues from the Iconic Books Project. From there I look at two approaches to materialism, offered by Raymond Williams and Crystal B. Lake, to help us locate the concept of materialism more generally as a useful tool within the human sciences. At the end of the chapter, I present the key aspects of my conception of material scripture, which will set us up to enter Part Two of this book, where I present four theses that attempt to illustrate these tactics in practice.

Readers familiar with materialist discourse will certainly see in what follows the intellectual debt I owe to thinkers in the Hegelian tradition, such as Ludwig Feuerbach and Walter Benjamin, as well as the Frankfurt School and its development of critical theory. Some of those lines of influence are explicitly named in what follows, while others simply haunt the text. Some of the concepts and ideas introduced in earlier chapters also find their way into the conversation as the chapter progresses, particularly the Jewish concept of tikkun olam, Franz Rosenzweig's ideas about modesty (tzniut), and Larycia Hawkins's notions of embodied solidarity. My hope is to weave this all together, not in order to present some new Big Idea, but to offer a set of coherent tactics for navigating situations structured by violence, using the objects we call bibles.

Using materialist forms of analysis to explore and understand what we read in the objects we call our bibles is nothing new, of course. In the nineteenth century, the Young or Left Hegelians such as David Friedrich Strauss and Ludwig Feuerbach, writing in the wake of Hegel's death to stake their claim on the theological implications of his project, offered one strand. Both thinkers made the shift in foundation from the spiritual to the material as their starting point for analyzing the processes of Christian religion, reversing Hegel's assumption (that spirit precedes matter) and paving the way for the spiritless and metaphysically resistant materialism of Karl Marx and those who took up Marxist-inspired forms of analysis in the human sciences. Such practices peaked rapidly and, especially in the case of Feuerbach, receded quickly.[1] They were soon all but eclipsed in much of North American and European twentieth-century biblical scholarship.[2]

In the 1970s and 1980s a pair of books reanimated discussions of materialism in biblical studies. The first was Fernando Belo's *A Materialist Reading of the Gospel of Mark,* followed a decade later by Michel Clévenot's *Materialist Approaches to the Bible.* By this point, a century of Marxist discourse had cemented a particular approach to the meaning of "materialism" and what it could offer. As Clévenot's translator, William Nottingham, puts it:

> a materialist approach does not allow for interpretations of life and experience from the standpoint of eternal truths or the will of God or abstract ideas working themselves out in daily life. The materialist approach means that a basic assumption about

> methods of historical understanding has been made, consisting of the attempt to discern how power is used overtly or subtly to dominate, brain-wash, or exploit classes of people.[3]

What I present in this chapter parts ways with many central aspects of the Marxist paradigm of materialism. Nevertheless, a key point from Nottingham's remarks should be highlighted: A materialist biblical analysis steers us away from "eternal truths." We are not looking for some "view from nowhere" when exploring the objects we call bibles.

Despite a notable trend in various liberation theologies to utilize aspects of Marxist analysis without explicitly naming it as a source, by the 1990s we observe an overall retreat from the methodologies of Marxist social theory in biblical scholarship. Scholars were certainly still interested in material culture but were looking for other foundations for their analysis. For example, Colleen McDannell's *Material Christianity* takes a comprehensive and well-illustrated view of American Christian mass culture, but it does so with only one reference to Marx and two to the neo-Marxist Frankfurt School, all in the introductory chapter. Notably, McDannell's materialist analysis draws less from the sociological traditions and more from the anthropological ones. Her approach looks at Christian religious practices and objects as forms of "unwritten text," and she seeks to read these texts in a manner that sidesteps the more explicitly political and economic interpretations of class and power that are found in Marxist materialists such as Belo and Clévenot.[4] This anthropological vein draws from works such as Thomas Schlereth's *Material Culture: A Research Guide* and focuses on insights from subdisciplines such as cultural geography, vernacular architecture, American studies, the history of technology, the decorative arts, and folklife studies. Thus we begin to see an expanded landscape of materialist analyses, grouped under the sometimes distinct and sometimes overlapping headings that include *dialectical materialism, material culture,* and *cultural materialism.*

It was into these clashing conceptions of materiality that my Iconic Books colleagues and I waded in the early 2000s. Iconic Books attracted a large web of scholars who brought with them a variety of materialist approaches.[5] To give some examples, S. Brent Rodriguez-Plate cofounded the journal *Material Religion: A Journal of Objects* and served for many years as its managing editor. He also wrote *A History of Religion in 5 1/2 Objects* and edited *Key Terms in Material Religion.* James Bielo undertook an ethnographic analysis of American evangelical communities, looking specifically at their material interactions with bibles, which resulted in his 2009 book *Words upon the Word.* Timothy Beal explored the overlap of materialism and media culture with the edited volume *Mel Gibson's Bible* (2005). Beal also served as editor in chief of the *Oxford Encyclopedia of the Bible and the Arts* and offered his own reflections on the materiality of bible objects in his 2012 work *The Rise and Fall of the Bible: The Unexpected History of an Accidental Book.*

Building on this momentum in conversations and publications, in 2010, Dorina Parmenter, James Watts, Timothy Beal, James Bielo, and I put together a wildcard panel at the annual meeting of the Society of Biblical Literature under the title "Material Scripture." Two major items emerged from that session. The first was a powerful essay from Beal, "Reception History and Beyond: Toward the Cultural History of the Scriptures," which was an expanded version of his conference presentation. Especially promising in Beal's essay was a strident call to bible scholars to turn from hermeneutical interpretation to questions of cultural production, which to my thinking moved his inquiry away from the anthropological approaches of Schlereth and McDannell and closer to what I mean when I use the phrase "material scripture."

The second outcome of that panel was Parmenter being asked to write an entry, "Material Scripture," for *The Oxford Encyclopedia of the Bible and the Arts*. Her analysis in that article may be the most comprehensive treatment of the subject to date. The definition she offers there is worth noting in full here:

> "Material scripture" refers to an interdisciplinary perspective toward the study of religious books and texts that considers the roles of the physical elements of a text's manufacture, transmission, use, and display and the effect of these roles on the production of authority, semantic interpretations, and ideologies attributed to scriptures. It is not a clearly demarcated field of study, but a point of emphasis used by a variety of scholars for the purpose of balancing the traditional predominance of textual interpretation without regard for material context in studies of the Bible. Other terms that have been used to analyze issues of material scripture include the iconic dimension of scripture and the artifactual use of scripture.[6]

Parmenter's definition is useful on a number of fronts. Like Beal's essay, it indicates a movement toward the question of scripture as a matter of cultural production. Also, it anticipates the position of this present chapter when noting that the questions and methodological approaches of material scripture are far from settled. Parmenter's definition invites us to continue to inquire, refine, and redefine the ideas we might use in exploring the materialist landscape.

It is in the spirit of such an invitation that I undertake in the remainder of this chapter to offer my own thoughts about how we might approach a practice of material scripture. I have rehearsed the history above to make clear that what I offer is part of a much larger mosaic of reflections and methodologies. Beal, Parmenter, Bielo, Watts, Plate, and the many others who have enriched these conversations may well disagree with me about where emphases should be placed and what material scripture can and should mean. Further, even where they might find points of agreement, I am mindful that scholars like McDannell and Schlereth (and perhaps also Belo and Clévenot) certainly will find points of substantial departure from my thinking here. I encourage readers to explore all these intersections and disjunctions, and to join our conversations as they are able.

One of the most important figures in my growing understanding of materialism has been the Welsh cultural theorist Raymond Williams, along with those who have taken up his ideas in the project that came to be called cultural materialism. In his seminal work *Keywords: A Vocabulary of Culture and Society,* Williams offers an extensive entry on materialism, in which he suggests that materialism, and its cognates *materialist* and *materialistic,* are "complex words." Williams then provides three conceptual subdivisions for thinking about the complexities of the varieties of materialism we encounter.

First, Williams notes, materialism may refer to "a very long, difficult and varying set of arguments which propose matter as the primary substance of all living and non-living things." Second, it might refer to "a related or consequent but again highly various set of explanations and judgments of mental, moral and social activities." Finally, materialism might refer to "a distinguishable set of attitudes and activities . . . which can be summarized as an overriding or primary concern with the production or acquisition of things and money."[7] That is, materialist approaches prioritize *physicality,* often as a way of grounding mental events, metaphysical claims, and spiritual experiences (to the extent a particular strand of materialism does not deny them outright), and are at times also connected to—or dismissed as being merely—self-focused and antisocial behaviors such as greed and consumerism.

Williams notes that, especially since the eighteenth century, materialism has also been understood to be arrayed against the formal, the ideal, and the spiritual.[8] Materiality, coupled especially with the rising currents of empiricism and scientific thought, brought a check against the grand systems of metaphysics that offered rival causal explanations for events in the world.

The danger, of course, is that such a binary risks having materialism collapse into a kind of clockwork determinism, a mechanical universe with no room for mental or spiritual affairs. Without following Thomas Hobbes and other British materialists of the eighteenth century fully into the assertion that our descriptions of the world must be limited solely to physical mechanics, I do share their hope that materialism might provide a check against the invocation of metaphysical or abstract entities as a kind of black box, proffering overly simplified solutions to complex questions. Williams shared this hope, too. Material analysis of "specific and indissoluble real processes" is the key here for Williams.[9] It helps us resist our urge to turn materialism itself into a general or abstract entity, "to propose that it is a system like others, of a presumptive explanatory kind."[10] In this sense, across numerous writings, Williams asserts again and again that he resists looking at materialism as a system, but rather deploys it *as a strategy* that always seeks to ground and reground analysis in specific histories and contexts.

These "real processes" are not just relations for captains of industry, kings, or battlefield generals. Every single one of us is and can be engaged in the processes that shape and move cultures in creative, unexpected directions. These real processes offer a kind of *natality.* That is, our material work can help to birth new and unexpected situations and processes into the world, where "in the inevitable tensions of new kinds of argument and new kinds of claim, the defenders of reason and education become open to new and unfamiliar relationships."[11]

These diverse voices of everyday lives, who have so often been overlooked or muffled by social and institutional structures of exclusion, are the ones the Christian tradition has often called the "least of these" and whom Howard Thurman referred to as "the disinherited." These teeming masses are, for Williams, the very motor force of *cultural* history, and through their struggles to create relationships and meaning in their lives, *new* cultural possibilities arise. We will return to this idea of natality in a moment.

What attracts me especially to Williams is his exploration of a materialism that avoids grounding in a mechanized or teleological determinism. He sought methods to understand culture, not as something created by elites or foreordained by base and superstructure, but rather as a social-material activity in which all humans participate, even if many do so at only an unconscious or a reactionary level. The study of culture is not simply the study of so-called high culture. Rather, as Williams often put it, *culture is ordinary.*

As opposed to those who believe, for example, that culture should celebrate and reproduce social inequalities and what results from them, Williams holds an entirely different view: Culture is and should be democratic and foster democratic practices up to its horizons. Since cultural production should include as many participants as possible, an ever-expanding and emancipatory franchise, Williams was interested in strategies that expand and support the agency of as many people within a given cultural moment as possible. As he once put it, "I've often defined my own social purpose as the creation of an educated and participating democracy."[12]

Williams thus combines the material analysis of culture with practices that welcome those on the margins into agency within concrete cultural arrangements. As I think about tactics of material scripture, I am mindful that abolitionist thinkers such as Ruth Wilson Gilmore have used Williams's work to explore the processes by which concrete cultures—not simply in the form of texts and artifacts, but also in the form of land, social relations, and human bodies—are alienated and redirected toward marketable ends. Specifically, they are redirected as land, social relations, and human bodies *to be sold.*

For me, material scripture is a set of tactics for thinking through the relationships and structures that are (re)produced around the objects we call bibles. These relationships and structures themselves are employed to (re)produce concrete social relations that aim at restriction or liberation. Williams is thus a core resource for the material criticism of what the abolitionist Frederick Douglass and (echoing him) the contemporary theologian Kelly Brown Douglas have termed "slaveholding Christianity."[13] We explore this concept more in later chapters.

As our brief look at Raymond Williams suggests, materialism has often been tied to the question of human agency. In her book *Artifacts,* Crystal B. Lake observes that over the centuries, material analysis returns "again and again to both historical and philosophical conflicts . . . over who as well as what had the power to initiate, control, and *take action.*"[14] In some interpretations, agency has been removed entirely: Think of Sir Isaac Newton's clockwork universe restricted to only physical cause and effect. Such arrangements leave no room for choice, and thus materialism manifests as a grim fatalism. In contrast, the kind of materialism that we focus on here is not tied to deterministic outcomes. Following Williams, our focus is on the prospect of natality, and the possibility that material structures can be reformed through processes of direct action and democratic change.

With that said, I find some arrangements of material agency more compelling than others. In particular, recent thinkers such as Bruno Latour, Graham Harman, Jane Bennet, and Karen Barad, among others, have each in their own way developed ideas that have been described as "New Materialism(s)." As Lake notes, these thinkers "all share an interest in the qualities objects possess that we cannot perceive and the way that objects *act on their own,* without us."[15] While I find these explorations very interesting, I wish to push analysis in the opposite direction. I am more interested in exploring the agency humans display in their use of objects, rather than exploring the agency objects might display apart from humanity. Lake observes that New Materialist approaches help us to see "what's at stake when we claim that objects are speaking or giving evidence of themselves."[16] At least in the ways I deploy material scripture here, I want to emphatically resist the notion that objects speak "for themselves." As we explore in later chapters, there can be a great danger when we ascribe a personality to an object such as a bible, to the point where we imagine that this object *wants* or even *demands* some action from us. In this sort of *parasocial* relation, we can create all manner of justifications for extreme violence, to the point where we imagine that we ourselves are mere accessories to the crime that the object itself commits. The aim of my materialist approach here is to radically *deflate* the mystification with which we enshroud objects. I seek to decrease the parasocial agency we might grant to objects as containers of agency or meaning. I seek instead to increase the material and social agency of human persons, particularly those who have been historically disenfranchised and disinherited.

In my life and in my scholarly work I remain committed to a certain form of what we might call Enlightenment hope. Put simply, this is a hope that we might achieve better local situations—and to the extent such narratives are still possible, thereby achieve a better world—through words, rather than through the organized exclusions and abandonments I have here called violence. I see in this Enlightenment hope a family resemblance to the idea of tikkun olam, the repair of the world, which was introduced and explored in previous chapters. We accomplish repair in local spaces by structuring and restructuring the relations and material conditions in those spaces until everyone—literally everyone—is able to say, of their own accord, "I feel safe here."

Enlightenment hope creates a tremendous pressure of unfinished business. I and we are constantly collapsing that hope into more efficient structures of social organization, which means we are always downshifting into arrangements where we have made peace with organized exclusions, even those exclusions that lead to premature death for the least of these among us. So we find ourselves convinced by arguments of expediency and limited resources to resort once again to violence instead of words, to the world as it is rather than the world as it might be, and to a locality where those around us cannot say "I feel safe here."

This book, *The Accessorized Bible,* is not a book about general social hope. It is a book about the objects we call bibles. So the shape of our inquiry into those objects, in the spirit of this Enlightenment hope for tikkun olam through words rather than through deadly arrangements of exclusions, takes the form of a particular method. We might ask, What are some ways we can engage with, read, and interpret the objects we call bibles such that, over time, those around us—even and especially the least of these among us, those whom Howard Thurman called the disinherited—might say, of their own accord, "I feel safe here"?

The kind of materialism we seek here should not, indeed cannot, be of the mechanistic or deterministic variety. When someone names the wound of their circumstance to us, when someone calls out for their world and our world to be healed, we cannot simply fall back on a materialism that would say, "These are our circumstances; they cannot be changed." So it is not just *any* style of Enlightenment materialism that will help us move forward here. In a similar fashion, I am wary of New Materialism's renewed interest in the inflated agency of objects; at present the various New Materialist approaches risk the dilution of social and political solidarities of human persons in their (in my view) overemphasis on object-agencies.[17]

I seek after a materialism that can help us analyze contexts and conditions, yes, but also aid us in shifting and reconfiguring those conditions when we are interrupted by the disinherited, or when we ourselves have been disinherited. We could call this a responsive materialism, a responsible materialism, or even a response-able materialism. It would resemble what Marx W. Wartofsky, in his analysis of Ludwig Feuerbach's influence on Karl Marx, has called a *critical* materialism, "whose objects of criticism are 'here below,' [and] whose attack is on the mystification and alienation of everyday life, in the human, political, and economic realm of ordinary existence" that so often results in suffering, lack of safety, and organized abandonment of many, particularly the disinherited.[18]

Years ago, while doing research in the library for my dissertation, I happened on a book called *Cultural Materialism: Theory and Practice,* by Scott Wilson, which introduced me to the work of Raymond Williams, Jonathan Dollimore, and Alan Sinfield. Wilson's book hit me like a lightning bolt. It showed me there were scholars asking questions about the ideological influences at work in book production, and how famous and influential books—like a Shakespeare play, or a bible, or a lexicon—might be viewed as products of manufactured culture. It also let me know that they were pursuing the answers to these questions in departments far outside of seminary faculties. Though these kindred thinkers were linguistic philosophers and literary critics, not theologians or biblical scholars, I began incorporating their writings alongside my reading for theological studies. Through Wilson's book, I learned about other books and thinkers, particularly Dollimore and Sinfield's volume of essays *Political Shakespeare: Essays in Cultural Materialism.* Dollimore and Sinfield suggest that cultural materialism explores

> [a] combination of historical context, theoretical method, political commitment and textual analysis. Historical context undermines the transcendent significance traditionally accorded to the literary text and allows us to recover its histories; theoretical method detaches the text from immanent criticism which seeks only to reproduce it in its own terms; socialist and feminist commitment confronts conservative categories in which most criticism has hitherto been conducted; textual analysis locates the critique of traditional approaches where it cannot be ignored. We call this "cultural materialism."[19]

Cultural materialism takes a broad and intentionally interdisciplinary approach to critical projects, not just asking *what* texts might mean (the question of hermeneutics) but exploring as well the complex (and often hidden) mechanisms and power relationships that operate behind these *cultural* productions of meaning. In this light, cultural materialism provides a useful method to begin to answer that basic question presented by Watts and Parmenter of the Iconic Books Project above, namely: *How* do books matter?

For this reason I view cultural materialism and Iconic Books as complementary projects. Returning to the "Three Dimensions" essay mentioned earlier, Watts invites us to imagine beyond the limits of the purely semantic dimension of scripture (interpretation, commentary, study) and beckons us explicitly to turn to the material nature of the objects we call holy books. In a parallel move, coming from literary studies, Dollimore and Sinfield invite us to consider the material conditions that lead to the reproduction of ideologies that both fund and depend upon the existence of "great" works of art, while simultaneously obscuring the social and political costs of such ideologies. In my reading, both Iconic Books and cultural materialism seek to unravel *how* the objects we call books come to be illuminated and obfuscated in these ways. Both seek to clarify, rather than mystify, the relations between material production and cultural capital.[20]

Watts's explorations of the iconic and expressive dimensions of scripture, as we have noted, introduce a field of analysis that looks at scripture in its cultural entanglements: visual presentations, theatrical and cinematic interpretations, and so on. Further, according to Watts, these dimensions have long been hidden in the shadow of the *semantic* dimension. (Recall that the semantic dimension is rooted in those aspects of the book that are specifically textual and interpretive, rather than material.) By implying that the semantic is the *only* dimension worth considering, those communities that foreground the semantic dimension benefit from epistemologies that are leavened with a naive metaphysics. "Meaning" and "interpretation" in such arrangements can thus be understood to exist "out there," in some intangible and idealized realm that transcends the particularities of time and place.

As a check against this mystifying, metaphysical turn, both Iconic Books and cultural materialism offer methods to reengage with the material nature of the book on the table in front of us. As Dollimore writes, "Materialist criticism refuses to privilege 'literature' in the way that literary criticism has done hitherto . . . this approach necessitates a radical contextualizing of literature which eliminates the old divisions between literature and its 'background' text and context."[21] Again, in what I see as a complement to this assertion, Parmenter and Watts's call to address the iconic and performative dimensions of scripture, and to interrogate *how* these books matter in our liturgical communities (collapsing an arbitrary distinction between text and context), reminds us not only that our holy books *are books* but that books have an irreducibly material *provenance.*

For Iconic Books, then, scripture is not a mystified theological category but a distinct set of social practices. The parallel I see is that for cultural materialism, literature is demystified and seen as a social practice. Both schools of thought seek to deploy methods that allow us to inspect the material conditions that anchor these social practices. These material conditions, moreover, can and should be interrogated to determine their ideological allegiances and effects.

In their explorations of cultural materialism, Wilson, Dollimore, and Sinfield (along with Williams and the Frankfurt School before them) help us see that our cultural industries are engaged in the preferencing and foregrounding of certain texts over others. In their view, "classics" and "canons" and culturally significant works do not achieve importance because of an inherent set of essential qualities, but rather through a complex network of interactions and assumptions (which shift in time and context) that move some works to the spotlight and others (the majority of others) to the margins. Even though the process is not essentialist, neither is it random. It involves the cooperation of (financial and cultural) funders, gatekeepers, and (in our latter days especially) tastemakers. In this understanding, all cultural labor—whether my work as an academic, or the work of a critic, or the value of an Instagram celebrity—is participation in the functioning of cultural (re)production. That (re)production is tied up with the claim that certain cultural products are naturally central and essential. To say it in another way, the product we all help (re)produce is a *canon:* a set of texts that serve as the material artifacts of an ideology that holds that these "naturally" core texts are to be viewed as "masterpieces," or "culturally significant," or representative examples of "genius." As Dollimore and Sinfield have foregrounded, William Shakespeare's works are not simply a part of culture, but are also part of this *culture industry.*

As with the works of the Bard, so also the objects we call bibles. Both are examples of cultural nodes, where a sense of vitality and importance has coalesced. We don't quite have a word for this phenomenon in English, but in German (following Franz Rosenzweig, as mentioned in Chapter 1) we'd call a work that becomes culturally central and determinative in this way a Schriftsprache.

When I imagine "material scripture," I think of a democratic and human-centered (rather than book-centered) process of interpretive negotiation. I would like it to be a practice that real living, breathing people use to become less isolated from and find more solidarity with each other. This might mean that, whatever material scripture is in a given time and place, it will probably look different from other practices that consider themselves to be material scripture in other times and places. Perhaps material scripture, as I imagine it, is a strategy of solidarity rather than a proper theory of interpretation.

The foundations for this strategy diverge from what physicist Chanda Prescod-Weinstein has termed "white empiricism," or "the phenomenon through which only white people (particularly white men) are read as having a fundamental capacity for objectivity and Black people (particularly Black women) are produced as an ontological other."[22] Instead, I find myself compelled by interpretive strategies championed by women of color, in particular Musa W. Dube, Kelly Brown Douglas, and bell hooks, among others. As we have seen, Musa Dube is a proponent of "trickster" readings, which draw from indigenous African storytelling traditions. Dube invites us to "read from the perspective of the vulnerable and in solidarity with them" and to commit ourselves to those reading practices that allow us to "retell any text from the perspective of the powerless and the vulnerable and to change its outcome completely."[23] Kelly Brown Douglas agrees, suggesting that "we are constrained to always find the liberative strand of the Bible in relation to the struggles of others. We are to resist any temptation to do otherwise."[24] Finally, bell hooks invites us to commit to reading *as an act of love,* which arises "only as we let go of our obsession with power and domination [and embrace] a global vision wherein we see our lives and our fate as intimately connected to those of everyone else on the planet."[25]

These three thinkers point us to an ethic of reading and interpretation that coheres well with the idea of tikkun olam, of healing the world, that I mentioned above in the discussions of Scriptural Reasoning. It constitutes a material engagement to read not only with the vulnerable and on behalf of the vulnerable, but in such ways that *change outcomes* for the vulnerable, both on the page and in the world. What I have in mind is an observation from historian Michelle Murphy that our acts of interpretation can be *infrastructural,* which is to say that our "knowledge making can install *material supports* into the world—such as buildings, bureaucracies, standards, forms, technologies, funding flows, affective orientations, and power relations."[26]

Particularly when we read and interpret the objects we call bibles, we participate in webs and networks that have invested for centuries in building and reinforcing certain types of infrastructures. As we imagine biblical stories mapping onto our lives, or ourselves mapping to the stories in the texts, we invest and are invested in very concrete outcomes that take shape in our shared world. Family planning, state welfare, border policies, the choice to go to war or refrain from war, incarceration, and even the meals we eat or the clothing we put on our bodies (or allow others to put on their bodies) are all pulled into the orbit of what we imagine this object we call a bible might "want" from us. Each of these material outcomes can be "read" in ways that pull us more toward violence or healing, incarceration or liberation, revenge or repair. Reading with an ethic of tikkun olam, therefore, is to read in a manner that is both *critical* of the existing infrastructures of harm and violence that presently exist and *committed* to building new and different life-giving material supports for the vulnerable.

Within my thinking about material scripture, I have sought to materialize and concretize my thinking about "the vulnerable" (who risk vanishing into abstraction) by thinking in terms of "the breathing reader." Following the insight of Emmanuel Levinas, mentioned in the previous chapter, this is the reader for whom *life is a sincerity,* who "breathe[s] for the sake of breathing."[27] But this is also the reader whose breath is *under threat,* whose breath may cease prematurely or be snuffed out as a result of personal or infrastructural neglect and violence. The breathing reader is always situated in a particular time and place, in contrast to the abstracted space of the "ideal reader." A breathing reader never offers a "view from nowhere," but always rather a view from somewhere. Often, in fact, the breathing reader offers us a view from *precarity,* a view from the space where one's back is against the wall.[28] Material scripture is an attempt to center the breathing reader in every encounter with the biblical texts, even if it means sacrificing scholarly rigor for the sake of moral seriousness and solidarity. Said another way, following the philosopher Judith Butler, this commitment of material scripture to solidarity with the breathing readers is an affirmation that "we have the power and the freedom to make more livable lives for ourselves, where bodies can be *more free to breathe,* to move, to love, without discrimination and without fear of violence."[29] It is this commitment to embodied solidarity, rather than "right reading," that forms a core tenet of strategies of material scripture.

So as I am using the term, material scripture is not a mechanism for getting the object we call the bible "correct," on its own terms. Rather, it is a commitment to active and intentional *misreading.* We become willing to misread and misinterpret whatever is on the page, in the narrative, rendered into our theologies, *until* those misreadings and misinterpretations point toward life, not death. We misread and misinterpret our way to the creation of ever stronger material supports for the vulnerable, on behalf of the "least of these" among us. Following an insight of New Testament scholar Love Lazarus Sechrest, this is a "refusal to excuse the text" when an established or "doctrinally correct" reading is used to support harmful policies or infrastructures of violence.[30] In this refusal, material scripture attempts to follow the example set by Jesus in the Gospels, where expectations of bodies, laws, and institutions are reversed. In Matthew 12, Jesus feeds and heals in violation of the Sabbath, and in a cognate story in Mark 2, Jesus proclaims that the Sabbath was made for humans, not humans for the Sabbath. From this example, material scripture derives its core ethic: Instead of breaking the reader for the sake of the reading, we break the reading for the sake of the reader. Instead of breaking the body of the breathing reader for the sake of the institution, we break the institution for the sake of the body of the breathing reader. In material scripture, we bring these ethical commitments *to* the text, rather than binding ourselves to the ethical structures we might imagine we encounter *in* the text. My hope is that such a strategy bears more than a passing resemblance to the sort of trickster reading suggested by Dube above.

To give a concrete example of what I mean by this (mis)reading and (mis)interpretation on behalf of vulnerable bodies, let us conclude with a brief look at Deuteronomy 21:18–21:

> If someone has a stubborn and rebellious son who will not listen to his father or mother, and will not listen to them even though they discipline him, his father and mother shall take hold of him and bring him out to the elders at the gate of his home city, where they shall say to the elders of the city, "This son of ours is a stubborn and rebellious fellow who will not listen to us; he is a glutton and a drunkard." Then all his fellow citizens shall stone him to death. Thus shall you purge the evil from your midst, and all Israel will hear and be afraid. (NABRE)

The plain sense of the text is stark. If a child repeatedly disobeys his parents, he risks not only discipline but *capital punishment* at the hands of the citizenry. Now, if we read this passage under the mystification that the object we call a bible not only wants, but *demands* certain actions from us, then we might apply the plain reading of this text into our infrastructures, yielding punitive and carceral policies that increase the possibility that our children will be put to death for all manner of "disobedience." Further, much like the story of Abraham told in Genesis 21, a reader might imagine that God, *through* this object we call a bible, demands this capital punishment as a sign of faith. Thus we might create entire institutions of death, based upon a very literal and plain reading of the biblical text.

I am intrigued, however, by what the rabbinic traditions have done with this passage. If we look to the Talmud, we find an extended discussion about how to interpret this text, and what we find can be well described as the rabbis intentionally (mis)reading and (mis)interpreting the plain sense of the text, with the intention of rendering it as *non*lethal as possible.[31] For example, the rabbis specify it must be "a son," and therefore no daughters are at risk. They then seek to limit the age of who can be considered a son. If the child is too young, they are not accountable for their actions. If the child is deemed too old, they are governed by different laws than those that apply to adults. The practical effect is that the age range for a son is reduced to the three months following the child's thirteenth birthday. The son will be considered rebellious only if he eats meat and drinks wine, both (not just one or the other) proving his gluttony. But then other rabbis insist that only *cheap* meat and *cheap* wine would count toward his rebellion. They then specify that it must be *both* the father and the mother bringing the accusation, for if one disagrees with the other, the son will not be liable. Finally, the discussion turns to exactly how many judges must be present, at what times, and under what conditions, for the strictures of pronouncing a death sentence to be met. After all these pages of discussions, the rabbis declare, "There has never been a stubborn and rebellious son and there will never be one in the future, as it is impossible to fulfill all the requirements that must be met in order to apply this *halakha* [Jewish legal teaching]."[32]

What this example shows us is that the various rabbis whose discussions are collected in the pages of the Babylonian Talmud were in this case committed to a very specific approach to the biblical text. They did not ignore it. Rather, they approached the text with a form of *moral seriousness* that allowed them to read, reread, argue with the text, misread the text, and reinterpret the text to the point of misinterpretation, until they reached a conclusion that pointed conclusively to life, not death. As I have mentioned, this practice echoes the hermeneutic of embodied solidarity modeled by Jesus when he fed and healed on the Sabbath. This commitment to life-giving misreadings, breaking institutions for the sake of the bodies within them, is the fundamental ethic of what I am here calling the strategy of material scripture.

II
Four Theses

4
First Thesis
A Bible Is a Book

Like a lot of folks, I have been a fan of Steve Martin for a long time. I haven't loved all his projects, but when they're good, they're really good. (My favorite is probably an old film called *Dead Men Don't Wear Plaid.* Great stuff.) Martin was a hugely successful stand-up comedian before he got into making films, and his 1979 bridge from stand-up to movies was *The Jerk.* The story of Martin's Navin R. Johnson, an unlucky buffoon, is loosely structured around vignettes of Navin making repeated attempts to better himself, and having those efforts go horribly wrong.

What I focus on here is a series of scenes from the first part of the film that take place when Navin gets his first job, as an attendant at a gas station. The job provides him income and stability, and that situation sets up the first gag. When the new telephone books arrive, Navin is ecstatic. Flipping through the pages to find his name printed among the many others, at last, he feels like he's "somebody."

As my older readers know, a telephone book was a large volume, printed on cheap paper stock, that listed the telephone numbers of everyone in the local area. Individuals were in the front, in the white pages, and businesses were listed in the back, in the yellow pages. That's really all it was: a big floppy book full of names and numbers, usually hundreds to the page.

It's also important to understand that, in casual conversation, a phone book would often serve as an example of the driest, most boring text you could imagine. As in, "That person is so charismatic, they could read the telephone book and I would stay interested." So the phone book in this scene is among the simplest and most pedestrian of texts. That's part of the gag: Navin getting excited about a telephone book just confirms the simple, unsophisticated person he is.

Soon after we witness Navin's excitement, we cut to another scene, again involving the telephone book. Here we see a character, referred to in the credits only as the Madman, who opens the phone book randomly and slams his finger down on the page. We cut to a close-up of the name next to his finger, and it is Navin's. The Madman then shouts, "Die, Navin R. Johnson!"

This is where I want us to linger, because in this moment, *a book is being used to make a moral choice.* Quite literally, a decision is being made about who should live and who should die. The Madman has said to the universe, "I am going to kill someone," and has then used some arbitrary external device to determine who the victim should be. In this instance, that arbitrary external device happened to be a book.

After we see this decision being made, we return to the gas station, where our hero is still working. Now the Madman takes up a post in a sniper's nest with a rifle and begins to shoot at Navin. In his simpleminded understanding, Navin at first believes that whoever is shooting intends to attack the oil cans behind him. Then it dawns on him that he is the target, and he flees the scene to find safety.

Here is where we reach the point. Some might argue that a telephone book was a "book" only in the loosest sense. Unlike a novel or a work of nonfiction, *or an object we call a bible,* this book is literally just a list of names and numbers. It has no plot, no action, no story of which we could speak. Nevertheless, in *The Jerk,* the Madman uses *the phone book* to make the most profound of moral decisions: who should live and who should die. If we had the ability to ask the Madman, "Why would you do this horrible thing?" it is very possible that his answer might simply be, "*Because the book told me to.*"

Now at this point, some might well protest, "But that's not what a telephone book is *for!*" A telephone book is made for cross-indexing names and numbers so you can call someone, and this new use (finding someone to murder) is clearly a perversion of its intent. Very well. We might say the same about the actuarial tables used by insurance companies, which are after all simply designed to statistically model various risk valuations for potential policyholders. Regardless of the intended use of these statistical models, however, insurance companies routinely use them to decide who gets access to care and who does not. In other words, they make the fundamentally moral decision of who should live and who should die. Insurance providers are not bound by the intentions of the statisticians who write their actuarial tables, just as the Madman using the phone book to decide whom to murder is not bound by the intentions of the telephone company.

Objects cannot have intentions. Actuarial tables and telephone books cannot have intentions. We cannot look at the actuarial table and say it wants us to do something. Rather, greedy or generous people consult the tables and interpret them to support the achievement of their greedy or generous ends.

The telephone book did not "tell" the Madman to go and kill Navin R. Johnson. *The Madman made that decision himself* and then used the phone book as a justification.

A reader with the intent of murder can come to any book, even one as deprived of narrative and action as the telephone book in *The Jerk,* and find a justification to carry out their dastardly intentions. Conversely, someone could have had the intention of giving away a sum of money, or paying someone's medical bills, or embarking on the chance of making a new friend and used the phone book in exactly the same way. *The book does not determine the moral outcome of the interaction;* the reader does. Saying "the book told me to" can never be a justification; it can only ever be an excuse.

As bible readers, we live *after* a certain kind of book, *after* certain kinds of books. We live in the wake of them but are not fully awakened to them. What does it mean therefore to say *a bible is a book?* For me, this is a fascinating and complex question. When we say a bible is a book, we might mean that a bible presents itself to us as an uncomplicated object, without guile or need for explanation. It may in such a view be the holiest book, or the greatest book, but it remains a book. For this reason it seems prudent, here at the beginning of our inquiry, to slow down the analysis. Before we rush to talk about an object we call a bible being an object we call a book, we might pause and explore what it means to say that *any* object "is a book." That is, what does the participation in such a category make plain, what is hidden, and what remains to be said?

One could be forgiven for assuming that a book functions as a kind of *container,* whether a physical container of words or a conceptual container of ideas, like jars on a shelf. My volume of David Hume's *Enquiries* is separate from my volume of Immanuel Kant's *Prolegomena to Any Future Metaphysics.* The two sit apart from each other in my bookcase, and this distance helps remind me as a reader that the thoughts and aims of these two thinkers are to be kept apart as well.

Due in no small measure to the fact that you and I are both participants in a literate culture, we understand *how to read.* But reading is not just a mechanical process, putting ideas into the jars and taking them out again. Reading is, but is not just, a neurological (re)cognition of written symbols. My friend, the author and publisher Jon Sweeney, once suggested that whatever we call a book might be less about the physical object and more about a peculiar way of paying attention. He was quick to add, however, that if the physical object disappeared from our cultural lives, then this way of paying attention would likely not be sustained for long.

Expanding on Sweeney's insight, I'd like to think about a book as a certain kind of *political arrangement.* Let's start by understanding that you and I, right now in this mediated interaction, are engaged in "my writing" and "your reading" as a set of relationships that do not simply depend on the two of us but also on an extended set of other organizational and logistical structures. Stephen King once said that he viewed books as a kind of mental telepathy, a mystical mechanism that takes thoughts from my mind and transfers them into yours.[1] In practice, however, this telepathy is more often presented (and distorted) into a form of *mind control:* You, the reader, should come away from the book with only exactly what I, the author, want you to think. Any deviation, in this model, is a form of perversion or failure on one or the other of our parts. In such a model, we understand that the social roles of "author" and "reader" imply that we are in a hierarchy. In spite of what I said above about telephone books, we both still might imagine that I am arranging words on a page with an intention to communicate some *meaning* to you, and that you, on the other end of this process, have the mechanisms in place to somehow *decode* that meaning. Moreover, we might imagine that my *intention* might (or should) limit or control the ways in which you do that decoding.

Let's dispense with that illusion as quickly as we can. Whether we're talking about a telephone book, or this book, *or any book,* the ideas I have for how you "should" use it actually hold no power of influence over you. As an author, I cannot control how you use these words. Books are not factories; in a factory, you can put in raw materials at one end and expect a certain predictable output of products and waste at the other end. As much as some of us might wish it were otherwise, ideas do not work like that. The author is not the master to which the reader is the beholden servant. I'm not the boss and you're not my employee. Rather, you and I are both protagonists in this encounter, and we are working out the trajectories of these ideas, separately and together.

Understanding and rejecting this model begins to touch on why I want to think about books as political arrangements. In using this phrase, I am not so much thinking of voting, elections, and governance—the sort of *overt* politics that functions as a kind of theater of security and control. Instead, I am thinking of "politics" here more in the manner of Hannah Arendt or Jürgen Habermas, who both have suggested that the political sphere is the space where we negotiate and work out unpredictable futures. Moreover, I am specifically borrowing the phrase "political arrangement" from comments made through the years by the late Chicago recording engineer Steve Albini as he reflected upon the different roles that evolve at various locations and times within musical cultures, especially when these cultures form themselves into organizations and structures such as "bands" and "record labels" within a "music industry."

So, for example, members of a rock band in the United States may choose to organize themselves simply as a hobby activity, or they may try to arrange their affairs such that playing music becomes their occupation. As should be clear, this simple decision between "we're doing this for fun" and "this is our job" will entail a vastly different set of legal, economic, and social obligations. Choosing one way or another means that the members, over time, will make decisions differently, utilize resources differently, and even participate in other social structures like families and taxation differently, depending on how they choose to define themselves as a band.

In a similar spirit, Albini, while consistently participating in work that is often associated with the recording and mixing of music for mass production and distribution, has consistently resisted being called a "record producer." He has said he prefers to be credited simply as a recording engineer, because he has made an explicit decision not to participate in certain decision-making and economic relations with the bands that he records. He actively resists arrangements that (in his analysis) have historically been part of a certain predatory relationship between musicians and a music *industry.* In a number of interviews over the years, Albini has repeatedly referred to these myriad relations (within bands, between musicians and music industry professionals, and between the music industry and the wider social sphere) using terms like "political organization" or "political arrangement." I see this analysis as being useful in helping us understand other cultural industries—such as the ones that produce the objects we call books—and this why I am using these terms here.[2]

Over the five-hundred-year history of the modern book, certain political arrangements have become so ubiquitous that they often operate without really being noted or even noticed. There are arrangements of *space:* a location (or locations) where the manuscript of a book is written, which is different from the location (or locations) where the manuscript is edited and assembled into its redacted form, and different again from the location (or locations) where the raw materials and parts that make up a book are manufactured, printed, and assembled. These various locations are different from the places where the finished products are warehoused and sold. Then you and I have a location (or locations) where we encounter a book, read it, think about it, discuss it, ignore it, or finally dispose of it.

Each of these stops along the journey of the life of a given book will involve a set of political arrangements. That is to say, intellectual and financial capital have been amassed and distributed. Social and physical properties have been secured to create space for its existence. Laws have been proposed, passed, and enforced for it to become possible—or impossible—for a book to reach markets and readers. In some cases, literal treaties have been negotiated around these objects and their movements across borders. Civic infrastructures are created and maintained and adjusted over long time periods that offer us libraries and bookstores and now online retailers, each of which is structured to get various books into our hands when we want them.

Personnel have been hired, trained, maintained, and compensated at every step of the process—not only to distribute and vend these books, but also to create the educational infrastructures that allow you to be able to read them. Moreover, it must be noted that during this half-millennium of the reign of the codex in the Western Hemisphere, there have been notable times when and spaces where certain books were not merely treated as commercial inventory, but instead became contraband objects whose possession carried criminal penalties.

No matter how simple the contents or unassuming the physical presentation may seem to the casual eye, every book is a highly complex assemblage of forces and factors that encompass geographies, markets, laws, and civic institutions. Each of these arrangements will present us, in the wake of our encounter with this object we call a book, with certain limitations as well as certain possibilities for action and interaction (and even, as we shall see, for *intra-action*). Every book has structured these complexities into the very possibility of its existence, and as such every book is irreducibly political.

Can you recall the first book you ever read? If so, can you recall what you were like the moment just before you read it? At that moment, you stood on the threshold, just outside of literacy. For most of us, of course, this moment happened so early that we really have no sense of what we were like before reading. We live *after* books. We navigate in the wake of them but perhaps not awakened fully to them. It is a paradox of our literate culture that talking about books is fairly common, but talking about how we talk about books is not. This occurs in part because we ourselves live *after the book.* We did not have to invent this object, this relationship, this interface, this technology. Rather, we are enculturated into a coexistence with books. We don't have to give an account of the mechanics of books for them to work; we are simply expected to learn to use them. If someone were to stop us on the street and demand we tell them how a book works, we might just *point them to a book.* "Look, here," we would say, as we show them the object, inviting them into a certain way of paying attention. "This is a book."

In this sense, if we stop and explain what a book *is,* we are doing it wrong. If we pause to step outside the enculturation of literacy to ask what or *why* or *how,* we risk being taken as foolish or *illiterate.* In a land of readers, everybody already knows what a book is, and there is no need to question further or more fully. After all, you're reading one right now.

I wish to understand books, so I turn physically to the examples in front of me and start there. I literally step away from the place

I am typing these words and I walk over to the bookshelf. First, I pull out Christopher Alexander's *A Pattern Language,* and then Frederic Jameson's *Postmodernism.* I choose these two books in part because they are at eye level on the particular shelf here in the room. More than this, I reach for them because something in their size and coloration appeals to my eye. Further, with Jameson's book in particular, I recall the enjoyment I felt upon discovering it and reading it for the first time a quarter century ago. Both the volumes have a pleasant weight to them; they feel substantial in my hands. I flip through them both—catch glimpses of phrases and illustrations. I return them both to the shelf. I notice that between them are other volumes I did not pick: Langdon Gilkey's *Naming the Whirlwind* and Karl Barth's *Theology and the Church.* I find myself wondering for a moment why my hand was drawn to the one pair, but not the other.

Let's begin here. A book is *sensory.* My interaction with these volumes on my shelf reminds me in myriad ways that I have a body. It is in particular a sensing body that comprehends shape, colors, and weight. It is a body that navigates the present with the aid of a set of stories I tell myself. I call this story the memories from my past, and in that story, the one who owns those memories is the person I call "me." I also navigate the present with a story that I call "my future." In this present, I feel desire and intention with regard to these volumes, in part based upon my knowledge of them—but that desire and intention are also strangely distinct from the volumes themselves. All I have done so far is to touch and scan these four books—to consider them, for this moment at least, as present at hand.

Let's think together about what it means to say *a book is an object.* Let's consider these four books as merely physical things. This is the approach taken by Keith Houston in his masterful book about books, *The Book: A Cover-to-Cover Ex-*

ploration of the Most Powerful Object of Our Time. There he tells his readers his study of books "is about the corporeal ones . . . the unrepentantly analog contraptions of paper, ink, cardboard, and glue that we have lived with and depended on for so long. It is about books that have mass and odor, that fall into your hands when you ease them out of a bookcase and that make a *thump* when you put them down."[3] Houston's physical starting point, for the moment at least, is ours.

So let us look at these four books first in their corporeal state, as objects in a physical world we share. Each of them has mass and inertia. I reach again for *A Pattern Language*. It's heavy. If I threw it, it would do some damage. I could also use it as a doorstop. I imagine it would be expensive to ship. I recall that in the past I have paid money over the course of several months to store this particular book (along with many others) in a different location than the house where I live. If I placed it in the hearth and set a match to it, I could burn it. In short, I understand that *A Pattern Language* participates in these and any number of other activities that we do in a world with physical objects.

Now let's take a step back and consider the physical materials that go into the construction and manufacture of a book: wood, flax, metal, carbon black, water, oil. To borrow the language of Russell McCutcheon, a book does not come to us sui generis.[4] A book is *manufactured*. The raw materials are put through some form of process or collection or refinement in preparation for use in the construction of a book. A book therefore is never an object that simply *occurs*. There is no book to be found without a number of social relationships always already preceding it—even if those particular relations are at present hidden from me. We must not assume a book to be natural. A book is always maintained. A book can be physical, but a book is never *exclusively* physical. Rather, when we speak of a book, we discover that it may involve itself with the physical and the sensory but is not bounded or encompassed by them. Therefore, when we speak of a book as an object, we actually mean that in a primary way, that a book is an irreducibly *social* object.

A social object will always emerge from a layered set of relationships, and there is no prior essence of the object to be discovered lurking behind those relationships. The prior components of a given physical book (such as wood, water, oil, and other natural objects) *occur,* and although in their occurrence they might be gathered, transformed, and arranged, these actions will always be managed according to various social relationships. The social object is not reducible to these elements, nor is it some essence that can be abstracted from their assemblage. Rather, there is an *intra-action* of these component parts that is anchored in the social. In this manner we can think of a social object as something that results from other objects that have been maintained for use in a social way.

We only ever come to possess a book by means of a chain of prior relationships; this is clear. But additionally, a book itself can exist only because of the provenance of previous relationships that have maintained certain objects and put them to use. Thus we can say that what a book *is* consists of this relational maintenance. As a fundamentally social object, a book *results* from relationships, and no book can exist apart from prior relationships. A book is irreducibly social.

Another way of saying this is that a book is an *indexical.* The meaning of a given book arises out of the context and the act of reading, and this indexical condition is demonstrated every time a reading takes place. The term "indexical" is borrowed from semiotics and linguistics, where indexicals are signs that refer outward to the direct context in which they occur.

For example, the semiotician can look at two signs that both read "Caution: Falling Ice" and suggest that each could have a different set of referents in the respective physical context in which it occurs. The two signs indicate differing concerns about where to look, and about what might constitute a danger in their given semantics and fields and physical environments. That is to say, there is no general case to be made for the sign "Caution: Falling Ice" in terms of an abstract meaning. In a similar fashion, for the linguist, words like "here" and "now" are indexicals, because they are deployed in such a way that their meanings are always context dependent. There is no abstracted *here* and no abstracted *now.* These words always participate in meaning-making with (and within) their context.

I am asserting a similar condition for any book. A book is indexical because it depends on conditions *external to the book* to function in the negotiated production of meanings. Take, for example, a book written in English. For this particular book to participate in a structure of possible meanings, we must assume that a reader or set of readers exists, first of all, who comprehend written English. Further, we must assume that conditions exist such that these readers would be interested in reading the book, and that the readers would exist in arrangements where the book would be available to them to read. All of these conditions are demonstrable *ad extra* to any book we might encounter, and yet we can readily understand that no book can be meaningful apart from these conditions of accompaniment. Furthermore, because of the indexical nature of the relations, all of these possible combinations will exist differently in differing contexts, and cannot be abstracted to some general case.

Again, a book is not a jar for meaning, nor is a book a black box that conveys meaning through telepathy. A book is not a stage-magic prop that produces effects without explanation. A book participates in meaning-making through readily demonstrable social and mechanical processes: You obtain the book. You open the book. You read the book according to the conventions of your given reading culture (though these do vary). At its core, for an object we call a book to participate in meaning-making, it must be read and interpreted by a specific reader at a specific time and in a specific place. Through such negotiations, both the book and the reader are changed.

Not all social relationships are the same, of course. We are shaped by both ideologies and localities, offering our imaginations both limitations and opportunities. So we can say that in our present context, when we encounter books as social objects, they will be objects that result from (and reproduce) these late-capitalist sets of relations. For those of us living in late capitalism, a book is an object *maintained in a certain way* within the boundaries of what Mark Fisher calls capitalist realism—the widespread sense that not only is capitalism the only viable political and economic system, but also that it is now impossible even to *imagine* a coherent alternative to it."[5] It is what Jonathan Beecher Field has characterized as "an ideology of unswerving loyalty to the logic of the market."[6] We can also encounter books that were produced and have existed outside our current sets of relations (e.g., produced and maintained within feudalism, mercantilism, Fordism, etc.). So we can be shown a hand-bound incunabular volume with vellum pages and be able to understand that this, also, is a book. However, even in its familiarity, it will also display to us alien qualities that can be examined, and these qualities will show that this object we are also calling a book is of its own time, and not of ours. A measure of translation will always be involved in speaking the words "This is a book."

Furthermore, in whatever manner we encounter these (alien) books, we encounter them from *within* the relations we have at present, and which at present *have us.* This is to say we are constrained. We think about the objects we recognize as "books from another time" through our understanding of "books at present," as objects maintained for use within capitalist realism. As biblical scholar Richard Horsley puts it, we form our concepts and make assumptions about our books from a location that is "deeply embedded in the assumptions of modern print culture."[7] We are biased to look at old books, and even ancient books, *as if* they were modern books, maintained for contemporary use.

These "assumptions of modern print culture" mean that when we speak of a book as a *social object,* we really and mostly mean that a book is a *commercial object.* This is to say, the social relationships that result in a book being maintained and used have a fundamental location as market relations. Within the present boundary of capitalist realism, an object we call a book will be maintained and used as part of a chain of relationships defined as a marketplace. Resources are diverted, maintained, and used through markets to make a book, and in turn, a book is produced to be an object to be diverted, maintained, and offered for sale in markets. Thus a given book's success *as a book* will be measured by its having been traded. Moreover, the very existence of a book (in terms of physicalities such as reprintings, warehousing, and eventual destruction) is governed in large part by market metrics, rather than by other forms of social evaluation.

A given book may be recognized as displaying great moral or literary value, but if it fails to be purchased, it is more likely to be remaindered (sold at deep discount), and the remainders of that printing are more likely to eventually be pulped. Meanwhile, a book that is recognized to be of lesser or even negligible literary or moral quality can expect not only to be maintained in stock but to enjoy multiple reprintings as long as it demonstrates consistent salability in the marketplace. The markets in which these phenomena occur can have varying characteristics. In some cases, the question might be whether or not a given book has been bought in sufficient quantities in a primary retail market. Or, in the case of a library, the maintenance of a given book will be a matter of whether or not it is in demand and circulating often among patrons. As social relations, these metrics are largely measures of a class of economic relations, or they are modeled primarily on such relations.

Note that these metrics are not deployed to measure whether a given book *has been read* (a social relationship we might understandably, but mistakenly, take to be primary), but rather whether the book *has been sold.* The books we encounter in our various social arrangements under capitalist realism are subject to what Mark Fisher called a *business ontology;* that is, they are all artifacts of the direct and indirect influences of markets, and these markets offer the limits and horizon of what an object such as a book *can be.*[8] Within these market paradigms, a small number of books become bestsellers, while the majority become instead remaindered or resold or swapped, with each new transaction serving as a derivative form of that primary social provenance.

These social forces that shape a book as a commercial object are political arrangements that shape all aspects of that book, in terms of physical form (e.g., hardcover, softcover, audio book, portable document format, etc.) as well as its content and reception. Here, *content* can include the text and the display, any graphic elements and illustrations, and paratext. Here, *text* denotes the body of continuous reading material, and *display* denotes the various enlarged elements of type, such as titles and drop-caps, that are placed around and among the running text. *Graphics and illustrations* are, as the terms indicate, the nonverbal and nonlexical visual elements that are placed amid the running text. Finally, the concept of *paratext* was first introduced by Gérard Genette as a way of accounting for all the additional text (such as footnotes and nonauthor prefaces), as well as the editorial actions that occur surrounding a running text.[9] Each of these italicized terms, it should be noted, functions within conventional practices of printing and bookcraft that have arisen over time.

It is possible to imagine other arrangements of structure and content that might arise, and indeed we can demonstrate a number of other forms of books that have been shaped by histories, geographic circumstances, and social pressures. Nevertheless, these are the terms for book structures that are most prevalent for us under the current "assumptions of modern print culture" where, as noted above, the prevailing ideology is Fisher's business ontology. Market expectations shape content via conventions such as total word counts and the possibility (or exclusion) of editorial apparatuses such as footnotes or indexes. Even the visual size of the printed words on the page is governed by the expected primary audience(s) in the marketplace.

For those who produce the varieties of books we consume in our present age of late capitalism, these social expectations are determined through a series of imaginative and metric exercises. Potential audiences are surveyed (directly and, increasingly, indirectly), and their demographic and geographic particularities are catalogued, mapped, and analyzed. Algorithms are created. Income level (and therefore purchasing power) is imaginatively identified and stratified. From this wellspring of data, book publishers turn to consultants, as well as to in-house and external publicists. These marketing specialists will create a series of imaginative avatars—a model set of idealized customers with catchy names like Helen Homemaker, Bill Breadwinner, and Sally Singleparent—that will embody a set of idealized social relations that map the most lucrative possible audiences for a given book.

If a reader has never thought about the social relationships that precede the object in their hands that we call a book, it might be of use to slow down for a moment and name some of them. To do this I draw from the main chapter headings of the table of contents of *Book Publishing: The Basic Introduction* by John P. Dessauer. In Dessauer's descriptions, we are told not only *How Books Are Created,* but also *How Books Are Manufactured.* In both of these chapters, Dessauer outlines chains of political arrangements that have less to do with the mind and experience of an author per se, and much more to do with the internal organizational charts of a contemporary publishing house. Dessauer's chapters go on to describe *How Books Are Marketed.* This is itself an extended process of multileveled social relationships that include not only wholesalers, distributors, and retailers, but also reviewers, elementary and secondary school teachers, and librarians. In the chapter on *How Books Are Stored and Delivered,* we then learn about the many political arrangements that subtend the creation, warehousing, transportation, and distribution of any object we call a book. Finally, Dessauer discusses in general detail *How Publishers Finance, Plan, and Manage* the books they produce. As you can see, within the overall structure of a business ontology, these myriad relationships create webs of interactions, such that an object we call a book is connected, visibly and invisibly, to so many other people beyond what we might at first imagine to be the simple roles of the "author" and the "reader." For a book to *be,* it must always already be social, indexical, *political.*

So, under current conditions, an object we call a book is very carefully measured and measurable as a market object. Beyond those metrics, however, this object is somewhat more difficult to define. Yet it seems fairly easy to demonstrate that a book is known and comprehended in a variety of locations and cultures. You and I are demonstrating right here and now, with this book here between us, that we both understand what a book is. Moreover, regardless of how you are interacting with my words at this particular moment of contact (ink on paper, pixels on screen, sound vibrations in air), at the end of that interaction I can ask you, "Did you enjoy my book?" and you would know what I mean. We can both understand a book as something positive, between us, even as a positive definition continues to elude us. That's not telepathy (in King's sense), nor is it mind control—you don't have to *know* what I mean for this interaction to yield meanings, and in the end the misunderstandings might be as interesting as the understandings, or even more so. As we both lean in to the *social* aspect of books as social objects, drawing upon the overlaps we share in this locality, this ideology, this context, we continue to recognize the *bookness* of the moment, the bookishness of the intra-action.

Let's take a moment to unpack that phrase, *the bookishness of the intra-action,* and why it is distinct from something like King's book-as-telepathy or a process of hierarchical mind control governed by the intentions of the author. This term *intra-action,* which I have been using throughout this chapter, comes from philosopher of science Karen Barad. In this neologism, an intra-action yields effects without prior isolated causes, or even effects that cause their causes. An intra-action denotes a mechanism that yields copies without the need for originals. As Barad notes in a 2011 article,

> what we commonly take to be individual entities are not separate determinately bounded and propertied objects, but rather are (entangled "parts of") phenomena . . . The notion of *intra-action* (in contrast to

> the usual "interaction," which presumes the prior existence of independent entities/relata) marks an important shift, reopening and refiguring foundational notions of classical ontology such as causality, agency, space, time, matter, discourse, responsibility, and accountability. . . . Intra-actions cut things together-apart (in one movement).[10]

I want to follow Barad and suggest that the object we call a book is always already constituted as a space of *intra-action.* When we look at an object and ask, "Could this be a book?" we are always already constituted by these intra-actions. As *possible* readers, we approach *possible* objects and bid them to intra-act with/without us into their bookness. As political arrangements, these states of intra-action are irreducible to stable essences, one apart from another, existing prior to being "cut . . . together-apart." Never a book without the possibility of a reader, never a reader without the possibility of a book. When we try to separate this intra-active entanglement, to chase toward a starting point, an origin, an essence, we find we are chasing our own language, our own selves. The separation of reader and book is possible only *after* an intra-action. There is/was simply nothing behind the intra-action, or prior to it. No intention, no meaning, no essence will bind or restrict the *sheer possibility* of book and reader, together, irreducibly.

I am reminded of a meme I once saw: a picture of a disgruntled driver, scowling while surrounded by a sea of cars on the freeway. The caption reads, "You're not stuck in traffic. You *are* traffic." This is the dynamic we are observing here with an object we call a book and the person we call a reader. It can seem like driver and traffic, book and reader, are somehow separate, but this is an illusion. They are separable only *after* their intra-actions, both the result of institutions, technologies, and political arrangements that make them inseparable and irreducible *prior* to their intra-actions. One giving rise to the other, constantly in intra-action, and no possibility of the one existing without the other, irreducibly.

The matters get more complex, of course, when we move from considering a contemporary book like this one shared between you and me (written, reproduced, distributed, and consumed all in a very advanced and highly developed stage of literate/print culture) and consider a book that we have denoted to be *a bible.* In that case, a book we call a bible is not just navigating the locality, ideology, and context of this late stage of print culture, but indeed it also has connections and relations to all previous stages of print culture(s)—the industrial, the colonial, the medieval, the incunabular (the period of transition from handwritten to mechanically printed texts), all the way back to manuscripts, scrolls, and tablets, and even (according to some) back to the stories passed by word of mouth, long before they were written in any form.

So when I say that a bible is a book, I mean that every object we might decide to call a bible is an object that is always already caught up in political arrangements at multiple stages of its existence—and in the case of many bibles, these political arrangements extend well beyond the roughly five hundred years of the modern printing industry, back through the incunabular, scribal, manuscript, and even oral periods of book history. We are inheritors of that complex lineage. Just as someone who drives a car is not required to understand the mechanics and history of the internal combustion engine, we are not required to become experts on all these political arrangements in order to become readers and successfully operate a book. Nevertheless, the genealogy of such political arrangements is there to remind us that an object like a bible is never available to us simply as an uncomplicated given, and any time we find ourselves falling into a reflexive simplicity about the object in our hands, someone may be in danger. That is to say, we ignore the effects of these political arrangements at our peril, or at the peril of others more vulnerable than we.

As we resist thinking of a book as only one particular sort of object or only one particular sort of political arrangement, we understand that an object we call a bible is not simply a codex, nor is a bible only a scroll. Further, a bible is not merely an idea in the mind of an author being deposited via telepathy or mind control into the mind of a reader. Because a bible is a book, a bible is not reducible to a single *meaning,* or an *intention,* or any abstraction. A bible is a book *indexically,* so it is always a set of interpretations taking place in a particular political arrangement. A given bible in a given place and time might attenuate some of these factors, or all of them, or none of them. As a book, an object we call a bible is always irreducibly an *intra-action.*

It is in this context that I turn finally to remarks made by New Testament scholar Bart Ehrman, who invites us to consider what it means to say a bible is a book:

> The question [in this case] is not whether miracles could happen or whether God could be behind the Bible or God has revealed his truth to his people. The issue is *how do we approach this book* that was written at a certain time or a bunch of different times, different places by different authors? Do we come up with a special way of interpreting this [book] that is [different from] any other book that we interpret? My view, when I was a Christian, was that . . . God had inspired writers to write books, and that . . . if God inspired writers to write books,

> *then he meant for those books to be interpreted as books.* He didn't provide some other medium for revelation. So if it's in a book, you need to study it *as a book* ... on the assumption that these are books that were written as books and are meant to be interpreted *as books.*[11]

If a bible is a book (and it is), then a bible can and should be interpreted *as a book.* Not as a special or exceptional case, but with the same mechanics and political arrangements available for understanding and meaning-making that accompany any object we call a book. The presence of the object does not cleanse our actions or absolve us of our responsibility for those actions. In the end, *a book is what we do with it,* and nothing more.

In the hands of the Madman in *The Jerk,* a telephone book became a tool of death. We can think of many examples, both on the screen and in the real world, where the objects we call bibles have been used to justify similar violent and destructive ends. When we do harm in the name of the object we call a bible, because the book "told us to," we may imagine ourselves to be among the saints, but we are instead among the sociopaths. The book may set before us death and life, the blessing and the curse, but the choice is only ever ours, the readers', to make. Choose life.

5
Second Thesis
A Bible Is a Platform

If a bible is a book, then any general claim about a bible must begin with the assumption that it functions like all books function, no more and no less. A book is socially produced and cannot be said to contain an essence or a meaning, but rather is always in the process of negotiations of meaning-making. So too a bible is an emergence out of a long chain of social intra-actions, where the object we call a bible and the people we call readers are irreducibly called forth by this entanglement of predication. As long as a bible is a book, it is a social object, and those objects that we name and predicate as bibles invite our active participation in a range of dynamics that include but are not limited to acts of interpretation.

The bookness of a bible allows us to focus on what is usually a very local intra-action: a solitary reader engaging with a single volume. However, if we understand a book not as a natural object, something merely presented by nature for our manipulation, but rather as a social object, then other dimensions are opened up for our analysis. For contemporary readers, a bible is a book (re)produced within certain types of markets, and these markets invite and (re)produce types of relationships and intra-actions that can be examined. This chapter and the next offer two approaches for the material analysis of the objects we call bibles, each of which moves beyond the narrow focus of book and reader. In this chapter, we consider what it means to say that *a bible is a platform.*

But first, a moment of interruption. In this analysis, we are not looking at a platform as an *ontology,* something of fixed state and clear and persevering definition. Rather, we explore the idea of "platform" as a set of sometimes overlapping and sometimes disconnected practices. If pressed, we might say that part of any definition of a platform is the fact that it does not itself offer definitions. Instead, when some arrangement *is acting like* a platform, that platform-like arrangement offers within its bounds certain possibilities for definition. The language here at the outset is a little convoluted, and it cannot be helped. I am attempting to write clearly about something that functions by deferring clarity to a future time. To focus *on* the platform in order to understand what the platform *is* would already indicate that I have misunderstood both what the platform *is* and *is for.* Instead of focusing on the platform, we should be paying attention to the *content* coursing *through* the platform. We are supposed to look at the spoilers and the paint job, and not think so much about the bare chassis below the surface.

A platform is a vague space. It is intentionally ill defined or underdetermined. A platform offers a structure and then invites various participants to fill that structure with content that is explicitly not the platform and not defined by the platform. Those who manage platforms will insist that the platform is not a publisher and that the actions of a platform cannot be editorial. At the same time, in practice, we can observe that a platform standardizes and limits what manner of content can be included, absorbed, and seen by others. Here, following a line of thought that spans from Gilles Deleuze and Félix Guattari through Jasbir Puar, John Phillips, and K. Wayne Yang, we might describe the platform as a space of *agencement,* "a term which means design, layout, organization, arrangement, and relations."[1] I like this term because it evokes (in English) the dual meaning of *agency:* both an individual latitude of unconstrained action and a corporate entity aligned toward specific business purposes. A platform *might* be an *agency* (a corporate body) where *agents* (collective and individual) discover and exercise their *agency;* or a platform might perform a *spectacle* of agency, where verisimilitude collides with an appearance of choice, while all the actual agency resides elsewhere. All of this and more is included in the semantic gesture agencement makes here. Yang pairs the idea of agencement with assemblage, a complex nexus of various objects, systems, and social possibilities. These assemblages are scalable and interlocking; thus a platform might be an assemblage of platforms, or itself a node in a larger platform.

A platform is a space—whether social, material, or political—that *maintains its vagueness over time.* It is a space that resists, or better still, *defers* definition until an explicit choice has been made, or until contents have been offered. Until the moment of choice occurs, until the flush and flow of content exerts its pressure, a platform remains in suspension, offering its structure as a pure form, as a field of opportunities rather than a list of particularities. Once the choice occurs, the vague haze of the platform condenses, concretizing into the particular and the individual. A vague platform can house many local practices that are themselves distinct, concrete, and individualized. In this manner, to the various participants, a platform can feel personally tailored, even as its underlying structures remain generic.[2]

Let's imagine a very simple type of platform: a raised flat wooden deck in a public park or town square. It doesn't have to be very large—think of the proverbial soap box—it just needs to get the speaker slightly above the crowd. The box *platforms* the speaker, but the box or the deck doesn't tell you what kind of speech you will hear. All it does is provide a structure where various speeches can occur, and the speakers themselves contribute the messages and content. This rendering has led some to insist that a platform is not a publisher but rather is a place where people publish; a platform does not act as a broadcaster but rather as a place where people broadcast. However, as we will see, the actual role of the platform (and of those who are invested in the platform) is more complex. True, a platform offers an open surface upon which one can exercise choice, but it also exercises its own forms of control.

Michael Hyatt is the former CEO and chairman of Thomas Nelson Publishers, a major Christian publishing house based in Nashville. As Hyatt was transitioning out of leadership at the company, he wrote a how-to manual for entrepreneurial self-promotion, which he called *Platform: Get Noticed in a Noisy World.* As the title implies, Hyatt's thesis is that everyone is overwhelmed with information coming at them from every direction. If you want to actually reach people with a message (whether for commerce or politics or evangelization), you have to find a mechanism to cut through the noise. "Very simply," Hyatt says, "a platform is the thing you have to stand on to get heard. It's your stage. But unlike a stage in the theater, today's platform is not built of wood or concrete or perched on a grassy hill. Today's platform is built of people. Contacts. Connections. Followers."[3]

Following Hyatt, then, we can explore the idea that a platform emerges when you have a particular set of social and political arrangements. Both a structure made of wood and a structure composed of people and relationships can function as a platform. Yet not every physical structure or social relation ends up being platform-like. We use platforms when we want people to interact in certain ways: to vote, to buy, or to bring forth materials that others might wish to see and engage with. To each of these potential actions and relations, a platform plays the role of matchmaker, midwife, intermediary. Platforms *mediate.*

When Henry Ford's motor company began using assembly-line practices to mass-produce the Model T, the cars that rolled off the line were as similar as possible. The Ford philosophy was to create an exact reproduction of the Model T, as perfectly, quickly, and efficiently as could be done. All the cars were the same color, with all the same parts machined to similar tolerances, and all assembled in the same order. Ford's competitors, however, quickly figured out that they could gain a market advantage by offering buyers some options. Those competitors would trade a bit of efficiency in order to offer their customers a bit of control over the final product. Instead of Ford's one-size-fits-all product, General Motors and other rivals began to offer a platform approach, a basic chassis that allowed for certain modifications during the assembly process. Buyers could specify not only different colors, but an increasing series of customizations that met an increasingly complex set of consumer demands. Years later, this dynamic played out again in the fast-food world, when upstart Burger King challenged the uniformity of the McDonald's hamburger with a platform approach that promised each customer "have it your way."

This is the basic logic of any platform: a balance of uniformity and flexibility. Platforms offer a set of standards upon which modularity and interchangeability can be exercised. Some of these modifications might be built into the product at the time of purchase. For example, when I bought the laptop I'm using to type these sentences, I was able to specify the computer's memory size and processor speed, both of which were added to the standard parts that come with every version of this particular machine. However, a series of after-market modifications can often be made as well. In the case of my laptop, I added a camera that works better than the one that comes standard on my machine. In the case of cars, a driver might choose a different stereo or a higher grade of tires, or might choose to make modifications that affect the performance of the engine. A platform demonstrates the dynamic between social objects and the desires of those who use and interact with those objects. The mediation of these dynamics occurs in our present context through a series of markets. Thus a new social dimension of objects can be demonstrated, where uniform market production is tempered with the increased ability to modify mass-produced objects in order to meet specific cases of use, taste, and desire.

Because it offers certain degrees of freedom, a platform can feel like a curated or expressive space. Within the platform, one might tend one's content like one tends a garden, resulting in a certain voice, a certain character, a certain style. A platform can open a space for the expression of a certain persona, a certain personality, and this expression may shift subtly or be wholly different in the context of a different platform. I may seem like a different person behind the wheel of a Porsche or BMW than I seem to be when driving a Mazda or Yugo. I may feel I am—or *need to be*—a different sort of driver in a Tesla than I do in a Prius. I might feel a dissonance between my ethical obligations to others and to the climate-imperiled world depending on whether my vehicle gets ten or ninety miles to the gallon, or uses no gallons at all. The simple act of moving to a different driver's seat in a different vehicle opens up certain options and eclipses others. I approach the road differently depending on the vehicle I am driving. I *feel* differently about the way I drive; one might even say *I feel my drives differently*, in that I feel dissonant possibilities, expectations, and obligations to self and others, depending on the seat in which I am sitting. This is the expressive power of a platform.

Such expression, however, comes at a price. As an assemblage, performing and (re)producing agencement, a platform is always a locus of *contested* agency. The users of Facebook (to take but one contemporary example) may feel like they have control over their content and their pages, until they wake one day to find that the developers at Meta (the company that owns Facebook) have (re)moved some core functionality or revised their terms of service (again), such that some previously extant bulwark of privacy or intellectual property protections has been rearranged or eliminated. Though the agencement of the platform may conjure feelings of agency, it is unlikely that those who maintain the platform will see participants as agents. Rather, it is much more likely that, from the vantage point of the platform, we are seen instead as *customers* or *employees.*[4] Following an insight from Wendy Brown, we might say that platforms "are much more concerned with free markets than with free people."[5]

Naming economic interest in this manner allows us to explore another dimension of the agencement of platforms. As noted by journalist and technology activist Cory Doctorow, "A platform is a firm that mediates between end users and business customers. Uber's got drivers and riders. Amazon and eBay have sellers and buyers. Google and Facebook have publishers and advertisers, and users on the other side. The platform sits between those two different groups and mediates between them."[6] From this position of mediation, Doctorow argues, platforms function as *gatekeepers* and *rent seekers.* That is, platforms interpose an exploitative and parasitic barrier between the relations of interested parties. The platform intercedes with an offer of convenience, often promising to introduce efficiency, consistency, or an economy of scale into the relationship, while extracting some (most likely unseen or hidden) value for itself. A platform allows those who run the platform to dictate certain limitations to participants, while reserving to themselves any number of liberties. Amazon, for example, controls what can be seen and what prices can be set for products, and takes for itself a portion of the profit on each transaction. Less tangibly, Amazon is joined by nearly every other online platform in mining the personal data of users for repackaging, resale, and profit. Increasingly, users not only provide the content that appears to be the product of the platform, but are themselves the product.

Finally, a platform creates a simulation of social organization. To create an actual community takes negotiation and patience. Communities form out of an abundance of deep interactions and long stretches of time. Participating in a community is an opt-in practice, where you learn (about) yourself by learning about others and learning with others. You have to put in the work. A platform, in contrast, is an opt-out scenario. As Doctorow observes, platforms are easy to join and hard to leave (a scenario he refers to as "high network switching costs"). Becoming part of a community is a slow and organic affair, whereas joining a platform is as simple as being swept into a sales funnel. Rather than being met as your whole self, in a platform you are assumed into a set of algorithmic and simplified identities and obligations that are legible to some larger organization and institution, and there is little or no space for negotiation. In place of a social contract, a platform provides users with its terms of service.

As airports go, the one in Charlottesville, Virginia, is a tiny one. But despite its small size, it has a pretty remarkable gift shop.

In addition to the standard fare of snack foods and sodas, the shop is stocked with local confections, regional wines, University of Virginia merchandise, and a mixture of historical memorabilia focusing on Thomas Jefferson, the third president of the United States.

Jefferson's final resting place is about a half-hour's drive from the airport. He is buried at Monticello, his Virginia plantation home. In addition to the plantation's buildings, Jefferson also designed the stone monument that marks his grave. On the marker, he chose to place the following words:

Here was buried
Thomas Jefferson
Author of the Declaration of American Independence
of the Statute of Virginia for religious freedom
& Father of the University of Virginia

The three items noted in the epitaph point to a certain thread that connects Jefferson's views on politics, philosophy, faith, and revolution. The Declaration of Independence proceeded from the assumption that his fellow citizens in the American colonies could rightly govern themselves. The Statute for Religious Freedom similarly proceeded from the assumption that every citizen would have their own opinion on matters of religion, and that the shared public sphere had enough capacity to accommodate them all, without rancor or need of violence. Finally, Jefferson's role in the founding of the university proceeded from the assumption that these civic virtues could be taught, and that future generations might grow to benefit as a result.

Jefferson's self-assessment makes for a compelling argument, to be sure. Of his many writings, we can understand why he chose the Declaration and the Statute to mark his legacy.

However, another curious document for which Jefferson was responsible deserves our attention here. While it was not penned by him, it is indeed the work and product of his hands, and also gives us insight into his core tenets regarding politics, philosophy, faith, and revolution.

This curious artifact is called *The Life and Morals of Jesus of Nazareth,* also known popularly as the Jefferson Bible. I first encountered it a little over a decade ago, in that airport gift shop. The book is tiny—almost pocket-size—with a pen-and-ink rendering of Jefferson's face on the cover. It's an intriguing little book. In fact, next to the Declaration of Independence, and despite his own notions to the contrary, *The Life and Morals of Jesus of Nazareth* might well be the most intriguing piece of writing Thomas Jefferson ever had a part in creating.

In their respective ways, both the Declaration and *Life and Morals* are thoroughly Jeffersonian documents. Both reflect the Enlightenment values that Jefferson championed, and both seem to share a spirit that continues to animate the discourse of American politics—one that seeks to include religious sentiments while simultaneously containing their wilder excesses. Certainly the direct effects of the Declaration are more clearly evident in our day-to-day lives, yet the themes and assumptions that helped shape *Life and Morals* cut to the heart of the Jeffersonian ideal we now refer to as the wall of separation between church and state.

The construction of *Life and Morals* was a twenty-year project, undertaken in Jefferson's limited spare time. His goal was to eliminate from Christianity all the vestiges of miracle and metaphysics, which he termed "ignorance . . . absurdity . . . untruth, charlatanism, and imposture," that in his view had accumulated over the centuries of telling and retelling the story of Christ.[7] This elimination was accomplished by literally cutting those vestiges out with a razor blade.

Using several copies of bibles, Jefferson sliced sections from each page of the Gospels and reassembled the remainder into a new, sleek narrative that begins with Jesus's birth (as a very human child to a very human Joseph and Mary) and concludes with Jesus's burial. "There they laid Jesus, and rolled a great stone to the sepulchre, and departed."[8] The end. Every trace of miracle and metaphysics has been eliminated. No walking on water. No healings. No encounters with demons. No proclamations of angels. No resurrection. "I have made a wee little book," Jefferson wrote to his friend Charles Thompson in 1816, "by cutting the texts out of the [New Testament] and arranging them on the pages of a blank book, in certain order of time and subject. A more beautiful or precious morsel of ethics I have never seen."[9]

The resulting "precious morsel" is a much slimmer volume than a standard collection of the four Gospels. Jefferson sought to give the reader the means to grasp Jesus as an exemplar of "the most sublime and benevolent code of morals which has ever been offered to man."[10] His was certainly not the first, nor will it be the last, to offer a revision of the Gospel writings. What Jefferson may have lacked in originality, however, he more than made up for in confidence. "There has certainly never been a shortage of boldness in the history of biblical scholarship during the last two centuries," writes historian Jaroslav Pelikan, "but for sheer audacity Thomas Jefferson's two redactions of the Gospels stand out even in that company . . . He was apparently quite sure that he could tell what was genuine and what was not in the transmitted text of the New Testament."[11]

In the end, Pelikan tells us, Jefferson "carved out a Gospel *for himself*, one whose witness he could respect and whose message he could understand."[12] Jefferson's boldness to "[carve] out a Gospel" in this manner makes clear that he likely did not view the pages in his hands as some inviolable or thematic whole.

Rather, he seemed to treat them as raw material to be ripped, rearranged, and even discarded, as his desires and ethics dictated.

Platforms allow for this kind of powerful flexibility. For example, only one small portion of the AR-15 military rifle—consisting of the handgrip, the trigger, and the chassis containing the firing mechanism where a serial number is stamped, collectively referred to as the "lower receiver"—is actually classed as a firearm from a legal standpoint. All the other aspects of the rifle, from the barrel to the sights to the shoulder stock, are technically not part of the gun. Instead (again, from a legal standpoint) they are considered components. The AR-15 is a modular platform that is built up from the lower receiver, with all other aspects being interchangeable. As journalist John Stokes puts it, "the AR-15 has evolved into an open, modular gun platform that's *infinitely hackable* and *accessorizable.* With only a few simple tools and no gunsmithing expertise, an AR-15 can be heavily modified, or even assembled from scratch, from widely available parts to suit the fancy and fantasy of each individual user."[13] This is a very important point: Platforms *encourage* rearrangement. When Stokes mentions *hacking* and *accessorization,* he's pointing us to a *modular* mindset, not a static one. The platform does not point us to an *essence,* but to a continued *engagement* with the object-as-assemblage. By participating in a marketplace of options, first as consumers, then as hackers, we exercise our agencement both *with* the platform and *through* the platform.

Now clearly, a bible is not a car or a rifle. Nevertheless, we see in Jefferson's example an embrace of this hacker ethos. He did not consider the text to be inviolable, or perhaps we could say it did not occur to him that his rearrangements could be considered a violation. In fact, according to Pelikan, one of the chief motivations of Jefferson's efforts to cut down and reform the Gospels was the desire to *improve* the text. Pelikan notes that Jefferson's aim was to eradicate all Pauline influences, which he saw as obscuring the true ethical message of Jesus. "Like other Enlightenment rationalists," Pelikan notes, "Jefferson was convinced that the real villain in the Christian story was the apostle Paul, who had corrupted the religion of Jesus into a religion about Jesus, which thus had, in combination with the otherworldly outlook of the Fourth Gospel, produced the monstrosities of dogma, superstition, and priestcraft, which were the essence of Christian orthodoxy."[14] For Jefferson and for those who thought as he did, orthodoxy was the *problem.* So he treated the Pauline elements, as well as other supernatural markers, as modular. They could be removed from the platform, and a more useful core would remain. Exercising his own agencement, Jefferson hacked his way to a solution.

Among biblical scholars the term for this process of cutting, pasting, and rearranging parts of a text to create new versions is called redaction. The contemporary interpretive practices known as redaction criticism and canonical criticism both attempt to account for the effects that centuries of editing and reassembly of texts have had on biblical versions, interpretations, liturgies, and theologies. The work of redaction and canonical criticism begins with the assumption that the form of the texts we have today does not reflect the earlier or earliest versions of those texts. From this assumption, it follows that the texts have been disassembled, recombined in new arrangements, and combined with other texts to reach the form we see in our present day. In other words, for the redaction or canonical critic, every bible we have is the result of processes not at all dissimilar to those of Jefferson and his razor and glue pot.

As Lee Martin McDonald has observed, this "relatively new [critical] approach . . . asks, in part, *which* form of the biblical literature is authoritative for the Church today. Should the Church accept as its inspired and authoritative literature the earliest form of the writing, or the later, redacted form, which we presently possess? In other words, is the Church's authoritative text the earliest form of a document or the final redacted form of it, which was passed on and developed in the Church?"[15] I understand the substance of this question, but I think it still relies too much on an assumption that an object we call a bible has a certain kind of *essence,* and that we know something *is* a bible by that essence, rather than by other factors.

This is why thinking of a bible as a kind of platform can be a useful and powerful aid to our understanding. Again, to go with our automobile analogy: When we look at two GMC Sierra pickup trucks, one straight off the assembly line and one with an after-market "lift kit" and oversized tires, we don't ask which is the *real* truck. Instead, we understand that the basic Sierra platform has been expressed in two different ways. Neither truck is more real than the other. In a similar fashion, thinking of a bible as a platform encourages us to avoid asking which object is the "real" bible and to focus instead on how and to what ends this object is being *used.*

When we adopt this platform mindset for our understanding of the objects we call bibles, we open ourselves to deeper and more imaginative connections to the communities that have engaged with, used, and shaped bibles throughout the past three millennia. For the objects we call Hebrew Bibles or Tanakhs, we see evidence of redactions as early as the eighth century BCE.[16] For the writings we now call the New Testament, and the various objects we now call Christian bibles, we see clear evidence that the process of redaction began in the earliest days of the Christian movement. Early practitioners and interpreters debated the inclusion or exclusion of the numerous letters, scrolls, and writings referring to Jesus that proliferated in the generations following his ministry and teachings.

There are many, many more of these writings than there are books in the New Testament, and those that were included in the text form what is called the *canon* of scripture, though exactly what this term "canon" indicates is a matter of ongoing discussion in biblical scholarship. To give a brief example, readers of the King James Version's rendering of 2 Timothy 3:16, "All scripture is given by inspiration of God, and is profitable for doctrine, for reproof, for correction, for instruction in righteousness," may feel reasonably certain that the "all scripture" in the passage refers simply to the writings contained between the two covers of the book they are holding. The readers, unlike their ancient forebears, do not have to grapple with the questions that frame what McDonald and others have referred to as the canon debate. In fact, McDonald argues, "the best available information about the earliest followers of Jesus shows that *they did not have such canons* as the church presently possesses today, nor did they indicate that their successors should draw them up."[17] Between the first communities of Christian believers and the readers of the present day stands a largely invisible history that results in this text from 2 Timothy being included in the Bible, while texts like the Shepherd of Hermas and the Letter of Barnabas are not.

Perhaps you have never heard of the Shepherd of Hermas. And even if you had heard the name, you might be hard-pressed to say what the book contains or what subjects it addresses. Because of the processes of canonization, and the results of those processes that we have inherited as readers, many of the writings that were contemporaneous with the various collections of texts that are currently referred to as the New Testament have, for all practical purposes, simply disappeared. Scholars are aware of them, certainly, but the everyday reader is not.

Much like the process that formed the Jefferson Bible, the formation of the canon of scriptures was, to a great extent, a process of cutting out texts that did not "fit" theologically. Communities and redactors continually exercised their own agencement, seeking to fit and refit canons of differing texts onto the platform, creating iteration after iteration of objects that they thought of, and increasingly referred to, as bibles.

Of course, what Jefferson did in taking a razor to the pages will seem to many readers less like an after-market upgrade and more like an act of sabotage. It is easy to look at the finished product and say with finality that whatever resulted from the application of Jefferson's razor, it is no longer an object we should call a bible. Yet at the same time, we, like Jefferson, yearn for a bible "whose message [*we*] could understand." In practice, we reject what Swiss theologian Karl Barth referred to as the "strange new world" that might confront us in the object we call a bible, in favor of a message that confirms our assumptions, our norms, and our comforts.[18] We often wish for a bible that might change *other* people's worlds, but not ours. We want a bible that will turn someone else's world upside down, leaving us affirmed, intact, and upright.

For a bible publisher it is always a delicate balance to strike between remaining responsible to the latest findings of textual scholarship and to the traditions and expectations of readers. As biblical scholarship continues from generation to generation, not only are new manuscripts unearthed, but old manuscripts' importance, veracity, and necessity are reconsidered. As a result, both across versions of bibles and also within various editions of the same version, a careful reader will find an ever-shifting assortment of these textual fluctuations. Unexpected words may be added, and it is just as likely that long-familiar phrases may slip from sight. The development of a "critical edition" of a biblical text from manuscript evidence is an exercise in cutting and pasting par excellence. It can be readily demonstrated that the scholars assembling these objects we call bibles, and the publishers who produce and distribute them, both exercise their agencement at key steps of the redaction, editing, and publishing processes, and treat these various elements as modular. All these individuals have excellent explanations for why they pull out one module and insert another, but at the core of the process the simple observation remains: A bible is not a solid essence of eternal and unchanged parts; to scholars and publishers alike, a bible is a platform.

A recent example of this phenomenon was documented in Peter J. Thuesen's account of the controversies surrounding the publication and subsequent emendations of the Revised Standard Version (RSV) in his book *In Discordance with the Scriptures.* In the chapter "The Great RSV Controversy," Thuesen recounts the outpouring of denunciation and suspicion that came from many quarters of American Christianity in the wake of the RSV's mid-twentieth-century publication and release. Detractors' hackles were raised over both the matter of copyright and fears of communist infiltration into the translation process.[19] The real lightning rod though, was the translation committee's decision—following the best scholarship and manuscript evidence available at the time—to make adjustments to the conventional rendering of the text of Isaiah 7:14.

The language of that passage was and is deeply familiar in the English-speaking world. "Behold, a virgin shall conceive and bear a Son," as it reads in the King James Version. In contrast, the words of the passage were rendered alien and incomprehensible to many readers of the RSV. There, instead of the expected "virgin," a "young woman" would conceive and bear the son: "Therefore the LORD himself will give you a sign. Look, the young woman is with child and shall bear a son, and shall name him Immanuel."

What was at stake, as Thuesen points out, was not merely the text's linguistic accuracy, but the very theological edifice built up to help support the claim of Christ's miraculous birth.[20] The response, from across the spectrum of evangelical and fundamentalist Christians, was swift and unilateral: Whatever this object was, the RSV was *not* to be considered a Holy Bible. It could only be an unholy one—a deceptive, satanic ruse deployed to confuse and distract Christians.[21] In the wake of the controversy, many Christian communities have championed other bible versions, whether centering themselves around the previously available King James Version or rallying behind alternate contemporary versions, such as the New International and English Standard Versions. Each of these has rendered Isaiah 7:14 with the more traditional "virgin" instead of the RSV's "young woman."

Thuesen describes in detail the reaction of one particular North Carolina pastor, Luther Hux, who went on the offensive against the RSV soon after the controversy erupted, publishing tracts and staging public protests against it. In a double-edged act that brings to mind Jefferson and his razor, Hux's first tract, *Modernism's Unholy Bible,* accused the translators of taking a penknife to God's Word. Hux's own subsequent reaction was to publicly rip the page containing Isaiah 7:14 from a copy of the RSV and burn it, proclaiming it to be "a fraud."[22] In other words, Hux's reaction to his perception that a bible had been "knifed" was to take a slice out of it himself.

Harry Rubenstein and Barbara Clark Smith write in their introduction to the Smithsonian Institution's facsimile of the Jefferson Bible, "we gain insight into just what teachings Jefferson prized from the four Gospels."[23] He took a razor to the text and excised the portions of supernatural narrative he found objectionable, leaving behind, according to Rubenstein and

Smith, what Jefferson considered to be the core of Christ's principal teachings about morality. Rubenstein and Smith go on to note that "Jefferson's library included volumes of moral teaching from classical philosophers, recent works by European thinkers, and multiple editions of the Bible. Yet *The Life and Morals of Jesus* may often have been his choice for such readings."[24]

I note Rubenstein and Clark's observations to emphasize that by all accounts, Jefferson undertook the task of revising and compiling *Life and Morals* as a *morally serious* endeavor. For more than a decade and a half—from 1803 to 1820—the project drew his continued attention, especially during the years of his postpresidential retirement. Jefferson clearly wished to know how to live a moral life, and he turned to the examples of Jesus Christ with painstaking attention in order to learn how to do so.

Along with these attestations of Jefferson's preoccupation with questions of biblical morality, let us not overlook the fact that during the period he was compiling *The Life and Morals of Jesus Christ,* Jefferson also owned some six hundred human beings as property. This fact is not mentioned in the essay by Rubenstein and Clark, though to me it seems to offer a significant context to the document in question. There is also no mention that, during this same period in which he was compiling *Life and Morals,* Jefferson had an ongoing sexual relationship of questionable consent with at least one enslaved woman, Sally Hemings, impregnating her multiple times.[25] Jefferson did not acknowledge his progeny with Hemings as his children, but rather viewed them as his property.

Jefferson did not simply cut out the supernatural portions of the text; his agencement allowed him latitude to read his own interests back into the object we now call the Jefferson Bible. The former president was certainly not alone in his capacity to read biblical texts with earnest seriousness in one moment and act with callous violence toward his neighbors in the next. Theologian Kelly Brown Douglas and others have referred to this habit as slaveholder Christianity, in which "a number of slaveholders found a way to participate in the business of slavery without denouncing their Christian faith."[26] We might just as easily call it empire Christianity, or colonial Christianity, or genocidal Christianity, for the root logic remains the same: An object we call a bible becomes an accessory to violent deeds, and violent deeds are accessorized by imagery and language borrowed from objects we call bibles. The slaveholders, Jefferson among them, saw no obstacle in the text. With the object they called a bible as the mediator of their violent desires, they could truly "have it their way."

I am strongly sympathetic with the projects of Douglas and other theologians in the liberation tradition who seek to examine these eruptions of violence within Christian communities and to empower sites of resistance to this violence. However, I disagree with their analysis, generally speaking, at one key point. The critics of slaveholder Christianity will often locate the distinction between slaveholder religious practice and liberator religious practice at the level of *interpretation.* So, for example, Kelly Brown Douglas notes that "slaveholding Christianity fostered a certain selectivity in interpreting the biblical message, so too did slave [liberationist] Christianity. Slaveholding Christianity avoided the Gospels [and] valued the epistles because of their emphasis . . . on obedience."[27] My hesitancy here is not in Douglas, whose work is meticulous. Rather, my fear is that some readers might come away from the work of Douglas and her liberationist colleagues with the conviction that the task ahead is simply to encourage the slaveholder to *read better.*

This, of course, is not the argument I find in Douglas, who is, rather, pointing to the historical data that both slaveholders and slaves were actively creating iterative communities of practice, as well as to the fact that the selective readings of certain portions of the objects they called bibles, and the suppression of others, was central to those iterative practices. As we analyze the materiality of those iterative practices—that is to say, as we look at the deeds they engender—it becomes more obvious why *better reading* will not save us. Well before we come to the act of interpretation, we have already become entangled in the agencement of the platform. That is, I might already be someone's customer, or someone's employee. I may feel like I'm the one in charge, but platforms can be deceptive.

In 2019 I had the chance to visit the Museum of the Bible in Washington, DC. I was there to see an exhibit titled *The Slave Bible: Let the Story Be Told.* The objects on display were books that had been printed in London in 1807 on behalf of the Society for the Conversion of Negro Slaves. The website for the exhibit notes that these books became known as "Slave Bibles" and that the "publishers deliberately removed portions of the biblical text, such as the exodus story, that could inspire hope for liberation. Instead, the publishers emphasized portions that justified and fortified the system of slavery that was so vital to the British Empire."[28]

In other words, part of the iterative practices of slaveholding did not involve simply *reading differently.* Rather, like Jefferson before them, these latter-day slaveholders took razors to the text, reshaping it in the image of their own violent desires. It is not a matter of reading the same object we call a bible differently. Instead, the very objects that are able to count as bibles at all for our various communities will be shaped and changed by interactions with those communities. We are reminded that reading is always a *material* act, and the material of the object being read is never natural. It is shaped by the iterative practices of communities. Whatever objects *we* might call a bible, that bible is always accessorized, algorithmic, modular. When we understand that a bible is a platform, we can begin to notice how different communities hack and recombine the object before us through an ongoing process of redactions.

When I stood in the room with the Slave Bible, I was face-to-face with racist ideology and colonial violence in a material form. But I would caution us not to fall into the essentialist trap of thinking that the Slave Bible is some deficient form of a "real Bible," an innocent bible that floats above violence and ideology. Rather, I would challenge us to look at the object we call a study Bible, or the object we call a Gideon's Bible awaiting us in a lonely hotel room, and ask ourselves, *Who has shaped this book, and why?*

We could explore other examples, but they would simply reinforce the main point of our analysis in this chapter. The bibles we encounter are demonstrably different, one from another. To the extent that observers insist on a unified identity that connects all these disparate types, I argue that it is not to be found in some essence of "bibleness." Rather, the feeling and perception of unity are explained by the thesis that a bible is a platform, and the variety we encounter is simply a reflection of the modularity with which every user and publisher approaches a bible. Like our laptops, our automobiles, and our weapons, we configure bibles to suit our various purposes, and reconfigure them to meet our various—and too often violent—desires.

6
Third Thesis
A Bible Is a Community

In both the theses we have considered so far, I have tried to demonstrate the difficulties that arise when anyone asserts that an object we call a bible is somehow simple, or easy to locate and define. Both of our previous reflections—that a bible is a book and that a bible is a platform—create dissonance around the predication of any object laying universal or essential claim to being "The Bible." In both of these prior reflections, I have tried to limit my thought to a certain realm of materiality. That is, while I do not think it is possible (methodologically or actually) to separate the physical and the social in these analyses, I have tried where possible to emphasize those physical aspects in the framing of these first two thesis statements. This analytic emphasis, however, should not be confused with an elimination of these social factors from consideration. The social dimension is in force at all levels of the analysis, and always alongside and interpenetrating any physical aspects that might be considered.

We can view the statement "a bible is a book" as an assertion about the bible's physical nature. Within that thesis are the claims that *every book is the result of various political arrangements* and that *every book requires interpretation:* two assertions about the social nature of a book. Recombining the social with the physical in continual intra-action helps us see that no book can interpret itself, no book functions as an object that presents a transparent meaning, and no book arrives sui generis in our hands.

Similarly, when we say that a bible is a platform, contained in that thesis is the assertion that *every platform we encounter offers us a series of modular (i.e., modal) choices.* In other words, any object we call a bible is an assemblage of numerous options included or excluded in a final arrangement, and that particular assemblage could have featured innumerable other arrangements different from those that have been chosen. The understanding of a bible as a platform moves us from an essential claim to a modal claim. Hence, the current arrangement that we might happen to be calling a bible is one of many *possible* arrangements that could also be predicated as a bible. The modal analysis asserts with humility rather than finality: This object is a bible, and we acknowledge that it could be otherwise. Choices, negotiations, and agencement have all played a role in the form the object takes at a given place and time.

In these next two theses I make an intentional analytic shift, from an emphasis on the physical aspects of the objects we call bibles to a more sustained focus on these social aspects. Again, I do not intend this shift in focus to imply that I think these aspects are exclusive or separable; it is my contention that they interrelate, overlap, and intra-act. However, I do think that, as is the case when one uses a flashlight to illuminate parts of a darkened room, every analysis can benefit from a sense of what it is highlighting, and what it is (therefore, in consequence) illuminating with less intensity.

When you read, it might be difficult at times to remember that *you are reading.* We get distracted by the relationships we form with the characters. Some part of our human wiring seems to make us very prone—at least in the West in the twenty-first century—to form fast and long-lasting relationships with imagined or imaginary people. These might be characters in a novel or in a television show, or they may be actual people (politicians, celebrities, victims of a tragedy) who have been presented to us primarily through the media. Over time, psychologists, media theorists, and others have begun to refer to these kinds of relationships, which are marked both by their asymmetry and by their intensity, as *parasocial* relationships.

The term indicates the many moments when a viewer or reader experiences empathy and relationship with a character, even though the character does not and cannot experience the same empathy and relationship with the viewer or reader. Despite this asymmetry, "the boundaries between self and other are transcended as the story receiver releases their own personality, identification, and belief system to take on those of the fictional persona."[1] With the rise of various forms of media in the twentieth century (particularly radio and television) and the explosion of the internet and "new media" in the twenty-first, human societies have reached the odd position where the majority of our relationships are parasocial in nature. This may be a result of the fact that most of our relationships with the world now come to us in the form of narrative. Sitcoms, dramas, and the news are all presented to us as narratives. When a friend writes a New Year's letter, it takes the form of a narrative. Because we are in fragmented contact with most of the people in our lives, our relationships are not so much with people but rather with our stories about those people. These relationships are asymmetric; even though we may feel the connection to the people mentioned with great intensity, these narrative relationships are parasocial.

So we spend each day awash in narratives, often crafted by professional storytellers aiming to create emotionally laden "driveway moments."[2] As a result, we are continually (re)forming empathetic bonds with people who are part of these story-events—but it is important to note that we are not bonding with them *as people*. Rather, we form one-way connections with them as *characters in the story*. In addition to these one-way relationships, I also find myself forming opinions about policies and contingencies regarding situations in which I may or may not have any stake whatsoever. All of these effects are forms of parasociality: Because we seem to be hardwired to form relationships, we can form them with almost anything in our social biome. Moreover, the bonds formed feel very real and very strong. We might even say they have a verisimilitude of sociality.

The most classic understanding of parasocial relationships has to do with the practice of forming strong and imaginative relational bonds with television or movie characters. For example, a popular television show with unconsummated romantic or sexual tensions between several characters might cause viewers to become " 'shippers." Here, 'ship is derived from *relationship*, and those who participate in these subcultures do so because they are invested in certain characters becoming more than just friends.

Progressing from this desire for two imaginary characters to have a romantic connection, some fans will not just pine for this sort of relationship; they will take matters into their own hands and begin to craft their own narratives. These alternate narratives are not limited to romantic imaginings, of course. All manner of new "amateur" storylines, called fan fiction or fanfics, can result. The pastime of crafting them has in some cases become a multimillion-dollar industry all its own, alongside and complementary to the more traditional channels of media creation and distribution. Perhaps the best-known recent example of bankable fan fiction is E. L. James's *Fifty Shades of Gray* trilogy, which began as a highly derivative fanfic based on another successful media property, the *Twilight* franchise.

Fanfics and 'shipping are part of a wider category often referred to as *head canon*. This term takes its cue from the more familiar notion of canon, which we encountered in the previous chapter.[3] In a biblical setting, canon refers to a body of writings that a given community considers to be scripture. In popular culture, say in reference to the *Star Wars* universe or other media franchises, canon refers to an interlocking set of narratives and data points that the creators and producers of the various intellectual properties agree are legitimately part of an ongoing story world. When fans engage with these story worlds, they inevitably discover that these narratives have certain gaps arising, perhaps, from breaks in continuity, revisions of previous storylines, or intentional unknowns put in place by the creators. The result of a fan community's attempts to reduce or remove the dissonance of those gaps in narrative by telling new (but notably "unauthorized") stories of their own is head canon. Head canon pushes against the authority of those positioned to declare things canonical—and becomes especially complex when stories last long enough for ardent fans to themselves become gatekeepers of the intellectual property.

While head canon is a way for fans to reach *into* their favorite stories and influence narratives, a parallel media trend involves characters sometimes reaching *back* into our world. This latter trend is often referred to as "breaking the fourth wall," where characters are written as if aware that they *are* characters and that they are being observed by an audience.

One show in particular that is written with a deep understanding of parasocial relationships is the sitcom *Community,* about a misfit study group at a community college in Colorado. The character Abed, written with the suggestion that he is somewhere on the autism spectrum, has been designed to emphasize the effects of parasocial relationships. Although he has difficulty reading the social cues of the other characters (who, within the universe of the show, are his "real world" companions), Abed shows a deep emotional connection to characters from movies and television shows (who, within the universe of the show, are considered "fictional"). At several points in the series, Abed is most charming and relatable to those around him when he is pretending to be a character from a movie or show he has seen.

Thus Abed functions as an audience surrogate. He is doing exactly what we, the viewers, are doing as we watch *Community:* He is forming deep emotional bonds with the characters, and he is crafting continual head canon, using his imagination to put those characters into new situations that have not been a part of the scripted canon of their respective programs.

Of course, Abed is also doing this *as a character* in a show of his own. *We* know that we are watching him. Strangely, however, Abed is written as if he is *also* aware he is being watched. Within the story world of *Community,* Abed the character treats his life *as if it were* a TV show. He seems to be aware of cameras that the other characters (who, from the perspective of his story world, are real people just like him) cannot see. He continually breaks the fourth wall and lets the viewers—us—know that he is aware that we are there watching him.

A technical word used in media studies to talk about the story world inhabited by characters is *diegesis.* One of the things

I really enjoy about *Community* is that once you accept the premise of its story world, it raises questions about where the diegesis of *Community* "ends" and the "real world" begins. In Abed's diegesis, his classmates all act as if there were no cameras. Only Abed seems aware that they are actually characters, and that they are all actually trapped in a TV show. They humor Abed but also find it increasingly eerie that he seems to know something they don't about the way their world works.

Let's think for a moment about our own diegesis—meaning, let's think about the world you and I share. Like Abed's friends, we are quite convinced this is a real world, filled with concrete objects and actual risks and rewards. Within our diegesis, we have stories we share. One example is a show like *Community,* where we can watch a character who is not a part of our real world, and we form bonds and relationships through our enjoyment of that character. Abed is not a "real person" in our world. He may feel real to us parasocially through the story we are told by *Community.*

The book you're reading right now is also a kind of story, one I'm telling through these words. I'm painting a bit of a world for you, a world of words that connects our two minds. You're not here with me, I'm not there with you. You trust that I am real, of course, and I trust the same about you. An author writing to a reader, sharing a world together. For both of us, however, this relation is parasocial. You imagine me as the author, writing these words, and I imagine you, my reader, receiving them and doing with them what you will.

Now let's make things a bit weird. I'm a religious person, a person of faith. Perhaps you are, too. As a person of faith, I have some sense of a transcendent reality, even with all my methodological hesitations about metaphysics. As a person who calls himself a Christian, specifically a Roman Catholic, I participate in a set of shared stories about this transcendent reality. These are stories where we use phrases and terms like "communion of the saints" and "angels" and "God." In this story, these are *characters* who are each part of this *transcendent* community.

In the way in which I understand this shared story of faith, at this point in our history, these various transcendent communities of saints and angels are oriented toward our current real world, our diegesis, as invested observers. This is to say, when I think of the communion of saints, I think of a structure of relationships similar in many ways to my relationship with the characters on *Community.* The transcendent community is an *audience.*

So here, in *my* so-called real world, here in *our* diegesis, I turn on an episode of *Community* and enjoy watching Abed interact with his fellow characters in *their* diegesis. Then, through Abed's breaking of the fourth wall, I enjoy his acknowledging me and interacting with me through the camera, *as if* he sees me. I then turn to the people watching the show in the room with me, and I enjoy interacting with them. I engage in a world of joys and frustrations, testing my possibilities and learning my failings in the process. Later, in prayer, I break the fourth wall of *my* diegesis, and I acknowledge and interact with my audience: the saints and the angels, who I believe are watching over me. I ask them to pray for and intercede on behalf of my fellow characters here in the diegesis I call the real world. Like Abed, I have a parasocial relationship with people who are not here in the world I inhabit but whose presence I sense in a manner not always obvious to those around me—almost as if it's fourth walls all the way down.

For Christians like (and even unlike) me, the most central of these fourth-wall-breaking interactions is with someone named

Jesus. At the moment, Jesus does not inhabit the diegesis with me. At least, Jesus is not in the world in the same manner that I am in the world, this diegesis in which I encounter and experience my fellow human beings. Instead, I interact with and know Jesus through *stories.* First and foremost, of course, Jesus is a character in these books that I call bibles. Also, when I am in Christian communities, these biblical stories are repeated, elaborated upon, and reinforced through preaching and all manner of cultural layering. I have read these stories, and experienced these reinforcements, and as a result over time I have formed a strong and even life-changing parasocial relationship with this character named Jesus.

Like Abed in *Community,* there are points where I confuse and even frustrate those around me, here in the diegesis we share, because I am getting information and making decisions from *somewhere else,* choosing my actions based on these stories about Jesus, rather than on the concrete data of the shared events unfolding around me. However—and I cannot emphasize this enough—as real as Jesus is to me in this shared world, Jesus is *not here* in this diegesis. Even when I go to mass and say a solemn "amen" to the wafer and cup, I do not encounter Jesus the way I currently encounter other people. I encounter Jesus in the most parasocial of ways: I form a relationship with this wafer *as if* it were a person. I form a relationship with the character of Jesus in a Gospel story or a sermon *as if* he were a person.

When I think of things this way, I find Abed to be quite a comfort. In the first episode of *Community,* one of his classmates in the study group observes that "Abed is a shaman."[4] I think that designation is useful. When we talk about stories, we're experiencing a kind of magic or alchemy. Similar to the manner in which Abed warps his world and our own, when Christians commit to the story of Jesus, or believe they have a relationship with Jesus, they are folding a diegesis within a diegesis, and breaking the fourth wall between them. In this parasocial relationship the borders keep shifting, pulling us into strange new worlds, and into relationships with characters from bible stories, with wafers and wine, and with invisible audiences of saints and angels. When I watch Abed in his diegesis breaking the fourth wall and winking up at me, in my diegesis, I feel a little better in my own world (the "real" one I currently share with you) when I break my own fourth wall, and look up, up, and out toward the transcendent audience I believe is watching us.

We must be cautious, however, because this experience of breaking the fourth wall can sometimes tempt us to be overconfident in our truth claims. To offer one example, on a spring day back in 2021, evangelical leader Franklin Graham paused for a moment during his lunch hour and made a post on a social media platform. It said, "The Bible alone is the absolute standard of eternal truth for every person in every age."[5]

Graham is the son of Billy Graham—perhaps the greatest American evangelist of the twentieth century. He is the CEO of the Billy Graham Evangelistic Association and its related ministry, Samaritan's Purse. He also, at the time of this writing, has nearly three million followers on that particular social media account. When he posts, he speaks to a great many people, and many of his followers likely take his words seriously. So here, Graham is making an assertion about his understanding of how an object he calls a bible works. For our present thesis, that a bible is a community, it is worth our time to give Graham's statement close attention.

I read this statement from Graham as a relatively straightforward assertion about how he thinks truth operates in our world. Therefore, I want to address his remark in what I take to be its plain sense. Graham's pronouncement—"The Bible alone is the absolute standard of eternal truth for every person in every age"—is making a claim about knowledge, about the world, and about every person who occupies the world. In other words, I read Graham here making a claim he holds to be indisputable and universal, without qualifiers or irony.

Graham's claim has a *nomological* character.[6] That is to say, Graham offers the statement with the same force he would use in proclaiming something a natural law. Nomological claims assert their principles as givens, rather than as claims derived through evidence or argument. A nomological claim allows only one possible state of affairs. Think, for example, of the inverse square law: Newton's classical mechanics posits that the gravitational attraction between two masses is directly proportional to the product of their masses and inversely proportional to the square of their distance. The assertion of this mechanical effect allows for no other possible state of affairs. The inverse square law is assumed to be the case for all available points in the universe, without an alternative.

In contrast to a nomological claim, we can understand two other types of claim. The first is a *modal* claim, which also makes a strong assertion about a state of affairs in the world, but as one among several *possible* states, or within several *possible* worlds. For example, the claim that the Allies won the Second World War states a fact about our world, but unlike the inverse square law (which assumes no otherwise is possible) we can readily imagine a state of affairs in our world where the Allied victory is *not* a fact. The second alternative to the nomological claim is the *testimonial* claim. This is the type of claim made in a court of law. A testimonial claim posits facts about the world that are understood to be personal and in direct dispute with competing claims about those same facts.

To return our focus to the nomological, we can understand a nomological claim to have two analytic characteristics: It is a claim that is both *totalizing* and *predictive.* A nomological claim is totalizing because it asserts a uniform claim on all possible conditions and entertains no exceptions to its general case. As mentioned above, in Newtonian (classical) mechanics, the force of gravity is totalizing in the sense that it operates in all frames of reference and at all possible distances and locations. In the Newtonian view, earthly gravity was no different from celestial gravity, at least regarding its mechanisms of operation.

Further, the totality of Newtonian gravity allows one familiar with its equations to make predictions about objects at any point in space, whether in the present, past, or future, as long as one has data about the initial positions and velocities of those objects. Because of these totalizing and predictive capacities, nomological claims give us confidence in our knowledge. However, they also possess a serious weakness: If a counterexample to the nomological claim can be found, the totality collapses. And along with that collapse comes a deflationary effect on the claim's predictive power.

We can assume that Graham's assertion, "The Bible alone is the absolute standard of eternal truth for every person in every age," was made with moral seriousness. That is, Graham was not joking or speaking ironically, and his intention was to exhort others to a mechanism for the acquisition of real and certain knowledge. The claim has a clear nomological structure. It makes a totalizing assertion of one absolute standard that applies to all possible participants in the pursuit of knowledge leading to truth. Further, the statement makes an undeniably predictive claim. *In every age,* says Graham, whether the present, past, or future, this same standard, and no other, shall be found to apply.

I realize that many individuals who post on social media do not use the medium to make totalizing epistemic claims. Rather, many do so ironically or hyperbolically. They may make grand or universal statements, but within contexts or while making use of subtexts that allow these statements to be interpreted as being playful rather than plain-sense, morally serious claims about the nature of the world. So there is always a possibility that Franklin Graham's post was made with some different intention than my reading of it here. I am *choosing* to read Graham's statement as if it is an epistemological claim made in a mindset of moral seriousness. I am reading Graham as if he is trying to communicate something about the world in plain language, something that he wants us to take seriously in shaping the way we understand truth and human knowledge in the world.

When I say knowledge, what I have in mind is something like the criteria set out by A. J. Ayer in his 1956 work *The Problem of Knowledge.*[7] Ayer holds that knowledge is not simply a matter of being sure that something is true. Rather, knowledge arises when this assurance is accompanied by the circumstances *such that one is entitled to be sure.* Ayer gives the example of someone who has been convinced of a mathematical proposition by way of an invalid proof. Even if the proposition were true, those using the invalid proof could not be said to *know* that it is true, given Ayer's strictures. In other words, we can be sure that something is true but lack the *right to be sure* of that truth. In such cases, following Ayer, we cannot be said to know the thing but are still in the realm of a strong bias or sentiment. Now, given the strength of Graham's claim (and again, assuming the best possible intentions involved in his having made it), there can be no doubt that Graham is sure. With Ayer in mind, however, we can further ask—in addition to his assurance—whether Graham also has the *right* to be sure in this case.

Graham speaks of an "absolute standard." As I read his statement, he does not mean "standard" in a casual way. It is not the "good enough" standard of my twelve-inch ruler but something more exacting and inflexible. The achievement of a standard like my ruler is fairly easy, but it is also hyperlocal. If we wished to achieve a standard that could be generalized, let alone universalized, that standard would be subject to deep and extended negotiations. In other words, the more *common* the standard, the more we depend on *communications* and especially *community*.

For example, for more than a century, the mass of a kilogram was set by correspondence to a heavily guarded object known as Le Grand K, the International Prototype Kilogram: a cylindrical slug of an alloy of platinum and iridium. It was stored behind lock and key in an underground vault in France, and a duplicate was stored under similar conditions at the National Institute of Standards and Technology (NIST) here in the United States.

I say the standard kilogram "was" set by this cylindrical slug, because as of this writing that particular standard has been abandoned. The kilogram was the last metric unit to be fixed to a physical object—and this particular configuration caused increasing problems. As technologies grew more dependent on exacting measurements and the need for increasingly precise tolerances around these measurements, the kilogram became unnervingly unstable. Though they were designed to be identical, the standard kilograms in France and the United States diverged from one another over time. Even in the most ideal conditions, they differed from each other by a few parts in a billion. While this discrepancy may have been acceptable by nineteenth- or even twentieth-century standards, it became unworkable as new twenty-first-century technologies came to the fore.

As a result of the need to correct these discrepancies, scientists from around the world met at the General Conference on Weights and Measures in Versailles, France, in November 2018 and voted to change the definition of the kilogram. The new standard was no longer dependent on a fluctuating physical object but became tied instead to the Planck constant. The standard for the kilogram now reads: "The kilogram, symbol kg, is the SI [International System of Units] unit of mass. It is defined by taking the fixed numerical value of the Planck constant h to be $6.626\,070\,15 \times 10^{-34}$ when expressed in the unit J·s, which is equal to $kg \cdot m^2 \cdot s^{-1}$, where the meter and the second are defined in terms of c and $\Delta\nu_{Cs}$."[8]

I mention this matter to illustrate the difficulty of reaching an absolute standard in actual practice. If we deploy the word "standard" uncritically, it can *seem* accessible, simple, and universal. However, when we describe the practices of organizations such as NIST that actually propose, maintain, and guard the standards that make the commerce of contemporary life possible, it becomes clear that *any* standard (let alone an *absolute* one) can be demonstrated to be vanishingly elusive, and difficult to maintain. Moreover, it is often the case (as it was with Le Grand K, at least until the committee voted to change its definition) that standards can be shockingly local. In other words, standards often function more as aims or ambitions, aspirations rather than actualities. A durable standard is the result of a group or several groups working hard and patiently over time to reach their agreements. A standard is social, and in many respects a standard is political. In short, the achievement of a standard presupposes a community.

A cognate difficulty arises when we think about Graham's use of the phrase "for every person in every age." In order for these words to mean what I believe Graham sincerely intends them to mean, we find ourselves caught in a paradox. It can be readily demonstrated that a bible cannot be the standard for every person in every age because of the simple fact that there was a time before these texts existed. Moreover, I must insist that there are many people, with us in the world here and now, for whom something other than a bible functions as a standard. It may be convenient in the short term to act as if such people do not exist, but in the long run it is not intellectually honest. Just given the example of Le Grand K above, what would it mean to suggest—seriously—that a bible is the sole standard of truth for NIST?

Even if we bracket out scientific discourse from religious discourse (as in, a bible is the absolute standard, yes, but only for religious discourse), difficulties can still be demonstrated. Morally serious Muslims or Sikhs or Hindus might listen to Graham politely but would still turn back to their own texts. Such communities are often aware of the object Graham calls a bible, but they are simply not compelled by it. Graham may be prepared to say that their experiences, their cultures, their texts are unworthy of consideration, but I do not agree that this is a position that should be held by a person who aspires to intellectual—and especially to moral—seriousness.

Thus, in order for his statement to be understood with the seriousness and sincerity that I believe he meant it to possess, Graham must appeal to a tightly focused semantic community that is trained to recognize what he means when making his nomological claim. This appeal is necessary since we can demonstrate that without such a semantic community, his claim quickly decays to a contingent modal claim at best, or is simply a subjective testimonial claim.

To form such a semantic community, we need to create a subcategory of speakers who are trained to recognize (and will understand as a first category of their interpretation) that when Graham says "standard," he means something other than what SI or NIST means by a standard. When he says "absolute," he means something different from what physicists mean when they say absolute. And when Graham uses the phrase "every person," he means something different from what linguistic anthropologists mean when they observe speakers in general using the phrase "every person."

You will note that this again creates a paradox, because from within this tightly knit community of understanding, where his words mean something different from what the same words mean in other communities, Graham is making what are unmistakably universal, totalizing, and nomological claims. If I take his statements seriously, then when Graham says "standard," I acknowledge that he does *not* intend to mean standard only for his community. Rather, he means standard for all times, cases, and people. Yet, as we have shown, it is demonstrable that his words do *not* mean these things for those outside his catechized community of understanding.

Thus we return to the strictures Ayer places for us in *The Problem of Knowledge*. There is no doubt that Graham means what he says, and that he is absolutely sure of what he says. However, for the reasons I have touched on above, I remain unconvinced that Graham is *entitled to be sure* of the nomological claims he seeks to make here. Assuming (as we are) that his statements are made in a spirit of moral seriousness, then Graham's statements in their plain sense are demonstrably incorrect. Or rather, they may be *locally* correct—within his community of catechized understanding (more on this in a moment)—but they are untenable as *universal* claims.

In the end, Graham cannot be making a serious universal nomological claim. Rather, his most serious intention seems to be to establish a political arrangement: He seeks a community whose claims can exist without being questioned or subjected to close analysis. To borrow a phrase from media theorist Dan Olson, Graham's assertion that "the Bible alone is the absolute standard of eternal truth for every person in every age" is not actually an attempt to explain the world. Rather, it functions as an attempt to *un*explain it, "because the explanations—the real explanations—have become inconvenient to [Graham's] politics."[9] Were we to grant Graham's claim the universal and totalizing status he seeks, we would have to grant him (and those who think like him) a special dispensation, the intellectual equivalent of a get-out-of-jail-free card. We would have to grant that Graham and those in his community occupy a privileged position of interpretation, a position unlike any other. That is a leap that some may indeed be willing to make, but I am afraid that at this time, I cannot follow.

As you may recall, Scriptural Reasoning posits three "spaces" where the preparation and production of its discourses occur: the House, the Academy, and the Tent. In the SR model, the House is the space of catechesis. That is where we learn to be members and practitioners of our particular faith traditions. The Academy is a space of play that disturbs these specific and localized revelations. It is a space where the truths that are solid and undisputed in our House are questioned, scrutinized, and analyzed. For this reason, there is a longstanding and understandable tension between Houses and Academies.

Although this tension between House and Academy is palpable and enduring, it can also be demonstrated that the House is dependent on the Academy in many ways. For example, many congregations require their professional clergy to have a graduate education, and this occurs in the space of the Academy. More specific to our discussions here, it is the members of the Academy who are often deeply involved in the processes that lead to the critical assembly, translation, and editorial shaping of the objects we call bibles.

Further, it is the role of the Academy to invite participants to shift from a mode of justification by revelation to a mode of justification by shared evidence. In this environment, some claims that operate very comfortably in the context of the House encounter difficulty maintaining their nomological character, while other claims that originate in the House find the environment of the Academy more congenial.

It is in these senses that the practitioners of Scriptural Reasoning find the discourses of both the House and the Academy to be types of "preparatory reasoning" that must be prior to the engagements that occur in the Tent of Meeting. The agreed-upon protocols of conversation that occur in the Tent assume that every SR participant has been catechized in a set of nomological claims that obtain in their particular House, and has deeply studied and understood how these truth claims survive the challenges of the Academy.

The protocols of engagement in SR further assume that all claims that participants bring with them into the Tent will be treated as modal for the duration of the conversation, meaning they have agreed (at least within the space of the conversation) that all their premises and givens could be otherwise. In practice, then, SR stands or falls on the willingness of a Christian participant to see their Muslim and Jewish companions as bearers of truth, and vice versa.

If we take the example of Scriptural Reasoning seriously, treating it as a morally serious space, then it teaches us something about how truth claims work with regard to these objects we call bibles. The practice of SR does not deny that there are places and times where engagement with objects that various communities call scripture will yield nomological claims. However, SR practice also makes clear that these claims will only and always manifest in a local and limited way. That is to say, within the House, we can and do make universal claims about reality. Yet the threefold nature of SR is predicated on the idea that in the Tent of Meeting, the ultimate question of which claim is "true" is left unresolved. When we enter the hospitality of the Tent, we are obliged to say to any claim that seeks to *end* the conversation, "Yes, and yet it might be otherwise."

Returning to the objects we call bibles, we can see that different Houses will catechize themselves around differing collections of objects and stories that members of a particular House will recognize as scripture. When you put one House next to another, of course you can demonstrate the difference between the nomological claims each House might make about what is and is not scripture. What you cannot do, however, is to create a neutral space between the various Houses, where you could adjudicate which version is the real or authentic scripture. To do so would be to confuse the neutral space with a space that has collapsed into one of the various Houses, and that has thus adopted the nomological claims of that particular House.

We can take away several items from this revisitation of the ideas of Scriptural Reasoning. The first is that the House, the Academy, and the Tent never refer to physical spaces. They are not geographic, in the sense that the communities to which they point do not simply map on to a location. Rather, I suggest we think of the House, the Academy, and the Tent as communities of practice.

This concept was originally introduced by Jean Lave and Etienne and Beverly Wenger-Trayner and was later developed in the work of Penelope Eckert and Sally McConnell-Ginet, among others. As the Wenger-Trayners put it: "A community of practice is not merely a club of friends or a network of connections between people. It has an identity defined by a shared domain of interest. Membership therefore implies a commitment to the domain [of the practices], and therefore a shared competence that distinguishes members from other people."[10]

In their work, Eckert and McConnell-Ginet have shown that these communities of practice do not just develop recreational or vocational affinities, but also grow to share common linguistic patterns, views of the world, and deeply rooted ideologies.[11] In other words, your communities of practice shape how you speak about, think about, engage with, and present yourself to the world in a repetitive, everyday way. In this sense, the concept of communities of practice engages with and complements the concept of *performativity* articulated by Judith Butler. For Butler, performativity is "not a singular act, but a repetition and a ritual, which achieves its effects through its naturalization in the context of a body, understood, in part, as a culturally sustained temporal duration."[12]

Taking these ideas up into the present discussion, it is within a House that we learn, practice, and repeat the performatives that install us into identity and ideology. In the context of discourse about belief, it is in the House where we learn to "be" not only Christian, Jewish, or Muslim (among other faiths), but also the specific instantiations of these identities. So Jewish believers learn the performatives that construct their identity as Orthodox or Conservative or Reformed as well as deeper particularities that might mark and differentiate belonging to a particular style of those communities. So too practitioners who are performatively Christian might practice and repeat the performatives that develop their identity as a Protestant rather than a Catholic, or a Cooperative Baptist rather than a Southern Baptist. The power of the analytic is that it can be deployed at many levels of magnification, allowing us to understand the differentiation of communities within a larger community, on the basis of differentiated practices performatively iterated over time.

The further advantage of this analytic is that it allows us a path to understand the existence of epistemic claims that are not grounded in essences. Practitioners in various communities will make nomological claims precisely because they have been inculcated into the practices of that community in performative repetition. When among the community of dedicated practitioners (when in the House), it makes sense that such claims would be received with nomological force, because receiving the claim with nomological force as a performative over time is part of the practice that is constitutive of "belonging" to a given House.

Part of understanding that we are shaped in these ways by a community of practice is the recognition that there are other communities. These communities may hold different allegiances than we do, and may claim different revelations than we do. At the same time, and in the face of these differences, there may also be deep commonalities. Members of these other communities love their children and have hopes and aspirations, like we do, and they work to build strong when they build, just as we do. There is difference, and there is common ground.

This is the wisdom we learn when we take the risk of stepping out of our House and entering the Tent of Meeting. We learn to appreciate the difference and the sameness that gather there. This is the wisdom of a practice like Scriptural Reasoning, whose goal again is not the production of a certain kind of knowledge but rather the enactment of a certain sort of healing. It is a healing that arises out of deepening relationships and a sincerely practiced hospitality.

When we imagine a Tent of Meeting, we are mindful that the very function of a tent is impermanence. It is designed to be a flexible and temporary space. Even with this caveat, however, it is possible for a tent to offer a space of hospitality, and even warmth and comfort. This is the goal of SR practice, certainly. Again, as we explored in earlier chapters, the animating idea of SR is not to destabilize texts or to create a new way of doing scholarship. The goal of SR is tikkun olam, the healing of the world. This healing will not happen in some abstract realm of theories. Rather, it will and must happen in the solidarity of flesh-and-blood people and the possibility of learning better and more hospitable modes of disagreement in the midst of enduring difference. So the tent is a vehicle, not a destination. The destination, if it is not too strange a word to use, is *friendship.*

This brings us to a deeper way of thinking about and understanding our thesis. A bible is a community because a bible arises out of a community and only ever finds a specific meaning *within* a specific community. More than this, however, we glimpse the possibility that a bible might be the ground of healing within a community.

So there is no doubt that an object we call a bible has the power to gather. We must also ask, however, what the purpose is for which we are being gathered. Is it for life and shelter, or for violence and exclusion? As we read together, what would it mean to commit, in every moment, to readings that heal?

A bible is a community. It never stands alone, nor can it act alone. As they say, "It takes a village"—to produce a bible, to distribute it, to read it, and to interpret it. Once these dynamics are in motion, so many things can happen. So many possibilities.

7
Fourth Thesis
A Bible Is an Accessory

I find myself thinking from time to time about a scene from the 2006 film *The Devil Wears Prada,* in which Meryl Streep's character lectures Anne Hathaway's character about a blue sweater. "What you don't know," Streep begins, her voice dripping with ice, "is that that sweater is not just blue. Not turquoise, not lapis. It's actually *cerulean.*" She then goes on to describe the 2002 haute couture season in which Oscar de la Renta and Yves St. Laurent introduced cerulean garments into their runway lines, and then traces the influence of these designers down into the bargain bins of discounted fast-fashion clothing shops. There is something Hathaway's character has failed to grasp, Streep continues: "That blue represents millions of dollars and countless jobs, and it's sort of comical how you think that you've made a choice that exempts you from the fashion industry, when in fact, you're wearing a sweater *that was selected for you* by the people in this room" (my emphasis).

The scene lasts all of three minutes. Streep never raises her voice. The effect of her words, however, is kinetic. You watch all the other characters in the room recognize the power of what is being said, and by the end of the short monologue, Hathaway's character seems to feel the effect like a bomb blast. She's not exempt; no one is. Such is the power of fashion.

"Fashion is a form of social production," writes Tansy E. Hoskins. "It is everything that *goes around* clothes that makes them fashion. Catwalks, media prestige and hype, and elaborate shops combine to create a *false religiosity*."[1] She goes on to note that this false religiosity "exists to help the fashion system produce maximum profits for corporations," while the fleeting pleasure it brings to consumers "does not actually afford an escape from the very things that make us seek pleasure in the first place."[2] Hoskins challenges us to ask, *In this society, what is fashion for?* "Is it for fun or to protect and enhance the body? Is it to act as a creative outlet, to represent culture and history, to seduce or repel, to showcase and celebrate difference, to express moods or the phases of the moon, to bring joy?"[3]

I like the stark clarity of Hoskins's questions because they are the same sorts of questions that we can and should bring to whatever object that we call a bible. *In this society, what is a bible for?* Will it be used for life or for death? Will it be used to enhance bodies or to shame them? Will it be used to celebrate difference, or in an attempt to expunge it? Will this object we call a bible be used to bring sorrow or joy into our aching world?

Jennifer Croll notes in *Bad Girls of Fashion* that "throughout history, people—especially women—have used fashion to shape the way other people think about them. *That's partly because it was one of the only ways they could.*"[4] Croll goes on to note, however, that "some women realized how *tactical* fashion can be—how powerful a tool it is for shaping opinion and challenging the status quo."[5] Again, as with Hoskins, what Croll says about fashion is precisely what we should be observing about the objects we call bibles. They are *tactical.* We use the objects we call bibles to shape the way other people think about us, and how we think about ourselves. Moreover, for good or ill, the objects we call bibles have been used through the centuries to challenge the status quo, sometimes pushing for a more inclusive society in the name of justice and mercy, though often pushing for the opposite as well.

All of these reflections up to this point have suggested something that I now wish to make explicit. The theses we have deployed—that a bible is a book, a bible is a platform, and a bible is a community—are not simply matters for abstract analysis. Rather, they point us to matters of material consequence. This is to say, *it matters* when you identify a certain object as a bible and exclude another object. *It matters* when political arrangements are made for the production and distribution of such objects. *It matters* when certain performatives are iterated over time, resulting in communities of practice that imagine themselves above, beyond, or in opposition to other communities of practice. Each thesis helps us understand how an object we call a bible can shift someone's thinking, someone's actions, and can be used in a tactical manner to help shift the status quo.

Several years ago I sat down for an interview with Wayne Hastings, who at the time was the senior vice president and publisher for the Bible Division of Thomas Nelson Publishers in Nashville. During our conversation, he made it clear that these connections between fashion and bible production are not arbitrary. Rather, when producing a line of bibles, the same sorts of questions that arise in clothing design also arise for publishers. "From my perspective," Hastings said, "it's all based on the customer need and filling a gap. . . . there's a desire for intimacy between that customer and God, and God's Word. So now you start asking questions of the customer . . . to help facilitate that yearning."[6] Over the years, listening to customer needs led Thomas Nelson to branch out from traditional "black-bonded" bibles (with their plain calf-grain covers and onion paper pages) into several lines of "designer" bibles. These included several "bible zines"—versions of the Old and New Testaments that were packaged for teenagers and had the look and feel of a high-end women's or men's magazine, such as *Vogue* or *GQ*. "You take a look at what young girls ages 11 to maybe on the stretch 16 are reading today and then you compare that to a black bonded Bible . . . there's a gap," Hastings said. "The truth is, they're going to be embarrassed to carry it. It doesn't match what they're already reading. And so our goal was to take something that was very familiar to the average young teenage girl, and then wrap in that the Bible text."

Later in our conversation, Hastings explicitly named the connection to fashion. "It's such a crass word sometimes, but it's the look and the feel of the product," he said, that sometimes builds the bridge with the customer. To illustrate, he mentioned a story he heard from a bookseller about a woman who came into the shop looking specifically for a bible with a lavender cover to match her Easter outfit. "The Bible as fashion doesn't dilute the message at all," Hastings continues. "It's just making that customer much more comfortable carrying it. And it sounds funny, but that's exactly how they feel. They want something that is appropriate to either style or color or something that . . . gives them a level of comfort."

Throughout the interview, Hastings moved between the frames of mission and marketplace. Producing bibles was core to evangelization, getting the "Good News" into the world, but that also depended upon a steady and dependable revenue stream in order to fund the mission work. A concrete example Hastings mentioned was the synergy between the selling of high-end "designer" or "fashion" bibles and the so-called Million Bible Challenge. This was a Thomas Nelson project that offered full bibles for around a dollar apiece and challenged Christians and their congregations to buy cases and basically give them away to new believers and the unchurched. By all metrics, the campaign was a wild success, meeting the one million goal within five months, and a total of six million bibles sold by the end of the first year.[7]

In another interview, I spoke with Tom Ciesielka, a public relations consultant based in Chicago who worked closely with Thomas Nelson on the Million Bible Challenge. "It was getting close to Christmas, and we came up with the PR campaign," Ciesielka said. "*For less than gift wrapping a bow, you can give someone eternal life* . . . all about the fact that whatever you give somebody this year as a present, you can also give a Bible with it."[8] Like Hastings, Ciesielka sees the need to cut through the noise of the marketplace, and using the techniques of fashion—including fashioning bibles to interest distinct demographic groups—can help with that. "You have to earn someone's ear," Ciesielka said. "They don't know the Lord, or they're not particularly religious, or, you know, they may be a nominal Christian, and they're a fireman or a golfer or . . . police officer or something like that. [A bible made specifically for them] might pique their interest."

I'm lingering on these questions of fashion because they open for us the first way of thinking about the thesis of this chapter: *A bible is an accessory.* In the same manner that "fashion is a form of social production," we can also say that an object that we call a bible is a form of social production. However, as we see in the comments from Hastings and Ciesielka, a bible is never *just* a bible, or *simply* a bible. Rather, it always appears as a *bible, and.* Those who produce these objects are always trying to earn someone's ear, always trying to forge a parasocial connection between the characters in the biblical stories and the readers, consumers, citizens of the community.

In the intra-actions of object, text, and breathing reader, we find undulating levels of agencement at work. To the extent that we reflect the styles found in and around these objects we call bibles, they accessorize us, and we become accessorized.

Looking at its etymology, the word "accessory" shares a family resemblance with the words "accede" (to give consent, approval, or adherence) and "access" (to approach). Our word "accessory" hovers in this neighborhood, loitering before and after the fact, adding to the whole, but also often claiming to add *nothing.* An accessory is a strange beast: something added to a system, to a machine, or to an outfit that has a *useful* or *decorative purpose.* Or again, an accessory is something that *improves* or *completes* that thing to which it is added.

So I began our reflections in the world of fashion, where accessories form part of a rhythm of product renewal and the constant market pressure for the new. Accessories are the "add-ons" that orbit around the main designs: belts, shoes, hats, scarves, socks, stockings, and ties all are examples of items used to accessorize the basic clothing. As Walter Benjamin noted, these objects highlight how fashion teaches us about the material commodification of desire. Even though, Benjamin said, we are inclined to think of fashion as an expression of individual preference, it is very much a social force.

Benjamin saw fashion as a *dialectical* phenomenon, to the effect that fashion manifests as a form of class struggle, perhaps even as an eruption of class warfare. It is the social means by which the aristocracy differentiates itself from the bourgeoisie. This is most evident for Benjamin when we look at mass fashion, as distinct from haute couture—the endlessly repeated iteration of prepackaged "style" as opposed to the one-of-a-kind garment. Thus, for Benjamin, looking carefully at the social rhythms of fashion can help us to understand why, with the advent of mass production, it became important to create the *sensation* that *certain* objects are *special.* This is not individuality, but the verisimilitude of individuality.[9]

So we can look at the structures of fashion to help us understand how and why a publisher might add things to an object we call a bible, even when the rhetoric of that object communicates that it supposedly needs nothing to make it truer or more desirable. For a bible-object to *function* in a marketplace, it must be *desired.* Desire manifests as a *need to own this specific object.* The object we call a bible is accessorized to heighten our desire and is accessorized by our desire.

In the material rhetorics of fashion, clothing is worn so as to create a gesture of coherence, an "outfit" that relates to contextual expectations and (for most of us) the uniformity of what can be bought off the rack. In these spaces, an accessory plays at the edge of uniformity and individuality, adding to the outfit, and in some aesthetic sense completing the outfit. So when we look at this form of the semantic field of accessories, we are looking for something philosophically akin to what occurs in fashion. If we were to think, then, of an object we call a bible in terms of the tropes of fashion, how would we begin to think about it in terms of *accessory?*

We could begin with its physicality. Taking this object we call a bible, we can illustrate it, or set the type in new and innovative ways, or give it a unique binding (tortoise shell, for example), or wrap the existing binding into an additional slipcover.[10] We can gild the edges of the pages. We can add appendices, charts or maps, other additions that help to bring the reader into the field of history, and information that provides context for and understanding of the text. These are all ways we physically accessorize an object we call a bible.

Diving between the covers, in terms of the text itself, we can add footnotes and explanations, or elaborate on points in an interlinear way, with pull quotes and reference boxes, asking study questions or giving some added explanation. All of these in-line accessorizations create an *experience* for the reader that is not to be overlooked.

We can also think about more ontological styles of accessorization. Following the examples discussed above with Wayne Hastings and Tom Ciesielka, it is no longer simply an object we call a bible. It is now a *study* bible, or a *life application* bible, or a *women's* bible, or any number of ontological wrappings we might conceive. We imagine that these titles place the object we call a bible into a certain state of being, in relation to a certain type of identity. It is now not just an object but an *evangelical* object, reaching out and "earning the ears" of those for whom it was designed, tailored, *fashioned.* These various demographic titles are not simply bolted on or added to the solid core of the bible. They are meant to inflect and intersect with our perception of the DNA of the bible itself. They alter the appearance of the bible in order to alter the experience of the reader, and what the expectations of the reader could and should be.

The *version* of a given set of objects we call a bible also invokes an ontology. It accessorizes the object by telling us where it fits in relation to the taxonomy of the family of translations that has spread and bifurcated over the centuries. This type of accessorization affirms certain communities of practice and disconfirms others. Whether King James, New International, or English Standard (to name but three), there are those for whom a particular version might as well be the only version. As we participate in distinct communities, we learn that certain objects are bibles (and others are not) because they *look* a certain way, they *sound* a certain way, and they make us *feel* a certain way.

These intra-actions with the object we call a bible open a field of effects that we might refer to generally as *para-biblical.* Everyday events and objects become imbued with an affective aura through their perceived proximity to whatever it is that we or our communities are calling "The Bible." A para-biblical geography maps an in-between space, a kind of marshy coastline (neither fully land nor sea), where the diegetic story worlds of the biblical texts leak into our world, and our world in turn is captured by the tidal currents of the biblical text. In the way an accessory both is and is not a part of the outfit, the para-biblical accessorizes both biblical and secular geographies through ongoing agencement and intra-action.

This observation gestures toward a wider swath of material accessorizations: the ancillary and secondary markets that are built up around the objects we call bibles—Christian music, T-shirts, statuary, jewelry, and a huge number of other objects that amplify a kind of bible-like presence, a bible vibe, found not only in bible-themed or Christian-themed bookstores, but also on spin racks at roadside truck stops, in Walmarts, in antique shops, and in airports.[11] We have an entire subculture of bible accessorization that inhabits a substantial corner of the marketplace.[12]

Accessorized para-biblical objects are legion, but geography and history are also repackaged in ways that are both material and marketable. Whether we consider a worship space like a European cathedral or museum space like the Museum of the Bible in Washington, DC, each exists largely to accentuate the experience and veracity of the bible—but they also risk becoming a kind of biblical Disneyland.[13] Labyrinth walks and pilgrimages like the Camino de Santiago are also accessories to this idea of a para-biblical space. They become events and experiences that evoke the verisimilitude of *bible-like* aesthetics. We might feel like we are in touch with the transcendent, or are touching some sort of history, when we partake of what these spaces offer. The effects are reciprocal—not simply flowing out of the object we call a bible, but pulling us back into the parasocial diegesis of the texts. Through this kind of accessorization, we might feel we can experience more fully the words on the page. The connection *feels* more *real* when we imagine we possess the objects, and explore the places, that the wor(l)ds on the page supposedly describe.

Again and again, we observe that an object we call a bible does not present meaning simply as an entity contained in itself. Rather, a bible is always already an entity in relation to other entities, and it is in these relationships that we can understand its meaning. So, for example, the assertion by a given community of practice that there is an *authentic* bible presupposes the comparative existence of *inauthentic* bibles. A bible object that is utilized by a certain community as expressing the truth of their faith presupposes the comparative existence of bible objects that give false accountings of faith.

We see an example of this dynamic in microcosm in the first two chapters of Paul's Letter to the Galatians. Paul at first condemns the presence of a "different Gospel" (*heteron evangelion*) than the one he preached to the Galatian community, and then immediately declares that it is not even possible for this alternative Gospel to exist at all. It could only be a perversion (*metastrepsi*) of the Gospel. Though the language is elliptical and perhaps even cumbersome in Galatians 1:6–7, Paul is not simply playing word games. He is deploying his rhetoric to distinctly political ends. Following a reading of Galatians offered by New Testament scholar J. Louis Martyn, one can see that Paul considers himself to be in a winner-take-all battle to shape the practices of the community in Galatia. As Martyn notes, "Paul has no intention of seeing a compromise formulation."[14] To use the language of our analyses above, Paul's intention is to shape the Galatian community of practice as a House founded around distinct and nonnegotiable nomological claims. Paul's desire is that the community not only profess *a* Gospel, but that it profess *Paul's* Gospel, which is not actually Paul's Gospel but is in fact the Gospel *of Christ.*

This is, I suggest, an example of when a community of practice becomes *accessorized.* Paul is not interested in the Galatians simply following a certain fashion, but rather in their becoming willing *accessories*—accomplices to Christ, not just in word but *in deed,* visible in the world. That is why looking at something like the social effects of the communities of practice around a particular version is so important, because accessorization, here understood using the language of fashion, plays in that marshy horizon, on the edge of our perception of the identity of the objects we call bibles, and the para-biblical events and objects that orbit them.

We would be hard-pressed to find an aspect more central to the bible than the language with which it speaks—and yet, in realizing that the version of translation also becomes a fashionable choice for the consumer, we understand that even *this,* the very language of the text itself, is an accessorization. The biblical texts do not reside in English or Syriac or Hebrew, Greek or Latin. Each language offers a unique space of hospitality to the texts, but none can claim to be their fatherland or their mother tongue. So it goes. There is no magical core that an object we might call a bible lives in or hides behind. There is no golden island of stability waiting for us to discover. It is all just a continued assemblage of accessorizations, all the way down.

We find a notable point of connection between fashion and para-biblical accessorization in the story of the eighteenth-century Quaker abolitionist and activist John Woolman. Born in 1720, he was a simple and prayerful man who was raised on a farm and spent his early adult years as a merchant and tailor. In his *Journal,* which has become an American classic, he notes an early childhood experience where he passed a mother robin sitting on her nest. Alarmed by his approach, the mother bird "flew about, and with many cries expressed her concern" for her "young ones." But the young Woolman picked up stones and threw them at the bird for sport, eventually striking and killing her. His feeling of accomplishment quickly turned to horror, however, as he realized his casual pleasure had now left a nest full of baby birds with no hope of surviving. As he reports, he then "climbed up the tree, took all the young birds, and killed them, supposing that better than to leave them to pine away and die miserably."[15] Woolman reports that in that moment, he reflected on a line from the twelfth chapter of Proverbs: *The tender mercies of the wicked are cruel.*

That Woolman chose this story to begin his *Journal* gives a frame for what follows. Woolman understood that he was in a position to exercise a thoughtless and casual violence in the world, and even when he could imagine his actions were (relatively) merciful, he was still implicated in pain and death. Thus began Woolman's lifelong and prayerful extrication from these mechanisms of violence, avoiding them when possible, but moreover devoting his life to naming them explicitly for himself and for others, so that his witness could become a quiet beacon, a lighthouse leading to less dangerous shores.

Woolman made the decision to leave his work in commerce and to devote himself full time to antislavery work. Stories about Woolman, as well as his own *Journal,* show us a man of gentle and singular purpose, traveling up and down the eastern seaboard, as well as to England, on behalf of the abolitionist cause. He was not a fiery orator; rather, he made visits to the homes of slaveholders to engage them in conversation.[16] His efforts, as reported in the *Journal,* were not always successful, but it seemed that even his most ardent opponents were struck by his gentleness of spirit and singleness of vision.

Though it later became a more widespread practice among the Religious Society of Friends, Woolman's fellow Quakers often looked askance at his appearance because of his habit of "dressing in the grey." As Woolman entered his forties, he made the choice to forego certain types of clothing, particularly garments that had fabrics or dyes that could be associated with the slave trade.[17] As one commentator notes, Woolman "renounced the use of dyed cloth because the dyes used in clothing originated from the West Indies' slave plantations. To use or wear such products, in Woolman's opinion, was to condone and endorse slavery."[18]

Two centuries later, the Catholic theologian Karl Rahner highlighted similar connections to the ethical implications of our participation in the marketplace. In his book *Foundations of Christian Faith,* Rahner invited his readers to consider the purchase of a banana. For the person making the purchase, everything that person needs to know is contained in that one transaction. The buyer gives the clerk the money and leaves with the banana. End of story. Rahner reminds us, however, that the interaction is not actually so simple. That banana did not just appear in the grocery store by magic. It has a history. The banana took a journey from its home country to the shelves of the store, and along the way, that banana got caught up in centuries-old commercial policies between the United States and South and Central America. The banana has passed through relationships that involve inequity and injustice toward the pickers and the packers of the fruits we eat. So while buying the banana in itself is not a sinful action, at the same time, the banana is a focal point for these social and systemic forms of sin. As Rahner asks, "Where does this person's personal responsibility in taking advantage of such a situation co-determined by guilt end, and where does it begin?"[19]

Woolman and Rahner both frame for us the wider scope of what I am trying to analyze with this idea of para-biblical accessorization. After his violence done to the family of birds, Woolman's reflection on the passage from Proverbs drew him into empathy and remorse, and helped shape his life going forward. Later, while working for the cause of abolition, Woolman was able to discern the unseen connections between the violence of slavery and the seemingly innocuous choices of clothing and fabric dye. Rahner's example of the banana names this for us in our most banal of daily activities: *Where does our responsibility for the violence visited on others begin and end?*

This question becomes especially important when we reflect on violence that is so often done *in the name* of these objects that we call our bibles.

In an early scene in Goethe's *Faust,* the character Faust labors with translating the first lines of John's Gospel, which are usually rendered in English as "In the beginning was the Word":

> (He opens a tome [of the New Testament] and begins.)
> It says: "In the beginning was the Word [*Wort*]."
> Already I am stopped. It seems absurd.
> The Word does not deserve the highest prize,
> I must translate it otherwise
> If I am well inspired and not blind.
> It says: In the beginning was the Mind [*Sinn*].
> Ponder that first line, wait and see,
> Lest you should write too hastily.
> Is mind the all-creating source?
> It ought to say: In the beginning there was Force [*Kraft*].
> Yet something warns me as I grasp the pen,
> That my translation must be changed again.
> The spirit helps me. Now it is exact.
> I write: In the beginning was the Act [*Tat*].[20]

Faust rejects the notion that the beginning could be the *Word.* Then he travels through a variety of options: The beginning was the *Mind,* or the beginning was *Force.* As he finishes his struggles with the text, however, he lands on the notion that the beginning of the cosmos was something else. *Im Anfang war die Tat:* "In the beginning was the *Act.*"

"Act" is the word chosen here by Walter Kaufmann in his translation. I would like to push back against this choice and instead read the line, "In the beginning was the *Deed.*" I make this choice both in the spirit of the passage itself (replacing one word choice with a different one), but also because the full import of the German word *Tat* here can be a little elusive to English-speaking ears, and "act" to me is too neutral and clinical. In German, *Tat* does not mean a simple deed, as in a neutral action. Rather, we should understand "deed" here in a slightly more expansive and even archaic sense. It is similar to the way we might have said in Victorian times that "he did the deed," a way of saying that "he committed the crime." *Tat* here can imply criminal intent. For example, in German, the term for a murder weapon can literally be *Mordwaffe* but can just as easily be rendered as *Tatwaffe,* "the weapon the killer used *to do the deed.*"

In Faust's wrestling with the first verse of John's Gospel, Goethe shows us a Faust open to the possibility that creation itself was a form of transgression, a violent act. It is perhaps even a *criminal act,* on the part of a perfect God, to create a world that is not itself also perfect. As creatures who literally benefit from this transgression (we have life despite our continued imperfection), we are, in Faust's translation, parties to this crime. We are—in legal parlance—*accessories* to this crime, after the fact.

Thus Faust invites us to return to the question raised above by Karl Rahner: *Where does our responsibility for the violence visited on others begin and end?* This question opens up another dimension to the idea of the para-biblical accessory. When we consider the various analyses that have been undertaken so far in *The Accessorized Bible*—when we think of an object we call a bible as a book or a platform or a community—the *material* question can remain somewhat deferred. As with Rahner's example of the purchase of a banana, or Woolman's example of the color of his shirt or coat, we might imagine that we remain untouched and disconnected from all the violence that we don't see. If we imagine that we have no connection, then we do not have to ask what effect this action or that choice might have in the world we share together.

However, as we saw from the examples of Wayne Hastings and Tom Ciesielka, those who produce the objects we call bibles do so—with great entrepreneurial imagination—because they want these objects to make a difference in the lives of people and, by those connections, change the world. If an object we call a bible is to *matter,* it will matter because it has affected some behavior, for better or for worse, within the world we share. It will matter to the extent that it has been a part of an effective change in some state of affairs, for better or worse, toward violence or toward healing. In short, the object we call a bible will have become an accessory to our deeds, or it will have made an accessory of us.

To explore questions of accessorization is to take identities and communities seriously. That is, when we approach a given community with a spirit of moral seriousness, we pay close attention both to how a given community describes itself and to how it uses its objects. When we focus on the objects that a community calls bibles, we can ask what effect the use of these objects will have on various members of that community. Does an object called a bible, acting as an accessory, "adorn the outfits" of certain members of that community, but not others? Do members of that community feel authorized to act as accessories to violence, authorized in some manner by their association with these objects they call bibles? These are serious questions.

When I speak of taking communities seriously, I have in mind both David Dark (whose thinking on moral seriousness has been referenced in Chapter 2) and Hugh Gusterson, a sociologist whose work has focused on the formation of scientific communities within the contexts of US and former-Soviet nuclear weapons facilities. Gusterson sees clear parallels between the types of socialization that occur when one goes from being an outsider to an insider at a top-secret nuclear lab, and the rituals of welcome and belonging that accompany the assimilation of a new believer into a religious community.[21] In Gusterson's analysis, this formative socialization is not simply a one-way push of indoctrination, but also a complex dance of negotiation, where some previously held truths are shifted and replaced as other ideological commitments move to the fore. As he describes the progression of his understanding of these dynamics:

> instead of thinking about the laboratory's integration solely in terms of its ability to recruit a particular type, I began to think about the practices through which the laboratory resocializes recruits and *actively produces new thinking, feeling, believing, acting selves* among its scientists . . . I began to see [these nuclear] scientists as united, not by a commitment to any overtly political program (for example, "push the Soviets out of Eastern Europe") but by a shared dedication to a technocratic program ("make sure the nuclear arsenals are safe and

> stable") that was avowedly trans-political. I began to think of the socialization of scientists into the laboratory as, in part, a process whereby political questions were transformed into technocratic questions, and I became interested in how this process was accomplished and experienced.[22]

It is this process of "actively produc[ing] new thinking, feeling, believing, acting selves" that I wish to identify as a set of iterated community practices of *accessorization.* What I am calling accessorization is a process that connects certain performative identities to specific *deeds,* which are authorized in some manner by their relationship to objects and practices related to that community. In the case of the communities described by Gusterson, the specific deed involved *creating weapons of mass destruction.* What Gusterson is describing is the complex process of *para-nuclear formation* by which these scientists—many of them self-described liberals, and some even pacifists, by his account—have become accessories to mass destruction. Accessorization is a complex interaction between communities, narratives, objects, and deeds. As Gusterson's analysis suggests, these deeds can and do include the potential for acts of tremendous violence. How does this occur?

When members of a community interact at a serious level with and within that community over time, the community will iteratively teach them (explicitly and implicitly) *legibility,* that is, the proper way to "see" objects, relationships, and other states of affairs. We may in fact take a given community so seriously that we (in the words of e. e. cummings) "forget to remember" that we have been taught (explicitly and implicitly) how to see these states of affairs. We may even eventually take a given community so seriously that the very structure of what we have forgotten to remember becomes the foundation of what we take to be natural in the world, shaped by these (implicit and explicit) teachings.

As I describe it, the process may sound very superficial. That is, one might think I am describing a brute force, a clumsy or ham-fisted style of propaganda that reprograms new members, as if we were talking about a 1970s-style cult. Certainly we can find examples of these kinds of communities, where the tactics of iterated and negotiated formation of identity take this form. However, I wish to be clear that the kinds of accessorizations I am thinking of are not restricted to this arsenal of superficial or brute-force tactics. Rather, I observe that many (if not most) communities undertake the socialization of members toward deeds with highly sophisticated, deeply embedded, and nearly unnoticed processes.

As an example of the sort of mechanisms I have in mind, let's consider a YouTube video, first released in August 2019 on the Folding Ideas channel and produced by Canadian media theorist and commentator Dan Olson. The name of the video is "Minecraft, Sandboxes, and Colonialism," with the subtitle "Oops! I Did a Colonialism in Minecraft!" As the title suggests, the video deals with some increasingly disturbing aspects of gameplay that Olson observed while playing the popular world-building game *Minecraft* with his friends. If you are unfamiliar with the game, *Minecraft* presents the players with a near-limitless game landscape that can be explored, exploited, manipulated, developed, rebuilt—and yes, mined—in various and increasingly complex ways. Depending on the server configuration, the game allows interaction with other players as well as nonplayer characters (NPCs). The manipulations of virtual landscapes involve the collection, alteration, and trade of resources including water, vegetation, livestock, precious minerals, and other analogues of commodities and objects in the real world.[23]

This includes human beings.

Olson's video begins with a suggestion from one of his fellow players that they find some feral cats and tame them to become pets. Olson then describes the lengthy process by which this would happen in the game, taking several rounds of play until a virtual cat "adopts" you. Though that process is rather simple, Olson explains that he and the other players also found it to be "kind of a hassle," since the random locations where the feral cats might be encountered made the overall process somewhat time consuming and inconvenient.

They soon figured out that the cat-taming process could be sped up if the villages where the feral cats lived were closer to the players' own settlements. But this presented a new problem: While *Minecraft* allows players to use resources to build a new village, the game will not automatically populate that newly created space with villagers. Olson points out that this limitation left the players with two options: Go to Hell, or do some slavery.

The first option, Hell, is a humorous and very elaborate journey to the *Minecraft* version of the underworld where you do some witchcraft that resurrects a dead soul into a villager. However, a lone villager will not reproduce, and thus the laborious underworld trip and resurrection scenario will have to be repeated a number of times to establish a growing population of villagers for your new, more conveniently located town.

As before, Olson and his friends don't really care about these NPC villagers. They just want some pet cats, and it seems they have now just traded one tedious obstacle (too much travel time to reach a distant village) for another (a village nearby that is very difficult to populate unless you are willing to do witchcraft to resurrect undead NPCs in the *Minecraft* version of Hell, over and over again). If all this seems too tedious, Olson reminds us, there is always the second option. And that option? Well for that, Olson deadpans, "You're going to need to acquire villagers from existing villages."

In other words, as Olson discovers to his growing horror, the *least inconvenient* way for players to get a supply of pet cats in *Minecraft* is to increase the village population by literally kidnapping the inhabitants of distant indigenous NPC villages. As Olson observes, "This interaction doesn't just mimic *kidnapping,* but more specifically the brutal relocation policies of *colonialism:* shove some people in a boat, translocate them off somewhere else, push them out and say, 'OK, this is your home now.'"

The point Olson is making is not that the game designers of *Minecraft* were somehow maniacally scheming to create chattel slavery in their video game. Rather, in Olson's analysis, *like any community of practice,* the game is in a dynamic state between the base assumptions of the game's structure, which cannot be altered by the players during the game, and the ludonarrative aspects, which are those portions of gameplay that a player can manipulate and control. In examining his enjoyment of games that involve metaphors of terraforming, building, and reshaping "uninhabited" wilderness, Olson understands that these games share a set of base assumptions that echo Manifest Destiny. In other words, they assume that the game landscapes (and their inhabitants) are there to be *colonized* and *used* in certain "productive" ways. Once these base assumptions are in place, alternative assumptions (e.g., that the player might move in a direction different from exploitation and colonization) become literally *unimaginable.* As Olson puts it, "It is certainly interesting that in a genre crowded with options, there are multiple games where the player builds vast labyrinthian factories to extract resources on an alien planet, and *not one* where the player *reclaims* a planet from the extractors, carefully balancing wetlands and ecosystems."

Whether a nuclear lab, a video game, or *a group gathered around an object they call a bible,* each milieu functions as a community of practice that operates using base assumptions and dynamic interactions. These interactions give rise to a number of expected outcomes (e.g., nuclear labs producing nuclear scientists and nuclear weapons) as well as a number of emergent, unanticipated outcomes (e.g., *Minecraft* players discovering that the *least inconvenient* way to get something done is to kidnap, relocate, and enslave native nonplayer characters). In each of these cases, the communities are producing a number of both planned and unplanned outcomes. In other words, these communities of practice are the sites where deeds happen, and these deeds are sometimes joyous (games played for fun), or horribly exploitative (as with slavery), or unspeakably monstrous (as with the creation of weapons of mass destruction).

It should be noted, however, that because the unplanned outcomes are often tied to the base assumptions of these communities of practice, the deeds they produce can be seen by those in the community as perfectly rational, or even natural, states of affairs. Moreover, the deeds resulting from the mixture of these assumptions and iterative practices may even be asserted as inevitable, because of either the misperception of the immutable status of the base assumptions, or an (un)intentional ignorance about the relation of these assumptions to dynamic emergent effects.

Nevertheless, it must be remembered that *no* community is natural or immutable in this regard. At all levels, whether those of assumptions, intentional outcomes, or emergent effects, communities can and should be interrogated and rigorously examined, *precisely* at those points where their base assumptions materialize in the shared world as deeds.

The apostle Paul talks about becoming all things to all people, in order that some might be saved. How we fashion ourselves, and are fashioned, is a result in part of our choices, as well as the influence of our communities. As Karl Rahner and John Woolman discovered, we are born into a world of tremendous violence. This violence is present in the food we buy, the clothes we wear, and even the games we play. Along with Faust, we discover we are *accessories* to this violence, even if it remains invisible to us. How shall we think about this object we call a bible, which—like Rahner's banana, Woolman's shirt, and Olson's game—is *fashioned* by these market forces, and which—through our para-biblical communities—*fashions* us?

When we at last realize that *we* are accessories, the para-biblical accessories, to these objects we call bibles, we must finally confront the question:

Where does our responsibility for the violence visited on others begin and end?

Conclusion
On Catastrophic Love

Among those of us who call ourselves Christians, we tell a story. It comes to us from the writings we call the Gospels. Like many old stories, this one gets told a number of different ways, with a mixture of details coming from the different versions. The story has a character named Pontius Pilate, the fifth governor of the Roman province of Judea, and in the story, we learn about a certain day when Pilate interrogates another character in the story, a wandering peasant mystic named Jesus.

The writers of the Gospels of Matthew, Mark, and Luke all tell this story in a similar way. They say the meeting between Pilate and Jesus takes place early in the morning. The night before, after praying in a garden, Jesus is taken into custody and brought before a council of leaders known as the Sanhedrin. There are questions and accusations, and finally, as dawn is breaking, Jesus is bound and brought before Pilate. It is here that this part of our story begins.

Pilate demands that Jesus give an account of himself against the charges made by the Sanhedrin. Jesus seems reticent to answer, and Pilate becomes frustrated. After their exchange,

Pilate presents Jesus to the crowd in the courtyard and asks them to choose whether he should spare the life of Jesus or another prisoner, a character named Barabbas. When the crowd chooses Barabbas, Pilate hands Jesus over to the soldiers to be tortured. He is whipped and scourged until he is dripping with blood.

With some variations, that's the story that comes to us across the three synoptic Gospels. The Gospel of John, however, adds an additional detail amid this flow of events: At the conclusion of their exchange, before he is to be taken to the courtyard and presented to the crowd, Jesus says to Pilate, "Everyone who belongs to the truth listens to my voice."

Pilate responds by asking, "What is Truth?"

Pilate's question chills me. It is the question of the philosopher, the metaphysician, and all too often, it is the question of the theologian. This is to say, as an academic and a theologian myself, I was trained to be *distracted* by this question: "What is Truth?" By *distracted,* I mean that when I was put face-to-face with the reality of suffering, I was trained *not* to ask, "Why is this person near me bleeding?" and I was trained *not* to ask, "Is it within my power to stop this suffering?" I was trained to hope that the bleeding and suffering might instead serve something abstract we had tacitly agreed to call *the Truth.*

In this story (that we tell and retell in communities that call themselves Christian), Pilate is face-to-face with a suffering human being, a human being in danger and distress. Pilate is well aware that in a few moments Jesus will be tortured, and in a few hours, Jesus will be brutally and publicly killed. With clear evidence of human extremity and vulnerability standing right before him, the question that preoccupies the mind of Pilate is not "How can I help this person who is suffering?" It is not "How can I use my influence and power to interrupt or end the violence unfolding here?" No. Pilate's question, instead, is one that steps aside from the suffering, vulnerable human being before him. Pilate asks instead, "What is Truth?" as if *this* were the most important question—as if there were an answer that could be shared by both the torturer and the tortured, between the condemned and the comfortable, between the subjugated and the colonizer—that would make everything all right.

A few verses later, in John's telling of the story, the character of Pilate is presenting the bloody and tortured body of Jesus to the crowd, and he utters this terse and curious phrase, *ecce homo*—"Behold the man." In other words, he says, *look at this.* And yet it is clear that Pilate himself has failed to do the very thing he has demanded of the crowd; Pilate does not look at the deed he has allowed to happen, the deed that was within his power to stop. Pilate does not look. Despite his command for others to do so, Pilate has failed to behold the man who is bleeding before him.

What is Truth? Indeed, to behold Jesus *in truth* in that moment would be to behold the bruises, the lash marks across his back and torso, the dripping blood. That question, *What is Truth?,* haunts this moment. Pilate calls others to look but remains himself distracted by his abstractions. To borrow a phrase from Travis Ables, at such moments an inquiry into "truth" becomes "a machine for neutralizing suffering by rendering it transcendent."[1] In the character of Pilate, we see the personification of the academic quest for Truth, blinded to its own complicity in brutality.

Pilate acts as if he bears no responsibility for the suffering of the bleeding human who stands before him. Indeed, in the Gospel of Matthew's version of the story, Pilate goes so far as to wash his hands, ritually cleansing himself of all attachment to the matter. Yet we who dwell in the words contained in the objects we call bibles are reluctant to allow Pilate such a clean break from Jesus. Pilate may think he bears no connection to the torture and killing of an innocent man, but we know that when the murder of Jesus took place, it happened with Pilate's full cooperation. *Pilate was an accessory.*

In the summer of 1987 I was at Duke University and enrolled in a philosophy seminar taught by Rick Roderick. The tables for the students were arranged in a U shape around the room, and Rick sat up at the front by the chalkboard. Most days he wore blue jeans and a Hawaiian shirt, although one blue pinstripe button-down inexplicably showed up in the rotation. Each day Rick sat back in his chair, kicked his feet up on the desk, lit the first of a fusillade of cigarettes, and lectured with West Texas humor and twang.

When I signed up for that course, there was no way I could have known what those afternoons would eventually do for me. I had arrived at Duke with plans to become a psychologist. I was young, politically conservative, and for a number of reasons, deeply empty inside. Yet as I listened, I became fascinated with the patterns that were being weaved before me. Through the haze of smoke and his thick Texas drawl, Rick lined up the building blocks of Western thought.[2] As the weeks unfolded, he helped me understand a deeper mystery: the mystery of clarity. Through the centuries, humans had stepped out of the darkness and done their tiny part to advance a bit of the brightness of knowledge. Goethe gave it a name. He called it *Enlightenment.* Kant gave it a rallying cry: *Sapere aude! Dare to know!*

In the middle of the twentieth century, philosopher and political theorist Isaiah Berlin was one of the thinkers who took up Kant's challenge, seeking to understand the mechanisms and limitations of the Enlightenment. In these analyses, he diagnosed a set of three presuppositions that led to what he described in various writings as monism, or the "Ionian fallacy."

I mention Berlin here because these three assumptions—that every question has a single answer, that there is a clear method for arriving at that answer, and that these answers fit together neatly into a whole—give us a succinct window into how academics like me have often been trained to attack the question "What is Truth?"[3] We undertake the tasks of inquiry, confident in a method that will yield an answer that is coherent and compatible with our other answers. In other words, Berlin gives me a shorthand to describe what I mean when I tell you I have been trained to look at situations, states of affairs, political arrangements, and conflicts primarily through the frame of *problems.*

Thus, when a particular state of affairs is failing to function as expected, it is "problematic." When I invite my students into the complexity of a question, I say I'm going to "problematize" the issue with them. My children come to me and I help them with their homework, where they solve row after row of math and science "problems." This is the linguistic reflex to which Berlin wished to draw our attention: We prefer things to be "problems" because *problems* are *questions with dependable, coherent, reliable answers.* This is our inheritance, as children of the Enlightenment. Our birthright, one might say. But Berlin knew what many of us have come to understand: Our faith in the *one true answer* can distract us from seeing the suffering right in front of us. Our commitment to the "Ionian fallacy" can lead us to a politics of comfortable violence.

Against this model of problems and problematics, we can turn to the insight of Franz Rosenzweig, who argued with his colleague Martin Buber about the necessity of tzniut, modesty, in our intellectual endeavors and our relationships. In the midst of the constant temptation to exert mastery and control, to classify and exclude, we are called instead to practice *modesty.*

Our encounters with others must be grounded—continually—in epistemic humility.

Tzniut reminds me that the other who confronts me (whether this is a text to be translated, a friend, a stranger, or the Divine Presence) does so with a wild genius and supply of mystery. That is, this other is never reducible to dependable, coherent, reliable answers. To think of the other in terms of *problematics* is to insist we will never be *surprised* by this other. They instead become our factory floor, our machine to produce predetermined outcomes. We insist they give us what we expect, and only what we expect, or we consider them to be malfunctioning. In the landscape framed by problematics, we have been taught we can love only that which can be predicted and controlled.

Against this tended hedge of management and expectation, Rosenzweig's tzniut seems to be a wild forest, teeming with the unknown. The clean factory floor gives way to an undergrowth of overlapping roots and a canopy of vines and branches above—alive, and so very out of our control.

Over the past decade or so, philosopher, public theologian, and self-avowed "bluesman" Cornel West has picked up on this critique of monism suggested by Berlin. West notes that academics and politicians are very comfortable with *problems* because problems exist *within* systems. The operating assumption is that solutions are to be found *within* those same systems. In this sense, a crisis experienced by some within the system is *domesticated* (my word, not West's) into a problem, and those who are suffering can be told, "We're working on the problem," as a *strategy* that maintains the overall structures of the system in which the problem occurs.[4]

We can return to Pilate's question—where he abstracts the search for "Truth" as a means to not-see the suffering person before him—as a kind of strategic practice. Pilate learned to do it the way we learn to do it: through repetition and reward. Considering Berlin's observations about Enlightenment presuppositions about how we *dare to know,* we can look all around and see it has become quite profitable to treat everything in our view as a *problem* to be solved within an unchangeable and unchanging state of affairs. Thus, we arrive at West's critical observation that we have inherited a certain *strategy* that is both tended and subtended in the Western philosophical traditions. The "monistic" approach of enlightened abstraction is preoccupied with (we might say distracted, or even bedazzled, by) crises that are reframed as problems. Structures of rationality and power are maintained and even strengthened in this process of abstracting complex material catastrophes into the problematics within a system—no matter if that system can be predicated as a philosophy, a reading, a community, or a culture.

In contrast to this logic of problematics, West gestures to an other-wise rationality of *catastrophe.* The *catastrophic* sensibility invites us to look at the bleeding and vulnerable human in front of us and—*Ecce homo!*—to behold that person in their fullness and extremity. This catastrophic sensibility enacts a morally serious commitment to look at the binding points within a system, and to *name them* and even *change them,* directly *in response* to the cry of the vulnerable person before us. To see this suffering person not as an *abstracted problem,* but rather in their *catastrophic particularity.* In their surprising demand, the vulnerable person is a luminous invitation to what we have seen Larycia Hawkins call *embodied solidarity.*[5]

The catastrophic sensibility arises when we finally understand that the solution to violence authorized by the system cannot be found within the system. The problematic is the motor action of bourgeois society. It is the discourse that takes place as an iterated practice in communities like Davos and the World Economic Forum, where the entire world is imagined to be a factory floor of managed outcomes. The catastrophic presents itself when we visit the underside of these polite venues. It is the reality of homeless populations in many cities that host major sporting events, such as the Olympics. For the polite competition of the sports arena to be presented to the world, the actual competition of suffering humans with a system that wishes for them not to exist must be hidden from view, out of sight, under a spectacular mirage: Before the games begin, the homeless are cleared from the streets.[6]

Pilate invites us to look at the bleeding and tortured body of Jesus but not to see the person issuing the invitation. The suffering body is present, and presented, as an unfortunate problem in the system, a malfunction of the machine. What Christ experiences as catastrophe—torture and the cross—is never acknowledged as a damning critique of that system. Everything appears to be running smoothly. Business as usual. Problematics are visible, catastrophes are unseen, because those with comfortable access to violence have the privilege to just *not see* them. Pilate is presenting us the bloody body of Jesus and saying, "*Ecce homo.*" Behold: *The system is working.* Everyone can look, but no one seems to see.

There are a lot of stories from that philosophy class with Rick Roderick that probably belong in a different sort of book, but there's one that fits here. It was midway through the summer, and I was writing my second or third short paper for the course. My task was to analyze and write a response to Saint Anselm's ontological argument for the existence of God.

If you have never encountered this beautifully polished little gem of reason, or it has been a while since you have, the argument goes like this: Anselm starts out with the premise that God is "the being the greater than which cannot be imagined."[7] Let's linger here for a moment. Close your eyes and imagine something good or powerful or beautiful. Now take that idea of goodness or power or beauty and blow it up. Expand it. Get a little bit of Boyle's perfect gas law going and let the ether of this idea grow to fill every crack and crevice of your imagination. Make the goodness, the power, the beauty you are contemplating rush and rise to become the greatest possible sense of that quality. You are still not there. Now combine each individual attribute, expanded to its maximum capacity in your thinking. Getting closer. We are in the regions now to which Saint Anselm is beckoning us. To understand the being the greater than which cannot be imagined, you first must radically stretch your imagination.

Now that you have pushed your mind's imaginings to their very limits, Anselm introduces the second step of his ontological proof. In addition to "God is the being the greater than which cannot be imagined," Anselm adds, "It is greater still to exist in both the mind and in reality, rather than in the mind alone." Such a subtle but deft move, this. Anselm has beckoned us to fill the mansions of our thinking to the brim, and then, when we have reached the very limits, it is as if he opens an unnoticed door in the wall to reveal entire ballrooms that we had not known existed, nor even contemplated. Because the greatest being we might *imagine* will always remain a lesser being if it dwells *only* in our imaginings alone. The greater being would be the one that dwells not only in our minds but also inhabits our reality, transcending the limits of our imagination.

This is the conclusion that Anselm himself reaches. If you have thought to your limits and imagined the greatest being you can, the only possible step to imagine a being still greater is to imagine something that would transcend the imagination. By this logic, Anselm concludes, "therefore God exists."

I still recall the paper I wrote that summer, because the image I had in my mind then has never quite left me. As I tried to understand Anselm's argument, I visualized my imagination as something like a large bowl, sitting on a table. I have a bag of rice. I lift the bag and begin to pour the rice into the bowl. It spills and fills the basin, and the rice level begins to rise along the sides. This is my mind's-eye vision of how I am filling my imagination, trying to get my thoughts to their limits. The rice level continues to rise as more and more grains make their way into the bowl.

Eventually, we reach a point where the rice has reached the very top. I am near the limits of my imagination. I pour carefully now, and the rice begins to rise into a mound above the rim. The rice becomes a little mountain of my imaginings, as I push the bowl to its natural capacity to hold the rice. Grain by grain, the level rises. In this vision, I am reaching the limits of what I can possibly imagine. I am now adding grains carefully, one by one, until the absolute limit of the bowl is reached.

Then a moment arrives, and the capacity of the bowl is finally, irrevocably transcended. A grain of rice hits the top, the pile gives way, and a cascade suddenly spills over the edge. We have stepped beyond the threshold of "what I could imagine," and now we are encountering that space occupied by that which is greater than what can be contained in my imaginings alone. The rice spilling out over the edge of the bowl is, in this Anselmian analogy, tumbling into the inevitability and the concreteness of *reality.* The rice has entered "the greater than which the bowl can comprehend," and it is greater to exist at the limits of the bowl *and* outside the bowl than it is to exist in the limits of the bowl alone. It is here that I fixed my concerns about Anselm's argument: In my paper, I confessed that I worried about what happened when that idea of God escaped the confines of the mind.

I did not know it at the time, but my paper was trying to describe the problem that computer scientists call *buffer overflow.* A buffer is a container for data and information. Different buffers are designed to have differing capacities for storage. The point is that it should be easy to get information in and out of the buffer and that ideally the buffers will work faster and more flexibly than the deeper regions of computer memory.

However, every buffer is finite and thus can be flooded with excess information. When this occurs, the excess data does the electronic equivalent of spilling over the holding capacity of the buffer. That overflow can be used as a kind of Trojan horse, to introduce malicious code or information into parts of the programs that normally could not be accessed. This is a real-world threat, a matter of cybersecurity. If we take it as an analogy, it can also help us think about the danger that I saw in Anselm's ontological proof.

Think of the human imagination as a kind of buffer. In Anselm's proof, the analogy is nearly perfect, because he stipulates that our imaginations have a finite capacity. That is to say, according to Anselm, we can imagine up to the very limits of our ability to imagine, and then we can also imagine transcending that limit. When we then imagine "the being the greater than which cannot be imagined," we have entered a state of buffer overflow: The rice is spilling out over the edge of the bowl. Our knowledge of this "greater than which" god is spilling out beyond the buffer, over the edge of our ability to imagine.

My worry when I was writing that philosophy paper was that, by definition, this space beyond our ability to imagine is an uncharted realm. The way Anselm has set up the logic, this buffer overflow is beyond imagining, and therefore noncognizable. Once the limits of the imagination have been transcended, we exceed our ability to measure or know any of the contents of the knowledge that sits beyond our limits of imagining.

In my paper, I suggested that it might be possible that out beyond that boundary are all manner of beings, and perhaps one of them is indeed the God that we profess. However, by Anselm's own logic, in that transcendent realm there would be no way for us to *imagine any difference* between one "greater being" and another. Once we enter the realm of buffer overflow, we become susceptible to malicious code. *Anything,* across the moral spectrum, *might be possible.*

Believing that we have found the true god beyond the limits of our imagining, we might find ourselves in thrall to *any* kind of higher power.

Commenting on my paper, Rick suggested that I had misunderstood the power of Anselm's ontological proof, and it is very possible that I did and do. My concern back then, however, was linked to the concern that animates the argument of this present project: I fear the unintended consequences of a buffer overflow—or worse, its intentional exploitation—toward malicious and violent ends, regardless of whether we are talking about our imaginings of a deity, a community, or an object we call a holy book.

Thus, I would like to linger with this concept of buffer overflow for a little longer. As was mentioned above, in the realm of computer security, a buffer overflow is a weakness that can be exploited for an attack against a system. It gains power from the confidence of the designers and users when they are convinced that all is in order and everything is fine. In fact, the very power of a buffer overflow attack comes about when the system is well understood and well defined. It is precisely at those well-defined points that an attacker can send in a swarm of new information, designed to overwhelm the buffer in a specific and predictable way, spilling information into other areas of the memory. This might destabilize the entire system or inject executable code into areas thought to be safe, even impenetrable.

A buffer overflow gains power from the gap that exists between what we think we know about a system and the actual mechanics that govern the outputs of that system. Operators and users expect that certain inputs will yield predictable and dependable outputs, but a buffer overflow attack creates conditions not anticipated by the operators. Moreover, if they do not suspect that anything is wrong, and especially if they trust the system and think that nothing *can* go wrong, it may be a long time before they finally understand that results coming out of the system are no longer properly connected to the data going into the system, and that the system has been turned toward malicious and even violent ends.

Now let's reverse this analogy with Anselm's ontological proof. The proof is a system designed to accept a series of inputs (*let's imagine how God might be*) and yield one and only one output (*God exists*). The mechanism is designed to produce a trustworthy knowledge that confirms the existence of a certain kind of God. In Anselm's architecture, if you put in the stipulated premises, namely that God is a being the greater than which cannot be conceived, and that it is greater to exist in the mind and in reality than in the mind alone, then Anselm's formula yields the logical conclusion that God exists.

There is a vulnerability in this system between the point where we exceed the capacity of human imagination and where we arrive at that which exists beyond the imagination alone. That is the range beyond the buffer of human knowledge. To comprehend something, we must be able to hold it in our minds, to imagine it within the schemata we use to build our sense of the world. The gap between our ability to know and measure something and the output that results causes me continued distraction. Ever since I first wrote about it in that paper, all those years ago, that gap has concerned me.

What I fear is the possibility that something else might work its way into that gap between our ability to measure the inputs and the output. Let's call it a kind of malware. In the case of a computer, it creates a possibility for security breaches and corrupted outputs. A system in buffer overflow still gives us answers, but it does so as a kind of black box. In the case of the ontological argument, my fear is that this gap creates a different sort of security threat. What sorts of gods lurk there beyond the one God we seek?

Anselm's ontological argument is more difficult still. By its own premises, to get to the sure result, we must introduce a moment into the process that by its very definition we cannot fully trust. We must relinquish not only our ability to fully know, but to imagine fully and adequately, at least for a moment. The God that Anselm seeks lives in that gap beyond imagination. But in that gap between imagination and beyond-imagining, we must concede that anything can happen.

It is the same for the objects we call bibles. They come from somewhere, don't they? They have been through a process that is much more commercial than it is divine. From that black box of production, they are assembled for us and offered in finished form, lined up in rows on shelves and websites for our choosing. Then once we get one in our hands, it is so easy to cry out "Lord! Lord!" and to forget all the steps that led up to this hallowed moment and made it possible.

In the preceding chapters, I have made attempts to slow down and review the tape regarding some of those steps. I want to do everything I can to make the dynamics and construction of the objects we call bibles visible and clear, because when we allow (or tolerate or ignore the introduction of) epistemic gaps, we introduce breaches in our security about the knowledge that results from our processes. Any moment that we step away from our understanding of the mechanisms that yield our claims to truth, we become vulnerable to idolatrous forces, to distractions masquerading as Truth, and gods masquerading as God.

I began thinking again about these ideas—about Anselm's ontological proof, the problem of buffer overflow, black boxes, and malware—because of a recent miniseries that aired on Netflix. The show was called *Midnight Mass,* and it is fair to say it caused a stir on social media among a certain subset of armchair theologians and religion scholars.[8]

The story of *Midnight Mass* concerns a dying Catholic parish, on an island with a dwindling community of fishermen and their families. The fictional island is thirty miles from the New England mainland, although the precise location is never quite specified. The parish has been served for decades by an aging and now ailing monsignor. As a thank-you for all his years in the pulpit, the parishioners raised money to send him on a pilgrimage to the Holy Land. While he was there, he encountered an entity that changed everything, for him and for his community back home.

A theme of addiction runs throughout the series, and several characters are addicts in recovery. In the initial episodes, this situation opens space for conversations among various characters and the priest about the concept of a "higher power." These characters discuss their orientation toward the "God of their understanding" and what it means to put yourself in a position of powerlessness in relation to this higher power. These early conversations serve to frame dilemmas that arise later in the series, as we discover that many in the community have indeed given themselves over to a higher power, but one that is arguably malevolent, violent, and antilife.

What struck me about the series is how it portrayed the eagerness of many members of the parish community to give in to this malevolence and give themselves over to these antilife powers. It is notable that the faith of the community is not depicted as being ironic or cynical, but deeply sincere. Despite the clear devotion of the parishioners portrayed in the show, however, they seemed to possess no bulwark whatsoever to protect them from becoming willing accomplices to the rapacious violence that eventually destroys the community.

While the motivations of several characters are obscured and open to multiple interpretations, the third episode of the series is focused on the monsignor and framed in such a manner that he explains his actions in plain language. It alternates between flashbacks and the narration of the priest as he speaks aloud to God in the confessional at the back of the sanctuary. The monsignor explains to both God and the viewers the actions he has taken and will continue to take through the end of the series.

In the flashbacks we see him on his pilgrimage. He becomes lost in a sandstorm and stumbles into an ancient ruin where he encounters a being, the greater than which he could not conceive. Though it is never named as such, the creature is, for all intents and purposes, a vampire. Throughout the story, however, the monsignor refers to this being as an "angel," despite the rising body count as the creature feeds its insatiable hunger by devouring the living creatures that inhabit the town. It is this malevolent higher power the monsignor has brought back to the village. The monsignor excuses all the violence (the creature's, and eventually his own as well) because he is convinced that the blood of the "angel" will revitalize this dying church and aging community with "eternal life."

As I watched *Midnight Mass,* thoughts of Anselm returned to my mind. In the story, I saw a clear depiction of the danger of buffer overflow. The monsignor entered a space of extremity and had a transcendent encounter with a being simply greater than he could possibly imagine. He was trained in his theology and in the iterated practices of his community to respond to this extremity *as if it were (of) God.* In the wake of that response, he began to countenance all manner of violence, eventually committing horrific violence himself, to serve this illusion of Godliness. The buffer overflow, in other words, opened the monsignor and his community to malicious attack. In his state of buffer overflow, a set of understood inputs (discovering that "a being greater than we can imagine" exists in reality) was hijacked, leading to unexpected ends.

In the logic of Anselm's ontological proof, when an encounter transcends not only our capacity to know but even our capacity to imagine, the danger is that in such a state we will have no remaining faculties for proper discernment. Once we enter that space of credulity toward extremity, *any* presence of sufficient grandeur, no matter how clearly malevolent, could exploit our trust. Indeed, it is exactly this chain of events we observe in *Midnight Mass,* where the "angel" offers a *kind* of comfort, community, and communion to those who are willing to be accessorized to its power—but only at great cost to their humanity.

Certainly, art imitates life here. We can readily demonstrate how, over the past hundred years, innumerable faith communities across North America and Europe have shown themselves to be willing accessories to all manner of violence and antilife allegiance. Their clerical structures proved no defense against such accessorization, nor did any of the objects they called bibles. It can be demonstrated time and again that faith communities (and here I speak especially of those communities gathered under iterated practices made in the name of Christ) have put themselves in the service of all manner of malicious and even violent sentiments. Gathered in the name of the Prince of Peace, the blood has flowed and flowed, and continues to flow.

So I am convinced of this ongoing structural weakness in the iterated practices of both our epistemic and communal life together. The evidence is overwhelming. Time and again, our communities demonstrate their susceptibility to this threat of buffer overflow, and we are slow to notice the threat, and even slower to respond. Vulnerable populations within and adjacent to our worship communities become victims of those people and institutions with comfortable access to violence.

Further, when the threat to the vulnerable is pointed out and named, the response too often is to blame or condemn the messenger. This makes a certain sort of sense to me. Institutions preserve themselves at the expense of vulnerable bodies and justify the preservation as an end in itself. To use the imagery borrowed from *Midnight Mass,* all manner of violence against human bodies can be excused if it means the institution of the church continues to "live." Again, this Faustian bargain offers a *kind* of comfort, community, and communion to those who are willing to be accessorized to its power—but only at great cost to their humanity. It is no longer the case that they will know we are Christians by our iterated practices of love, but rather we will be known by our performative allegiance to whatever malevolent power has possessed the ineffable space of the buffer overflow.

What if it were otherwise?

In 1964, James Baldwin published "Nothing Personal," a short essay to accompany a book of photographs taken by his longtime friend and colleague Richard Avedon. It is hard to describe what this essay means to me. It is a Chartres Cathedral of language, by which I mean to say, when the light hits just right, it can cause me, quite suddenly, to weep.

The essay is about twelve pages long, divided into four parts. The first time I sat down with it, it took me less than an hour to finish. Working through the ideas in it, though, has occupied the better part of my adult lifetime, and if I spend the rest of my days on it, it still might not be enough. Throughout the pages Baldwin is both diagnosing a sickness and suggesting a remedy, with a wisdom similar to what Fred Rogers—Mister Rogers—was drawing from when he suggested that "love is at the root of everything. All learning, all parenting, all relationships. Love or the lack of it."[9]

Love or the lack of it is what preoccupies the whole of Baldwin's attention in "Nothing Personal." He begins the essay with a litany of all the ways we have of distracting ourselves in contemporary society from the ever-presence of despair, and invites the reader to join him in examining both the source and the effects of this despair. Baldwin notes, however, that we have been well trained to resist such inquiries, indeed as if our very lives (though more likely our public identities) depend on it. "We are afraid to reveal ourselves because we trust ourselves so little," he says. "Therefore the truth cannot be told, even about one's attitudes: *we live by lies.*"[10]

Baldwin observes that we cope with this fear by externalizing it. We create scapegoats and invent enemies to move our nervous energy destructively outward into the external world around us. "It has always seemed much easier to murder than to change," he says. "And this is really the choice with which we are confronted now."[11] That is, the choice between remaining in our darkened tutelage of hateful ignorance, or daring to step out into new light. Baldwin draws out and deepens this moment of decision, casting it simultaneously as the most universal and most personal of experiences. He calls it the "four AM choice," after that bleakest hour of the morning, when the despairing soul literally decides between existence and suicide.

The answer to this choice cannot be more institutions, or more property—"placing things above people," as Baldwin puts it.[12]

No. There is no instrumental solution. As Baldwin points out, *we have already tried them all.* Then, when history has shown us that none of the instrumental solutions has worked, we tried to erase history itself from our lives. All to no avail, and we are left with what has ever been the only *possible* solution: We must, at last, allow ourselves *to love:* "One day, perhaps, unimaginable generations hence, we will evolve into the knowledge that human beings are more important than real estate," Baldwin says, "and will permit this knowledge to become the ruling principle of our lives."[13]

As we noted in our discussion of *Midnight Mass* above, institutions preserve themselves at the expense of vulnerable bodies, and justify the preservation as an end in itself. This is the endgame of "placing things above people," and, as Baldwin asserts, it ends in either the literal suicide of the despairing soul or "that death in the heart that leads not only to the shedding of blood, but reduces human beings to corpses while they live."[14]

Daring to love means doing what in our present state of affairs can only be described as irrational: We must preserve vulnerable bodies *at the expense* of our institutions, in the name of love. Further, this is not an abstract or philosophized sort of love, but rather a love that *listens* to the vulnerable beloved and asks, "Does my presence make you feel safer? Do my actions contribute to your flourishing?" Love builds only that to which the vulnerable consent and dismantles any structure that would do them harm.

For reasons I will explain in a moment, I have begun to call preference for the care of vulnerable bodies over the preservation of institutions "catastrophic love."

During that summer seminar back in 1987, Rick walked us through the history of Western philosophy, week after week, describing a way it might all hang together. Toward the end of the course, though, in the last couple of sessions, he shifted from the past to turn to the future. Drawing on the thread that ran from Hegel through Marx and the later critical theorists of the Frankfurt School, he suggested that the tensions of our present age would move, dialectically, to bring change. Rick was careful in his predictions, however. "I don't know what it will look like," he said several times. "I don't really know what to name it, so I just *call* it anarchy."

Here is what I think Rick meant: I believe he was telling us that, as wild as his imagination might be (and from the evidence shown that summer, it was pretty wild), his imagination was still conditioned and limited by capitalism and other ideologies. As a result, his very *I* was limited. So, as he thought to the very edge of his imagination—and beyond that edge—*he had no name for what was to come.* All he knew was that to us, it would look like anarchy, because that was the best word we have for something that is no longer governed by the power relations and exploitations of our current world. He was gesturing to a community of practices beyond his very ability to imagine. It was something yet to come, defined not by a set of names or doctrines, but by a fundamental change in material relationships. The entire world would be different in its wake.

For those committed to preserving the ongoing structures of our present age, when it finally comes, that thing Rick was talking about—whatever it is—will certainly feel to them like a catastrophe.

Not only in the Gospel of John, but in all the Gospels, the violence against Jesus is violence *in the name of* the status quo. It is violence *in the name of* religious stability. It is violence *in the name of* protecting what we—the comfortable—have already got. From the perspective of a community that has iterated a set of practices that include the power to do violence, the bloody and tortured body of Jesus is just one more problem to be solved, while the system that does the torture remains perfectly intact. That's the way the religious leaders want it. That's the way Rome wants it. And (let's be honest) that's the way we want it. Violence against the innocent and the vulnerable solves the *problems* of our system, in order that we may remain comfortable. That's the point.

So for German Christians in the 1930s there was a "Jewish Problem," but for the Jews living in Germany and annexed space at that same time, it was not a problem. It was a *catastrophe.* That is, the German Christians' "solution" to the problem was designed to leave the structures of their comfort intact and unquestioned. This problematic comfort, however, demanded the complete and utter destruction of Jewish cultures, relationships, and ultimately Jewish bodies.

This is the paradox: There is ample evidence that German Christians felt a deep love for each other and their country, but the problematic nature of that love allowed them to turn even the giving of bread to the poor into a callous act.[15] For Jews, in this example, the presence of the problematic love of German Christians ("problematic" here again meaning limited within and dedicated to the structures of German Christian *comfort*) was experienced not as love, but as a catastrophic violence.

But Jesus occupies the underside, burrowed beneath our comfort, and his language is not restricted to the rhetoric of problematics. His words inhabit the otherness of catastrophe. "Tear down this temple, and in three days I shall build another" is not a program of urban renewal. To tear down the temple is to uproot the axis mundi of a system that wishes to master the universe for the ends of comfort. It is a strike at the heart of the very economy of atonement. As Cornel West put it,

> The situation of poor people is catastrophic. Black people had slavery, Jim Crow, Jane Crow. Cat-

> astrophic. What was the response? It wasn't to create a Black Al Qaeda. It wasn't counter-terroristic. In the face of slavery, Frederick Douglass said . . . "We want freedom for everybody. We don't want to enslave others, just because we're enslaved." [We must respond] to the catastrophic with compassion, without drinking from the cup of bitterness. Not with revenge, but with justice.[16]

So the question arises: Is there a kind of love that does not maintain the oppressive structures of comfort for the few, but dismantles those structures for the flourishing of the vulnerable? This is what I think West is pointing to, and also what Rick Roderick was pointing to when he talked about "anarchy." Also, perhaps, what Jacques Derrida was talking about with his "democracy that is to come," and maybe even the apostle Paul's "already not yet."[17]

I am wondering aloud what our communities would look like if they were no longer organized around catastrophic violence, but rather toward iterative practices of *catastrophic love.* I imagine this is the sort of vision Hannah Arendt had in mind when she suggested that we should love the world enough to become responsible for it, that thought of hers that I introduced in the earlier exploration of moral seriousness (Chapter 2).

It may be a love that no longer assumes that the comfortable structures of our world will look or act the same after the loving has happened. Like Rick, like Derrida, we have to say to some extent that we have no idea what this will look like in practice, because our very imaginations have been limited by ideologies that make us more likely to imagine the end of the world before imagining the end of capitalism. Levinas calls it sincerity. Derrida calls it democracy. Rick called it anarchy. Jesus calls it the Kingdom of God.

We might test the limits of our vision by imagining that catastrophic love—in its very structure—is always rooted in solidarity with the experiences of those *already in catastrophe.* Not only Jews in Germany, but African Americans in the United States, LGBTQ+ people globally, the hungry and vulnerable and unhoused in our cities, and the poor that Christ told us would be with us, always. Our current iterated communities of neoliberalism treat these vulnerable people and populations as problems to be "solved" within a steady-state system of global capital. Bodies are broken so that systems might stay whole.

The hope of catastrophic love is that systems will be broken so that bodies stay whole. It also means that we must join in solidarity with the vulnerable in their catastrophic oppression, that we might also encounter catastrophic love—because at this point, you do not encounter the one without the other. There is no comfortable way to do this. Narrow is the way, as they say, and straight is the gate.

In the concluding section of "Nothing Personal," Baldwin describes what this reversal of bodies and institutions looks like in practice:

> Pretend, for example, that you were born in Chicago and have never had the remotest desire to visit Hong Kong, which is only a name on a map for you; pretend that some convulsion, sometimes called accident, throws you into connection with a man or a woman who lives in Hong Kong; and that you fall in love. Hong Kong will immediately cease to be a name and become the center of your life. And you may never know how many people live in Hong Kong. But you will know that one man or

> one woman lives there without whom you cannot live. And this is how our lives are changed, and this is how we are redeemed.[18]

What Baldwin describes on the personal level, in the one-on-one experience of the lover and the beloved collapsing geography and time to be together, is a species of what I am trying to describe in this idea of catastrophic love. "If your lover lives in Hong Kong and cannot get to Chicago, it will be necessary for you to go to Hong Kong. Perhaps you will spend your life there, and never see Chicago again," Baldwin says, concluding that against any obstacle, "love will simply have no choice but to go into battle with space and time and, furthermore, to win." Your love for the beloved draws you beyond the hedge, into the wild forest, beyond the predictable response, into the unknown future.

In other words, the lover described by Baldwin is the one willing to collapse every structure and every habit that forms an obstacle hindering proximity to the beloved. That is a *catastrophic* response to the obstacles that hinder the boundlessness of our loving. The beloved is not a problem to be solved, but rather presents for us a complete reorientation of what it means for us *to be*. The beloved exists for us in tzniut, in the freedom of surprise, and thus we exist for each other in a state of unpredictable vulnerability. We behold our beloved, and see that our love is vulnerable, and our beloved is vulnerable, and we are moved to respond. We find ourselves continually asking, "Do you feel life in abundance because I am here?" and "Does my presence make you feel safer?" and allowing our interests and our expectations to be interrupted and rearranged continually until the answer is and remains, "Yes."

How do we work for the safety and flourishing of our vulnerable beloved? It begins by listening to them when they speak of their experiences and struggles, and following their lead when they tell us what needs to be done. In the Gospel of Mark, chapter 2 (echoed in Luke 5) we hear of a paralyzed man who wishes to come close to Jesus but is unable to; he is unable to enter the house because of the crowds of able-bodied people who have filled the space. The story tells us that the advocates for the disabled and vulnerable man rip a hole into the roof of the house where Jesus is preaching in order for the man to get access to him. As the text puts it, they "opened the roof":

> When Jesus returned to Capernaum after some days, it became known that he was at home. Many gathered together so that there was no longer room for them, not even around the door, and he preached the word to them. They came bringing to him a paralytic carried by four men. Unable to get near Jesus because of the crowd, they opened up the roof above him. After they had broken through, they let down the mat on which the paralytic was lying. When Jesus saw their faith, he said to the paralytic, "Child, your sins are forgiven." (Mark 2:1–5 NAB)

When the house was built, it was not built for everyone, and so the most vulnerable in the community could not come close and hear the Good News. Instead of accepting their situation as inevitable, or just the way things have to be, the people accompanying the vulnerable man rearranged things so that not only was the house accommodating to his vulnerable body, but the paralytic man was now front and center—as close to Jesus as the most able-bodied person in the room.

Where might we find the suffering Christ among us? In the twenty-fifth chapter of the Gospel of Matthew, we are told to look among the hungry, the thirsty, the immigrants, the sick, and the prisoners. In other words, we are to look for Christ among the unwanted, among the ones whom those in our communities with comfortable access to violence would most like to make disappear.

In "Nothing Personal," Baldwin speaks of his own interactions with those who possess comfortable access to violence. "I am an old hand at this—policemen have always loved to pick me up and, sometimes, to beat me up," he says.[19] Later, he adds, "The America of my experience has worshipped and nourished violence for as long as I have been on earth. The violence was being perpetrated mainly against black men, though—the strangers; and so it didn't count. But, if a society permits one portion of its citizenry to be menaced or destroyed, then, very soon, no one in that society is safe."[20]

Baldwin helps us understand Christ's reference in Matthew 25. It is not that the suffering Christ will *only* be found among the hungry, the sick, the immigrant, and the prisoner. Rather, these are examples of those declared to be *the strangers,* the ones attacked by the comfortably violent to deny their own despair. The stranger is the one targeted by the comfortably violent for disappearance. They are the vulnerable beloved. They are the suffering Christ whom we are to seek, seeking them with a love that is catastrophic to all that wishes to menace or destroy them, as if they didn't count.[21]

I don't know what things will look like if we're doing it right, but I do know the house won't look the same when the loving is done.

What Baldwin describes on a personal level is the complete deconstruction of the habits and locations of the self, rearranged into new habits and new locations so that love might live and flourish. In the spirit of Baldwin, I invite the reader to take this wisdom and now expand it beyond the narrow focus of the one-on-one, the only-personal, and to imagine the corporate and the corporeal manifestations of such a love. Hold in your vision the possibility that entire social structures—communities, governments, and yes, even churches—might "move to Hong Kong," that is, abandon and dissolve themselves in order to rearrange and respond in comportment with the needs of the vulnerable beloved. Imagine that institutions might learn to completely deconstruct their habits and locations, so that the vulnerable beloved might live and flourish. This is no longer "love" in the abstract, as some principle or duty to which bodies are conformed, but is at last a material and practical loving, in which every abstract thing is conformed in a material way to the safety and flourishing of the vulnerable beloved, and to the care of the bodies that present the suffering Christ among us.

Here I need to my lay cards on the table, for though I have written this book in a way that will be of use to all readers, I am navigating these matters from a distinct perspective as a Roman Catholic who finds Pope Francis to be a compelling moral voice on these issues—two of his works in particular, *The Way of Humility*, written when he was the cardinal archbishop of Buenos Aires, and a speech he made before the United Nations in September 2015. These two works help to clarify my thinking about the scalability of Baldwin's one-on-one example of catastrophic love into a collective material space.

In *The Way of Humility*, Pope Francis draws an analytic distinction between sin and corruption. Sin here is the general state of fallen humanity—"we are all sinners," if you will—but not all who sin are corrupt. Instead, to use language deployed earlier in this project, corruption is made manifest as a *community of practice.* As Francis puts it, "Corruption is not an act but a state, a personal and collective state, to which people get accustomed and in which they live. The values (or non-values) of corruption are integrated into a real culture, with a capacity for its own systematic doctrine, its own language, and its own particular way of acting." Above all, Francis notes, these iterated practices "spoil and limit *a person's capacity to love.*"[22]

Again, Pope Francis's analysis oscillates between the personal and the systemic. Those with a *personal* habit of corruption seek out others with whom to build *communities* and *structures* of corruption. In parallel with Baldwin's observation above, Francis notes that individuals and communities in the throes of corruption protect themselves by strategically selecting "others" to attack as scapegoats, ending in a triumphalism "born of the feeling that one is the measure of all justice and judgement."[23] Corruption itself becomes both the institution and the justification for perpetuating the institution, and vulnerable bodies are sacrificed for the preservation of the false appearance of righteousness.

Francis wrote *The Way of Humility* when he was still the cardinal archbishop of Buenos Aires, but one imagines its themes were on his mind when he ascended to the world stage and addressed the United Nations in September 2015. During the early moments of the speech, Francis names explicitly his concern:

> In effect, a selfish and boundless thirst for power and material prosperity leads both to the misuse of available natural resources and to the exclusion of the weak and disadvantaged, either because they are differently abled (handicapped), or because they lack adequate information and technical expertise, or are incapable of decisive political action. Economic and social exclusion is a complete denial of human fraternity and a grave offense against human rights and the environment. The poorest are

> those who suffer most from such offenses, for three serious reasons: they are cast off by society, forced to live off what is discarded and suffer unjustly from the abuse of the environment. They are part of today's widespread and quietly growing "culture of waste."[24]

Here again we see West's notion of the catastrophic, now on a global and even an ecological scale. Pope Francis is naming a suffering that overflows the buffers of the imagination, pushing beyond the scope of problems with well-framed solutions. The scope is overwhelming. It seems impossible to push against these entrenched institutions, committed as they are to profit from corruption and comfortable violence. How would we even begin?

Ecce homo. We begin by looking at the vulnerable beloved and truly seeing them. Beholding them in their vulnerability and their suffering, we close our mouths and cease our attempts to tell their story for them. Instead, we listen, truly listen, as they tell of their suffering—even when they tell us plainly how our actions or our indifference have played a role in their suffering. We listen as they tell their story.

Tzniut. Pope Francis and Franz Rosenzweig both call us back to *modesty* and *humility.* In his 2015 speech, Francis put it this way: "To enable these real men and women to escape from extreme poverty, we must allow them to be dignified agents of their own destiny."[25] In other words, we must support those who suffer for our comfort in becoming the protagonists of their own story, rather than minor characters in our story.

Tikkun olam. This is Baldwin's *moving to Hong Kong* on a global scale. When we truly see the vulnerable beloved, bleeding before us, and truly listen as they tell their story of suffering at the hands of our institutions and habits of corruption, we might then be ready to tear the house apart. We might finally be ready to dismantle every bit of violence with which we have become comfortable, until at last our beloved can say, "I feel safe with you. I flourish because you are here."

I can't tell you what it will look like. Only the least of these can. Only the disinherited can.

What is a bible? Throughout this entire project, I have tried my best to avoid answering that question. Not because I don't think there's an answer—in fact, I think there are many answers—but because in the end I don't think that's the point. Try as we might to imagine otherwise, the objects we call our bibles cannot give us anything we did not already have in ourselves. Our capacity for corruption, and our capacity for love, do not come from outside us. Rather, in every moment, they are what we choose to do. Choices build up habits, and habits build communities, and communities include or exclude. No object in the universe chooses this for us. We do.

Let me say it plainly: Whatever object happens to be the one we call "The Bible," the only possible purpose of that bible is to get us to fall in love with the people around us. I mean catastrophically in love, the move to Hong Kong kind of love. So often—too often—we get this backwards. We mistakenly think the only purpose of the people around us is to get them to fall in love with our bible. But that's the triumphalism Pope Francis warned about. That just makes the folks around us into minor characters in our story when our job—our only job—is to help them be the dignified agents of their own destiny.

David Hayward is a cartoonist who worked as a minister for three decades. He now publishes a regular series of cartoons and commentary under the title *The Naked Pastor.* There's one of his cartoons that I particularly like, and I've kept a copy nearby for much of the writing of this book. It shows a simple line drawing of Jesus, standing on the right side of the panel, speaking to a group of modern-looking folks on the left side of the panel. Each figure on the left has a bible tucked under their arm. The word balloon above Christ's head says, *The difference between me and you is you use scripture to determine what love means, and I use love to determine what scripture means.*[26]

To recognize this requires that we participate in loving relationships. We must be in relationships of nurturing honesty with trust and permanence at their core. We must become vulnerable and be willing to listen to the vulnerability of our beloved. No amount of reading or study will supplant the basic necessity of these sorts of relationships. We must become absolutely serious—morally serious—about what an object we call a bible can and cannot do. Most important, we must let go of the idea that any object we call a bible could ever create a condition of absolute goodness, beyond the need for further examination, discussion, or interpretation. Books do not work this way. Platforms do not work this way. Communities do not work this way.

The object we call a bible does many things for us. When we carry it so the world can see, it accessorizes our identity. When we act in the world, it is the accessory to our benevolence, our violence, and our nonchalance. But it isn't the protagonist of our story. We are. It is the object *we call* the bible. In the end, it is *our* accessory.

James Baldwin said once, "If the concept of God has any validity or any use, it can only be to make us larger, freer, and more loving."[27]

That's it. That's the whole of it.

I've been wrestling with how to end this book, and I keep coming back to this one story. It's about the musician Julien Baker.

When I first read it, my heart broke in two different ways. The first breaking was from pain, but the second was from something I'd like to call hope, although I don't know exactly what hope looks like just yet. For a while I tried rewriting it in my own words, but I could never quite capture the simplicity and power of the original. So I'm just going to put the whole thing right here as I found it. I would ask you to read it like a kind of holy thing, like you would read a parable:

> When Julien Baker came out to her father at 17, he reached for his Bible.
>
> "I was like, 'I think I'm going to hell.' He said, 'Okay, stop,'" the now 20-year-old singer and guitarist remembers. "He went over and grabbed his Bible off the shelf and I was like, oh no, I think I'm about to get holy watered."
>
> Fair assumption. After all, hers was a churchgoing family—she considers herself nondenominational—living in the buckle of the Bible Belt: A 2013 Gallup poll of the most and least religious states in the country revealed Tennessee to be in the top ten, and Memphis, where Baker grew up, borders Mississippi, which claimed the number one spot. One of her friends was thrown out of his house when he came out, and another was shipped off to Love in Action, a "pray away the gay thing," as Baker calls it. But she was wrong about her father.
>
> "He spent the next hour saying, 'I'm gonna prove to you that you're not gonna go to hell.' I told my mom [I was] afraid and she was like, 'If I'm human and imperfect and I love you no matter what, how much do you think a perfect being loves you?'" Baker continues. "Here my parents are [say-

> ing], 'We love you. God loves you.' I think that's why I wanna talk about it so much. This exists. Tolerance exists."[28]

I would ask you to sit with this image for just a moment—Julien Baker and her father—with an object they call a bible, open between them. Open like a hand might be open, to help someone up, or like a door can be open, inviting in the poor and the stranger.

They are building a tent of hospitality, where the vulnerable are seen and sheltered. There's nothing grand about it. The space is small. For all I know, from a distance, nobody would notice this little light at all. Yet here we are, and for now my wish is that you and I linger with the two of them, father and daughter, in this space, without needing to say much more about it. We should just listen a while.

Every ending needs a beginning, and this—*this right here*—is where I choose to begin.

Notes

Introduction

1. I draw both of these ideas, and many more, from Adams, "Making Deep Reasonings Public."

2. Wittgenstein, *Philosophical Investigations*, 50.

3. I interviewed David Dark for my radio show *Things Not Seen*. Dark, "An Imaginary of Infinite Possibility."

4. Solnit, *Whose Story Is This?*, 134.

5. Neither this phrasing nor the intention behind it is original to me. Over the years I have heard this aim expressed by Richard Rorty, Nicholas Adams, and several other mentors and colleagues.

6. Baker quoted in Tolentino, "Raw Devotion of Julien Baker."

7. Fiasco, "Lupe Fiasco Presents."

1
Provenance and Terroir

1. "A fragment of a story, a fragment as a story." Ahmed, *Complaint!*, 15.

2. In making this reference to gleanings, I have in mind not only Leviticus 19 and Amos 8, but also the use Pope Francis makes of the idea in chapter 2 of *Laudato si'*. See Francis, "Encyclical Letter *Laudato si'*."

3. In particular, the metaphors of the wild forest from James C. Scott, *Seeing like a State*, and the rhizome/intersecting root system from Gilles Deleuze and Felix Guattari, *A Thousand Plateaus*.

4. The assertion comes from the description provided online by Eerdmans, the publisher of the ten-volume English-language set of Kittel; Kittel, *Theological Dictionary of the New Testament*.

5. Ericksen, "Theologian in the Third Reich."

6. Heschel, *Aryan Jesus*, 185.

7. Heschel, *Aryan Jesus*, 186.

8. Heschel, *Aryan Jesus*, 187–89.

9. Albright, "War in Europe," 165.

10. In addition to Susannah Heschel's excellent work on this matter, see also Ericksen, *Theologians Under Hitler;* and Hastings, *Catholicism and the Roots of Nazism.*

11. In Buber and Rosenzweig, *Scripture and Translation*, 47–69.

12. Rosenzweig, "Scripture and Luther," in Buber and Rosenzweig, *Scripture and Translation*, 52.

13. Rosenzweig, "Scripture and Luther," in Buber and Rosenzweig, *Scripture and Translation*, 64.

14. Rosenzweig, "Scripture and Luther," in Buber and Rosenzweig, *Scripture and Translation*, 66.

15. Eisenstadt, "Making Room for the Hebrew," 557.

16. Bloom, *Anxiety of Influence*, xviii—xix.

17. Bloom, *Anxiety of Influence*, xv.

18. I am deeply indebted to the work of Rabbi Zachary Truboff for the connection of tzniut to Rosenzweig's theory of translation. Of particular importance is his YouTube video lecture, "Translating the Other."

19. See "What Tznius Is Actually About."

20. Again, I express my indebtedness to Zachary Truboff for this insight.

21. Though I do not have space to develop it here, I am thinking of the work of Karen Barad and Donna Haraway when I invoke this word "diffraction."

22. Ochs and Levine, *Textual Reasonings.*

23. Ochs and Levine, *Textual Reasonings*, 4.

24. Ochs, "Introduction," in Ochs and Levine, *Textual Reasonings*, 4–5.

25. Ochs and Levine, *Textual Reasonings*, 6.

26. Ochs, "Introduction," in Ochs and Levine, *Textual Reasonings*, 6.

27. In making this assertion about the "goal" of the textual practices up to and including Scriptural Reasoning, I am mining a view that I find present throughout the early texts that speak of the development of the practice. In these sources, the hope for tikkun olam is explicit and repeated. I also acknowledge that a more recent generation of SR thinkers and practitioners has consciously stepped away from tikkun olam, specifically and explicitly on a species of *moral* grounds, in the spirit of antiproselytization and noncoercion. I commend to the reader especially Goodson, *Philosopher's Playground.* Goodson and I disagree vigorously regarding the place of tikkun olam in SR practice, but the process of thought he uses to reach his conclusion remains compelling and is worth sustained attention.

28. For an early example, see the reflections of David Ford, George Lindbeck, and Daniel Hardy, collected at the conclusion of Ochs and Levine, *Textual Reasonings,* 252–76.

29. Ford, "Interfaith Wisdom," 4. I highly recommend Ford's excellent essay, as well as the essay that follows it, "A Handbook for Scriptural Reasoning," by Steven Kepnes, for those readers unfamiliar with the history and mechanics of SR.

30. Nicholas Adams, quoted in Ford, "Interfaith Wisdom," 6.

31. The House, Campus, Tent model is explored in detail in Ford, "Interfaith Wisdom," 7–13.

32. Ford, "Interfaith Wisdom," 7.

33. See also Kepnes, "Handbook for Scriptural Reasoning," 24.

34. For the tendency to use the phrase "the text is our only host," see, for example, Dault, "Catholic Reasoning," 49; and Ford, "Deep Reasonings."

35. Kepnes, "Handbook for Scriptural Reasoning," 24.

36. These works are collected in the Comparative Research on Iconic Books and Performative Texts series, edited by James W. Watts and published by Equinox Press.

37. The history noted in this paragraph is drawn from both personal conversations with Watts and Parmenter and from Watts, *Iconic Books and Texts,* 1–3.

38. The ideas in this paragraph are drawn from Watts, *How and Why Books Matter,* 1–5.

39. Watts, *How and Why Books Matter,* 1.

40. Watts, *How and Why Books Matter,* 54.

41. Since my first exposure to these conversations (more than a decade ago, as of this writing), Watts, Parmenter, and the scholars who are part of the constellation of the Iconic Books Project have become my colleagues and friends. Together, we have worked to launch and grow an international organization known by the fortuitous acronym SCRIPT, which stands for the Society for Comparative Research on Iconic and Performative Texts. Through this organization, we continue to meet and delve ever more deeply into the questions that were raised in those initial symposia at Syracuse University and Hamilton College.

42. Note that, as mentioned later in this paragraph, in early versions of Watts's "Three Dimensions," the expressive dimension is referred to as the performative dimension. This change occurred in 2019.

43. Watts, *Iconic Books and Texts,* 16.

44. Watts, *How and Why Books Matter,* 53. My emphasis.

45. This issue has begun to be discussed and addressed in Iconic Books. James Watts has shared with me a copy of his article "Mobilizing the Social Power of Iconic and Performative Texts for Justice and Reform." I received it

too late to incorporate into the present analysis, but it suggests a very positive step in the development and maturation of the Iconic Books Project, and one that begins to bring it onto more of a parallel track that runs alongside the ethical focus of Scriptural Reasoning.

46. My most extended engagement with this claim to date is found in an article I wrote dealing with SR in specifically Catholic contexts. See Dault, "Catholic Reasoning and Reading Across Traditions."

47. Although this phrase has become common among SR practitioners, after speaking with them and engaging with them in a search of their published material, I have been unable to find who first introduced this phrase.

48. One of the clearest examples of this incorporation would be the work of Richard W. Newton Jr., particularly his *Identifying Roots.*

2
On Moral Seriousness

1. This date is contested by recent scholarship, which notes that the photo of Dorothy Counts was taken in September 1957. This means the dates of 1956 and 1957, recounted by Baldwin in his essay "No Name in the Street" (see pp. 476–77), which was first published more than a decade later in 1972, are incorrect. For narrative purposes, I have chosen to retain Baldwin's chronology of events throughout this chapter, despite this discrepancy.

2. Campbell, *Talking at the Gates,* 54.

3. Peck, *I Am Not Your Negro.*

4. Dark, *We Become What We Normalize,* 36.

5. Auden, *For the Time Being,* 124.

6. Dark, *Life's Too Short,* 134. Italics in original.

7. Here I am following the lead of Mathew Lu, who insists on the need to translate the Greek word *spoudaios,* particularly when it is found in Book I, chapter 7 of the *Nicomachean Ethics,* as "moral seriousness." See Lu, "Getting Serious."

8. Ma, "Nancy Hanks Lecture 2013."

9. I have Henri Nouwen in mind as I write these words, particularly his decision to depart from Harvard University to begin work with the L'Arche Community.

10. Hannah Arendt, "The Crisis in Education," in Arendt, *Between Past and Future,* 193.

11. Levinas, *Ethics and Infinity,* 99.

12. Derek Webb (@derekwebb), "why did I wear a dress to the dove awards?," Twitter, October 19, 2023, https://x.com/derekwebb/status/1715073827837788557?s=20. See also Stan Mitchell (@pastorstanmitchell), "Becoming an Ally," Facebook, November 17, 2019, https://fb.watch/n_oNX_z967/.

13. Lee, "Rev. Franklin Graham."

14. Merritt, "Franklin Graham's Turn."

15. Schulte, "Wheaton College Professor."

16. Hawkins, "Pragmatics of Embodied Solidarity." My emphasis.

17. Dark, *We Become What We Normalize*, 12.

18. Levinas, *Existence and Existents*, 36.

19. I borrow this language of protagonists from Pope Francis. I will return to this idea and its consequences in the concluding chapter of this book.

20. I am synthesizing a number of strands of Gilmore's thought here for the sake of space. Aspects of her thinking on "organized abandonment whose ultimate aim is premature death" can be found in both *The Golden Gulag* and *Abolition Geography*, particularly the final chapter of the latter book, "Abolition Geography and the Problem of Innocence."

21. Žižek, *Violence*, 1–5.

22. David Dark has explored this sort of bind, particularly with regard to his "robot soft exorcism" theory. See, e.g., *We Become What We Normalize*, 101–30.

23. Ahmed, *Complaint!*, 115.

24. Butler, *Force of Nonviolence*, 15.

25. This connection between Butler's and Gilmore's thought is my own, but I have since come to find that Butler also makes the connection in "Legal Violence." Although I happened upon this source too late to incorporate it into the present book, it will be included in my projects to come, which will explore more fully this idea of violence as organized isolation.

26. Butler, *Force of Nonviolence*, 72.

27. Arendt, *On Violence*, 56.

28. Arendt, *Human Condition*, 247.

29. I am indebted to my editor, Jennifer Banks, and her illuminating book *Natality: Toward a Philosophy of Birth* for helping me more fully understand this dimension of Arendt's work.

30. Butler, *Force of Nonviolence*, 148.

31. Dube, "Subaltern Can Speak," 54.

32. Although Mmulte is a specifically African character, those of us who grew up watching Bugs Bunny cartoons should have no difficulty imagining a rabbit in a narrative as a trickster figure.

33. "African trickster stories functioned among the enslaved Africans as a sign of hope in hopelessness. Despite the seeming powerlessness of enslaved people, the trickster stories continually said, 'you can resist, you can survive, you can get out, you can in fact beat the master.'" Dube, "Subaltern Can Speak," 56.

34. Dube, "Subaltern Can Speak," 58.

35. Dube, "Subaltern Can Speak," 69.

36. Dube, "Subaltern Can Speak," 70.

3
On Material Scripture

1. See the assessment of Feuerbach's waning prominence in Kamenka, *Philosophy of Ludwig Feuerbach,* particularly 25–32.

2. For the sake of space, I am moving somewhat quickly. It may be more accurate to say that the eclipse of materialist analysis (post-Marxist and otherwise) is evident in German and English biblical scholarship. Material analysis also remains at the heart of various liberation theologies, whether those arising among Spanish-speaking theologians or those increasingly emerging from within Francophone, Afrikaans, and English-speaking post-colonial contexts.

3. Clévenot, *Materialist Approaches,* ix.

4. McDannell, *Material Christianity,* 4.

5. For an updated list of Iconic Books approaches, including many materialist approaches, see the Iconic Books Project's regularly updated listing, "Categorized Bibliography."

6. Parmenter, "Material Scripture," 24–25.

7. Williams, *Keywords,* 146.

8. Williams, *Keywords,* 147.

9. Williams, *Marxism and Literature,* 82.

10. Williams, *Culture and Materialism,* 113.

11. Williams, *Culture and Materialism,* 9.

12. Williams, "An Open Letter."

13. Brown Douglas, *Black Christ,* 12–14 and passim.

14. Lake, *Artifacts,* 194. My emphasis.

15. Lake, *Artifacts,* 42. My emphasis.

16. Lake, *Artifacts,* 206.

17. Lake's afterword, "The Artifactual Form," offers an excellent discussion of both the political possibilities and limitations present in the various New Materialist approaches. My summary here has likely failed to capture her nuance, and it may yet be the case that such approaches will be useful to my own developing work. See Lake, *Artifacts,* 193–206.

18. Wartofsky, *Feuerbach,* 18.

19. Sinfield and Dollimore, *Political Shakespeare,* vii.

20. Sinfield and Dollimore, *Political Shakespeare,* viii.

21. Sinfield and Dollimore, *Political Shakespeare,* 4.

22. Prescod-Weinstein, "Making Black Women Scientists," 421.

23. Dube, "Subaltern Can Speak," 70.

24. Brown Douglas, "When the Subjugated Come to the Center," 42.

25. hooks, *All About Love,* 87–88.

26. Murphy, *Econimization of Life,* 6. My emphasis.

27. Levinas, *Existence and Existents,* 36.

28. I have in mind here both Howard Thurman's notion of the disinherited and the Nicaraguan farmers that sat with Ernesto Cardenal to read the Gospels. See Thurman, *Jesus and the Disinherited;* and Cardenal, *Gospel in Solentiname.*

29. Big Think, "Berkeley Professor Explains Gender Theory / Judith Butler," June 8, 2023, YouTube video, 13:23, https://youtu.be/UD9IOllUR4k?si=O5L4_i-dOi5pIzR-.

30. Sechrest, *Race & Rhyme,* 8.

31. Tractate Sanhedrin 68b—71a.

32. Tractate Sanhedrin 71a.

4
First Thesis

1. King, *On Writing,* 104–7.

2. There are many interviews and articles where Steve Albini discusses some aspect of his concept of political arrangements. Probably the most (in) famous introduction comes in his article "The Problem with Music." For Albini's more fully developed thoughts on political arrangements, see also his conversation with Marc Maron, "Steve Albini."

3. Houston, *The Book,* xvi.

4. I highly recommend readers take time and engage with McCutcheon's *Manufacturing Religion.* Its analysis of these matters is truly excellent.

5. Fisher, *Capitalist Realism,* 2. For Fisher's discussion of the concept, see 3–7.

6. Field, *Town Hall Meetings,* 4.

7. Horsley, "Oral and Written Aspects," 95.

8. Fisher, *Capitalist Realism,* 17.

9. I am gathering these terms from Glaister, *Encyclopedia of the Book,* and from Genette and Maclean, "Introduction to the Paratext."

10. Barad, "Nature's Queer Performativity," 125. I am deeply indebted to my dear friend Alexander Badenoch of the University of Utrecht's Department of Media and Culture Studies for bringing the article to my attention. Barad takes up the idea of intra-action more fully in the book *Meeting the Universe Halfway.*

11. Ehrman speaking in the video "Does Bart Ehrman Want You to Leave Christianity?" My transcription and emphasis.

5
Second Thesis

1. Yang, *Third University,* 62n12.

2. In the early 2000s, the set of customization options the online platform MySpace (capitalization later changed to Myspace) offered its users for each individual page bordered on the anarchic. Users could choose font and background options that often made their individual pages practically inoperable as websites, illegible and hardly navigable. Facebook, which offered a very different approach to content and aesthetics, lured the user base of MySpace to its own platform. The visual contrast between these two platforms could not have been starker, and yet in almost all respects, their core functions remained the same.

3. Hyatt, *Platform,* xvi.

4. I borrow this insight from Field, *Town Hall Meetings,* 4–5.

5. Brown, *Undoing the Demos,* 17, quoted in Field, *Town Hall Meetings,* 6.

6. Doctorow, "DEF CON 31."

7. Thomas Jefferson, personal correspondence to Charles Thompson, *Jefferson Bible,* 28.

8. Jefferson, *Jefferson Bible,* 147.

9. Jefferson, *Jefferson Bible,* 18.

10. Jefferson, *Jefferson Bible,* 17.

11. Pelikan, "Jefferson and His Contemporaries," 149.

12. Church, "Gospel According to Thomas Jefferson," 30. My emphasis.

13. Stokes, "AR-15 Is More." My emphasis.

14. Pelikan, "Jefferson and His Contemporaries," 153.

15. McDonald, *Formation of the Christian Biblical Canon,* 28–29. Emphasis in original.

16. For an overview of the basic understanding of redaction in the Hebrew Bible, see Müller, Pakkala, and Romeny, *Evidence of Editing.*

17. McDonald, *Biblical Canon,* 426. My emphasis.

18. Barth, "Strange New World."

19. Thuesen, *In Discordance,* 104.

20. Thuesen, *In Discordance,* 96 passim.

21. Thuesen, *In Discordance,* 97.

22. Thuesen, *In Discordance,* 97.

23. Rubenstein and Smith, "History of the *Jefferson Bible,*" 12.

24. Rubenstein and Smith, "History of the *Jefferson Bible,*" 12.

25. In my view, what was done to Sally Hemings by Thomas Jefferson should be regarded as rape. However, I am aware that there is a great deal of debate in recent scholarship around this issue, particularly regarding how

much agency Hemings was able to exercise. Thus, I have chosen the phrase "questionable consent" to acknowledge that, in the end, we cannot know the full extent of the relationship between Hemings and Jefferson from the limited evidence that has been preserved to the present day. For a recent overview of this matter, see Stockman, "Monticello Is Done."

26. Brown Douglas, *Black Christ,* 10.

27. Brown Douglas, *Black Christ,* 25.

28. Museum of the Bible, *Slave Bible.*

6
Third Thesis

1. Walker, "Between the Lines," 287.

2. See, for example, this self-referential story about the process: Hansen and Kern, "Crafting Radio's Driveway Moments."

3. For more detailed discussions of "canon" (particularly in a biblical sense), see McDonald and Sanders, "Introduction," and Rendtorff, "Importance of Canon." For a general discussion of the subject in extrabiblical contexts, see von Hallberg, *Canons.*

4. Russo and Russo, "Pilot."

5. Franklin Graham, "The Bible alone is the absolute standard of eternal truth for every person in every age," X, May 21, 2021, https://x.com/Franklin_Graham/status/1395793048135774208?mx=2.

6. I am aware that Carl Hempel has used the term "nomological" in his work, most specifically in "Deductive-Nomological vs. Statistical Explanation." My use of the term here diverges from his in ways that I hope will be clear.

7. I am drawing chiefly from Ayer, *Problem of Knowledge,* section V, "Knowing as having the right to be sure," for my comments in this paragraph.

8. International Bureau of Weights and Measures, *The International System of Units,* 131. I have gathered this information about Le Grand K and the move to a new standard measurement from a number of sources. The National Institute of Standards and Technology website is an invaluable source of information about the entire set of measurement standards and protocols known as the International System of Units (SI). You can find information there about the kilogram at "Kilogram: Introduction." I also drew upon Resnick, "World Just Redefined the Kilogram"; and "The kg Is Dead."

9. Olson, "In Search of a Flat Earth."

10. Wenger-Trayner and Wenger-Trayner, "Introduction to Communities of Practice."

11. See Eckert and McConnell-Ginet, "Communities of Practice."

12. Butler, *Gender Trouble,* xv.

7
Fourth Thesis

1. Hoskins, *Anticapitalist,* 7, 16. First emphasis in original, second emphasis mine.

2. Hoskins, *Anticapitalist,* 281.

3. Hoskins, *Anticapitalist,* 18.

4. Croll, *Bad Girls,* 2. My emphasis.

5. Croll, *Bad Girls,* 2. My emphasis.

6. Hastings, "Interview with Wayne Hastings."

7. Numbers are from Hastings, "Farewell Thomas Nelson."

8. Tom Ciesielka, interview with the author, July 11, 2018.

9. I draw the observations in these two paragraphs from Benjamin, *Arcades Project,* particularly pp. 43–74.

10. The tortoise shell example may seem oddly specific, but I have in mind an incunabular text I saw while visiting the Walter A. Maier Rare Book Archives at Concordia Seminary in St. Louis in 2010. It was a bible text bound in a tortoise shell cover. For more information and a photo, see Dault, "Report from a Visit."

11. There are some wonderful overviews that explore and explain the kind of "bible vibe" I reference here. See Bielo, *Materializing the Bible;* Bado-Fralick and Sachs Norris, *Toying with God;* Beal, *Roadside Religion;* and Wexler, *Holy Hullabaloos.*

12. Important work has recently been done on this subject by Daniel Silliman. Unfortunately, I encountered his masterful book *Reading Evangelicals: How Christian Fiction Shaped a Culture and a Faith* too late to incorporate properly into this project. It is my hope to give his ideas and insights the engagement they deserve in a future work.

13. I am thinking here in particular of the essays collected in Baudrillard, *Gulf War.* See also Thackaray, "Don't Turn Notre Dame into 'Politically Correct Disneyland.'"

14. Martyn, *Galatians,* 112. For a detailed discussion of the politics at stake in the Galatian community, see 106–36 in particular.

15. Woolman, "Abridgment," 163–64.

16. Woolman, "Abridgment," 171–72, 186, 192–93.

17. "John Woolman." See also Woolman, "Abridgment," 203.

18. Osmond, "Influence of John Woolman," 71.

19. Rahner, *Foundations of Christian Faith,* 110–11, 114. I was first introduced to this story by my friend Tyler Wigg-Stevenson in his book *Brand Jesus,* 87.

20. Quoted in Pelikan, *Vindication of Tradition,* 82. In *Faust,* the quotation is found in lines 682–83; they fall on pp. 114–15 of Walter Kaufmann's

translation, where they are rendered, "What from your fathers you received as heir, / Acquire if you would possess it."

21. Gusterson, *People of the Bomb,* xv passim.

22. Gusterson, *People of the Bomb,* 10. My emphasis.

23. Olson, "Minecraft."

Conclusion

1. Ables, *Body of the Cross,* 196.

2. Unfortunately, Rick Roderick published very little in his brief lifetime. However, toward the end of his life he recorded a number of lectures for video distribution, and these give a good overview of the methods of thought and connection he employed in the seminar I took. Many of these lectures are available on YouTube and can be found by searching Roderick's name. A thorough search of used booksellers might also yield a copy of his excellent *Habermas and the Foundations of Critical Theory.*

3. Joshua Cherniss and Henry Hardy describe Berlin's presuppositions:

> 1. All genuine questions must have a true answer, and one only; all other responses are errors.
>
> 2. There must be a dependable path to discovering the true answer to a question, which is in principle knowable, even if currently unknown.
>
> 3. The true answers, when found, will be compatible with one another, forming a single whole; for one truth cannot be incompatible with another. (This, in turn, is based on the assumption that the universe is harmonious and coherent.)

Cherniss and Hardy, "Isaiah Berlin." See particularly section 4.1, "Berlin's Definition of Value Pluralism."

4. West speaks often about this domestication, as well as about being a bluesman. For an accessible discussion, see his interview in Astra Taylor's 2008 documentary *Examined Life.* I am also thinking here of the work of philosopher Sara Ahmed. In her book *Complaint!,* she details the numerous strategies used by institutions, bureaucracies, and other systems to arrest the claims of those who are victims of systems. In this case, "We're working on the problem" would be an example of what Ahmed calls a *nonperformative,* an appearance of action that results in no action. Although Ahmed discusses the concept of the nonperformative throughout the text (and her work at large), see especially *Complaint!* 30.

5. See for example Hawkins, "Pragmatics of Embodied Solidarity."

6. For two brief examinations of this practice, see Gershon, "How Olympics Host Cities Hide Their Homeless"; and Willsher, "Thousands of Homeless People Removed."

7. For a discussion of the ideas found in this section, see Tillich, *History of Christian Thought*, 162–63.

8. Flanagan, *Midnight Mass*.

9. Neville, *Won't You Be My Neighbor?*

10. Baldwin, "Nothing Personal," 393. My emphasis.

11. Both quotations in this paragraph are from Baldwin, "Nothing Personal," 393–94, and (for the "four AM choice"), 395–99.

12. Baldwin, "Nothing Personal," 398.

13. Baldwin, "Nothing Personal," 399.

14. Baldwin, "Nothing Personal," 395.

15. See Mayer, "Caritas," 37–39.

16. "Cornel West's Catastrophic Love."

17. See Derrida, *Rogues*, 78–94.

18. This and the following quotation from Baldwin, "Nothing Personal," 399–400.

19. Baldwin, "Nothing Personal," 392.

20. Baldwin, "Nothing Personal," 394.

21. This perspective is not unique to Baldwin, of course. We find aspects of it in the work of James Cone, Kelly Brown Douglas, Miguel De La Torre, Larycia Hawkins, Musa Dube, Love Lazarus Sechrest, and many others. Christ actively identifies with those whom the people with comfortable access to violence seek to make disappear.

22. Bergoglio, *Way of Humility*, 45, 22. My emphasis.

23. Bergoglio, *Way of Humility*, 36.

24. Epatko, "Full Text."

25. Epatko, "Full Text."

26. Hayward, *Flip It like This!*, 110. My emphasis.

27. Baldwin, "Letter from a Region."

28. Haithcoat, "He Hears Either Way."

Bibliography

Ables, Travis E. *The Body of the Cross: Holy Victims and the Invention of the Atonement.* New York: Fordham University Press, 2022.

Adams, Nicholas. "Making Deep Reasonings Public." In *The Promise of Scriptural Reasoning,* edited by David F. Ford and C. C. Pecknold, 41–58. Malden, MA: Wiley-Blackwell, 2006.

Ahmed, Sara. *Complaint!* Durham, NC: Duke University Press, 2021.

Albini, Steve. "The Problem with Music." *The Baffler* 5 (December 1993). https://thebaffler.com/salvos/the-problem-with-music.

———. "Steve Albini." *WTF with Marc Maron.* Episode 650. October 29, 2015. https://www.wtfpod.com/podcast/tag/Steve+Albini.

Albright, W. F. "The War in Europe and the Future of Biblical Studies." In *The Study of the Bible Today and Tomorrow,* edited by Harold Willoughby, 162–74. Chicago: University of Chicago Press, 1947.

Arendt, Hannah. *Between Past and Future. Eight Exercises in Political Thought.* New York: Penguin Classics, 2006.

———. *The Human Condition.* 2nd ed. Chicago: University of Chicago Press, 1998.

———. *On Violence.* New York: Houghton Mifflin, 1970.

Auden, W. H. *For the Time Being.* London: Faber & Faber, 1945.

Austen, Jane. *Pride and Prejudice.* Oxford: Oxford University Press, 2019.

Ayer, A. J. *The Problem of Knowledge.* New York: St. Martin's, 1956.

Bado-Fralick, Nikki, and Rebecca Sachs Norris. *Toying with God: The World of Religious Games and Dolls.* Waco, TX: Baylor University Press, 2010.

Baldwin, James. "Letter from a Region in My Mind." *The New Yorker.* November 9, 1962. https://www.newyorker.com/magazine/1962/11/17/letter-from-a-region-in-my-mind?mbed=social_tumblr.

———. "No Name in the Street." In *The Price of the Ticket: Collected Nonfiction, 1948–1945*, 449–562. Boston: Beacon Press, 1985.

———. "Nothing Personal." In *The Price of the Ticket: Collected Nonfiction, 1948–1945*, 388–400. Boston: Beacon Press, 1985.

Banks, Jennifer. *Natality: Toward a Philosophy of Birth.* New York: W. W. Norton, 2023.

Barad, Karen. *Meeting the Universe Halfway: Quantum Physics and the Entanglement of Matter and Meaning.* Durham, NC: Duke University Press, 2007.

———. "Nature's Queer Performativity." *Qui Parle* 19, no. 2 (Spring/Summer 2011): 121–58.

Barth, Karl. "The Strange New World Within the Bible." In *The Word of God and the Word of Man.* Translated by Douglas Horton, 28–50. Gloucester, MA: Peter Smith, 1978.

Baudrillard, Jean. *The Gulf War Did Not Take Place.* Translated by Paul Patton. Sydney: Power Publications, 2012.

Beal, Timothy K., ed. *The Oxford Encyclopedia of the Bible and the Arts.* Oxford: Oxford University Press, 2015.

———. "Reception History and Beyond: Toward the Cultural History of the Scriptures." *Biblical Interpretation* 19 (2011): 357–72.

———. *The Rise and Fall of the Bible: The Unexpected History of an Accidental Book.* New York: HarperOne, 2012.

———. *Roadside Religion: In Search of the Sacred, the Strange, and the Substance of Faith.* Boston: Beacon Press, 2005.

Beal, Timothy K., and Tod Linafelt, eds. *Mel Gibson's Bible.* Chicago: University of Chicago Press, 2005.

Belo, Fernando. *A Materialist Reading of the Gospel of Mark.* Translated by Matthew J. O'Connell. Maryknoll, NY: Orbis, 1981.

Benjamin, Walter. *The Arcades Project.* Translated by Howard Eiland and Kevin McLaughlin. Cambridge, MA: Harvard University Press, 2002.

Bergoglio, Jorge Mario. *The Way of Humility: Corruption and Sin & On Self-Accusation.* San Francisco: Ignatius Press, 2013.

Bielo, James S. *Materializing the Bible: Scripture, Sensation, Place.* New York: Bloomsbury Academic, 2021.

———. *Words upon the Word: An Ethnography of Evangelical Group Bible Study.* New York: NYU Press, 2009.

Bloom, Harold. *The Anxiety of Influence: A Theory of Poetry.* Oxford: Oxford University Press, 1997.

Brown, Wendy. *Undoing the Demos: Neoliberalism's Stealth Revolution.* Cambridge: Zone Books, 2015.

Brown Douglas, Kelly. *The Black Christ.* Maryknoll, NY: Orbis, 1994.

———. "When the Subjugated Come to the Center." *Journal of Religious Thought* 52/53, no. 2/1 (1996): 37–43.

Buber, Martin, and Franz Rosenzweig. *Scripture and Translation.* Translated by Lawrence Rosenwald with Everett Fox. Bloomington: Indiana University Press, 1994.

Butler, Judith. *The Force of Nonviolence: An Ethico-Political Bind.* London: Verso, 2021.

———. *Gender Trouble.* New York: Routledge, 1990.

———. "Legal Violence: An Ethical and Political Critique." 2016 Tanner Lecture on Human Values, Yale University. June 30, 2016. YouTube video, 1:45:26. https://youtu.be/coBcQajx18I?si=dCNjyMofUMKhI_KC.

Campbell, James. *Talking at the Gates: A Life of James Baldwin.* Oakland: University of California Press, 2021.

Cardenal, Ernesto. *The Gospel in Solentiname.* Translated by Donald D. Walsh. Eugene, OR: Wipf & Stock, 2020.

"Categorized Bibliography." Iconic Books Project. Updated June 15, 2024. http://jameswwatts.net/iconicbooks/IB%20Bibliography.htm.

Cherniss, Joshua, and Henry Hardy. "Isaiah Berlin." In *The Stanford Encyclopedia of Philosophy* (Winter 2023 ed.), edited by Edward N. Zalta and Uri Nodelman. https://plato.stanford.edu/archives/win2023/entries/berlin/.

Church, Forrest. "The Gospel According to Thomas Jefferson." In *The Jefferson Bible: The Life and Morals of Jesus of Nazareth,* 1–31. Boston: Beacon Press, 1989.

Clévenot, Michel. *Materialist Approaches to the Bible.* Translated by William J. Nottingham. Maryknoll, NY: Orbis, 1985.

"Cornel West's Catastrophic Love." *BigThink.* November 3, 2009. 6:00. https://bigthink.com/videos/cornel-wests-catastrophic-love/.

Croll, Jennifer. *Bad Girls of Fashion: Style Rebels from Cleopatra to Lady Gaga.* Toronto: Annick, 2016.

Dark, David. "An Imaginary of Infinite Possibility: David Dark." Interview by David Dault. *Things Not Seen: Conversations About Culture and Faith,* January 1, 2024. https://www.thingsnotseenradio.com/shows/2301-dark.

———. *Life's Too Short to Pretend You're Not Religious: Reframed and Expanded.* Minneapolis: Broadleaf, 2022.

———. *We Become What We Normalize: What We Owe Each Other in Worlds That Demand Our Silence.* Minneapolis: Broadleaf, 2023.

Dault, David. "Catholic Reasoning and Reading Across Traditions." *Modern Theology* 29 (2013): 46–61.

———. "The Covert Magisterium." PhD diss., Vanderbilt University, 2009. https://ir.vanderbilt.edu/bitstream/handle/1803/11105/GDRDavidDault-Dissertation.pdf.

———. "Report from a Visit to the Concordia Seminary Rare Book Archives." *Material Scripture.* June 13, 2010. https://materialscripture.blogspot.com/2010/06/report-from-visit-to-concordia-seminary.html.

Deleuze, Gilles, and Felix Guattari. *A Thousand Plateaus.* Minneapolis: University of Minnesota Press, 1987.

Derrida, Jacques. *Rogues: Two Essays on Reason.* Translated by Pascale-Anne Brault and Michael Naas. Stanford: Stanford University Press, 2005.

Dessauer, John P. *Book Publishing: The Basic Introduction: New Expanded Edition.* New York: Continuum, 1989.

Doctorow, Cory. "DEF CON 31—An Audacious Plan to Halt the Internet's Ensh*ttification—Cory Doctorow." DEFCONConference. September 14, 2023. YouTube video, 45:42. https://www.youtube.com/watch?v=rimtaSgGz_4.

"Does Bart Ehrman Want You to Leave Christianity?" Video posted by Drew McCoy [Genetically Modified Skeptic, pseud.]. July 27, 2022. YouTube video, 29:21. https://youtu.be/KHC4mSUMrBk.

Dube, Musa W. "The Subaltern Can Speak: Reading the Mmulte (Hare) Way." *Journal of Africana Religions* 4, no. 1 (2016): 54–75.

Eckert, Penelope, and Sally McConnell-Ginet. "Communities of Practice: Where Language, Gender, and Power All Live." In *Locating Power: Proceedings of the 1992 Berkeley Women and Language Conference,* edited by Kira Hall, Mary Bucholtz, and Birch Moonwomon, 89–99. Berkeley: Berkeley Women and Language Group, 1992.

Eisenstadt, Oona. "Making Room for the Hebrew: Luther, Dialectics, and the Shoah." *Journal of the American Academy of Religion* 69, no. 3 (2001): 551–75.

Epatko, Larisa. "Full Text of Pope Francis' Speech to United Nations." *PBS News Hour.* September 25, 2015. https://www.pbs.org/newshour/world/full-text-pope-francis-speech-united-nations.

Ericksen, Robert P. "Theologian in the Third Reich: The Case of Gerhard Kittel." *Journal of Contemporary History* 12, no. 3 (1977): 595–622. http://www.jstor.org/stable/260042.

———. *Theologians Under Hitler.* New Haven: Yale University Press, 1985.

Fiasco, Lupe. "Lupe Fiasco Presents 'Rap Theory & Practice: An Introduction.'" MIT Comparative Media Studies/Writing. December 6, 2022. YouTube video, 1:29:45. https://youtu.be/zBHRsYhYb-0?si=7k2SCqkr5flsDKE2.

Field, Jonathan Beecher. *Town Hall Meetings and the Death of Deliberation.* Minneapolis: University of Minnesota Press, 2019.

Fisher, Mark. *Capitalist Realism: Is There No Alternative?* Hampshire: Zero Books, 2009.

Flanagan, Mike, dir. *Midnight Mass.* Intrepid Pictures, 2021. Netflix miniseries.

Ford, David F. "Deep Reasonings, No Map: Inter-faith Engagement as a Core Dynamic of Theology and Religious Studies." Cambridge Interfaith Programme 2013. https://www.interfaith.cam.ac.uk/resources/lecturespapersandspeeches/Deepreasoningsnomap.

———. "An Interfaith Wisdom: Scriptural Reasoning Between Jews, Christians, and Muslims." In *The Promise of Scriptural Reasoning,* edited by David F. Ford and C. C. Pecknold, 1–22. Malden, MA: Wiley-Blackwell, 2006.

Francis. "Encyclical Letter *Laudato si'* of the Holy Father Francis on Care for Our Common Home." The Holy See. May 24, 2015. https://www.vatican.va/content/francesco/en/encyclicals/documents/papa-francesco_20150524_enciclica-laudato-si.html.

Frankel, David, dir. *The Devil Wears Prada.* 20th Century Fox, 2006.

Genette, Gérard, and Marie Maclean. "Introduction to the Paratext." *New Literary History* 22, no. 2 (1991): 261–72.

Gershon, Livia. "How Olympics Host Cities Hide Their Homeless." *JSTOR Daily.* July 8, 2016. https://daily.jstor.org/how-olympics-host-citie-hide-their-homeless/.

Gilmore, Ruth Wilson. *Abolition Geography: Essays Toward Liberation.* New York: Verso, 2023.

———. *The Golden Gulag: Prisons, Surplus, Crisis, and Opposition in Globalizing California.* Berkeley: University of California Press, 2007.

Glaister, Geoffrey Ashall. *Encyclopedia of the Book.* 2nd ed. New Castle, DE: Oak Knoll Press, 2001.

Goethe, Johann Wolfgang von. *Faust.* Translated by Walter Kaufmann. New York: Anchor, 1990.

Goodson, Jacob L. *The Philosopher's Playground: Understanding Scriptural Reasoning Through Modern Philosophy.* Eugene, OR: Cascade, 2021.

Gusterson, Hugh. *People of the Bomb: Portraits of America's Nuclear Complex.* Minneapolis: University of Minnesota Press, 2004.

Haithcoat, Rebecca. "He Hears Either Way: Julien Baker Is Writing a New Gospel for Broken Hearts." *Vice.com.* April 20, 2016. https://www.vice.com/en/article/65z83x/noisey-next-julien-baker-sprained-ankle-interview-profile-2016.

Hansen, Liane, and Jonathan Kern. "Crafting Radio's Driveway Moments." *Weekend Edition Sunday.* National Public Radio, July 20, 2008. https://www.npr.org/templates/story/story.php?storyId=92716706.

Hastings, Derek. *Catholicism and the Roots of Nazism: Religious Identity and National Socialism.* New York: Oxford University Press, 2010.

Hastings, Wayne. "Farewell Thomas Nelson." 2009. Accessed July 26, 2024. https://waynehastings.com/leadership/farewell-thomas-nelson/ (site discontinued).

———. "Interview with Wayne Hastings of Thomas Nelson Publishers." Interview by David Dault. *Material Scripture.* April 8, 2009. https://materialscripture.blogspot.com/2009/04/interview-with-wayne-hastings-of-thomas.html.

Hawkins, Larycia. "The Pragmatics of Embodied Solidarity in Theopolitical Space." 2017 Greely Lecture for Peace and Social Justice, Harvard Divinity School. February 23, 2017. Internet video, 43:07. https://cswr.hds.harvard.edu/news/2017/02/23/video-pragmatics-embodied-solidarity-theopolitical-space.

Hayward, David. *Flip It like This!* Minneapolis: Broadleaf Books, 2022.

Hempel, Carl. "Deductive-Nomological vs. Statistical Explanation." In *Scientific Explanation, Space, & Time.* Minnesota Studies in the Philosophy of Science, vol. 3, edited by Herbert Feigl and Gordon Maxwell, 98–169. Minneapolis: University of Minnesota Press, 1962.

Heschel, Susannah. *The Aryan Jesus: Christian Theologians and the Bible in Nazi Germany.* Princeton: Princeton University Press, 2008.

hooks, bell. *All About Love: New Visions.* New York: HarperCollins, 2001.

Horsley, Richard A. "Oral and Written Aspects of the Emergence of the Gospel of Mark as Scripture." *Oral Tradition* 25, no. 1 (2010): 93–114.

Hoskins, Tansy E. *The Anticapitalist Book of Fashion.* London: Pluto Press, 2022.

Houston, Keith. *The Book: A Cover-to-Cover Exploration of the Most Powerful Object of Our Time.* New York: W. W. Norton, 2016.

Hyatt, Michael. *Platform: Get Noticed in a Noisy World.* Nashville: Thomas Nelson, 2012.

International Bureau of Weights and Measures. *The International System of Units (SI)*, 9th ed. Sèvres, France: Bureau International des Poids et Mesures, 2022. https://www.bipm.org/documents/20126/41483022/SI-Brochure-9-EN.pdf/2d2b50bf-f2b4-9661-f402-5f9d66e4b507.

Jefferson, Thomas. *The Jefferson Bible: The Life and Morals of Jesus of Nazareth.* Boston: Beacon Press, 1989.

"John Woolman." Quakers in the World. Accessed July 27, 2024. https://www.quakersintheworld.org/quakers-in-action/62/John-Woolman.

Kamenka, Eugene. *The Philosophy of Ludwig Feuerbach.* London: Routledge & Kegan Paul, 1970.

Kepnes, Steven. "A Handbook for Scriptural Reasoning." In *The Promise of Scriptural Reasoning,* edited by David F. Ford and C. C. Pecknold, 23–40. Malden, MA: Wiley-Blackwell, 2006.

Kepnes, Steven, Peter Ochs, and Robert Gibbs. *Reasoning After Revelation: Dialogues in Postmodern Jewish Philosophy.* Boulder, CO: Westview, 1998.

"The kg Is Dead, Long Live the kg." Video posted by Veritasium. November 15, 2018. YouTube video, 2:44. https://www.youtube.com/watch?v=c_e1wITe_ig&t=522s.

King, Stephen. *On Writing: A Memoir of the Craft*. New York: Scribner, 2000.

Kittel, Gerhard, ed. *Theological Dictionary of the New Testament*. 10-vol set. Eerdmans EBook. Accessed July 27, 2024. https://www.eerdmans.com/9781467422734/theological-dictionary-of-the-new-testament-10-vol-set/.

Lake, Crystal B. *Artifacts: How We Think and Write About Found Objects*. Baltimore: Johns Hopkins University Press, 2020.

Lee, Carol E. "Rev. Franklin Graham: Islam 'Evil.'" *Politico Now Blog*. October 3, 2010. https://www.politico.com/blogs/politico-now/2010/10/rev-franklin-graham-islam-evil-029683.

Levinas, Emmanuel. *Ethics and Infinity: Conversations with Philippe Nemo*. Translated by Richard A. Cohen. Pittsburgh: Duquesne University Press, 1985.

———. *Existence and Existents*. Translated by Alphonso Lingis. Pittsburgh: Duquesne University Press, 1988.

Lu, Mathew. "Getting Serious About Seriousness: On the Meaning of *Spoudaios* in Aristotle's Ethics." *Proceedings of the American Catholic Philosophical Association* 87 (2013): 285–93.

Ma, Yo-Yo. "Nancy Hanks Lecture 2013: Yo-Yo Ma." Americans for the Arts. April 8, 2013. YouTube video, 1:26:22. https://www.youtube.com/live/TWsdrjUhol4?si=kSmqLKcn2EcwznFa.

Martyn, J. Louis. *Galatians: A New Translation with Introduction and Commentary*. Anchor Yale Bible Commentaries. New York: Doubleday, 1997. Reprint, New Haven: Yale University Press.

Mayer, Milton S. "Caritas." In *What Can a Man Do? A Selection of His Most Challenging Writings*, edited by Eric Gustafson, 36–43. Chicago: University of Chicago Press, 1964.

McCutcheon, Russell. *Manufacturing Religion: The Discourse on Sui Generis Religion and the Politics of Nostalgia*. New York: Oxford University Press, 1997.

McDannell, Colleen. *Material Christianity: Religion and Popular Culture in America*. New Haven: Yale University Press, 1995.

McDonald, Lee Martin. *The Biblical Canon: Its Origin, Transmission and Authority*. Peabody, MA: Hendrickson, 2007.

———. *The Formation of the Christian Biblical Canon*. Nashville: Abingdon, 1989.

McDonald, Lee Martin, and James A. Sanders. "Introduction." In *The Canon Debate*, edited by Lee Martin McDonald and James Sanders, 3–20. Peabody, MA: Hendrickson, 2002.

Merritt, Jonathan. "Franklin Graham's Turn Toward Intolerance." *The Atlantic*. July 19, 2015. https://www.theatlantic.com/politics/archive/2015/07/franklin-grahams-turn-toward-intolerance/398924/.

Müller, Reinhard, Juha Pakkala, and Bas ter Haar Romeny. *Evidence of Editing: Growth and Change of Texts in the Hebrew Bible.* Resources for Biblical Study. Atlanta: Society of Biblical Literature, 2014.

Murphy, Michelle. *The Econimization of Life.* Durham, NC: Duke University Press, 2017.

Museum of the Bible. *The Slave Bible: Let the Story Be Told.* Washington, DC. https://www.museumofthebible.org/exhibits/slave-bible.

National Institute of Standards and Technology. "Kilogram: Introduction." Last updated February 22, 2023. https://www.nist.gov/si-redefinition/kilogram-introduction.

Neville, Morgan, dir. *Won't You Be My Neighbor?* Focus Features, 2018.

Newton, Richard W., Jr. *Identifying Roots: Alex Haley and the Anthropology of Scriptures.* Sheffield: Equinox, 2020.

Ochs, Peter. *Religion Without Violence: The Practice and Philosophy of Scriptural Reasoning.* Eugene, OR: Cascade, 2019.

Ochs, Peter, and Nancy Levine, eds. *Textual Reasonings: Jewish Philosophy and Text Study at the End of the Twentieth Century.* Grand Rapids: Eerdmans, 2002.

Olson, Dan. "In Search of a Flat Earth." Folding Ideas. September 11, 2020. YouTube video, 1:16:16. https://youtu.be/JTfhYyTuT44.

———. "Minecraft, Sandboxes, and Colonialism." Folding Ideas. August 23, 2019. YouTube video, 15:00. https://www.youtube.com/watch?v=d6i5YluomgM.

Osmond, Winston Stanley. "The Influence of John Woolman on the Quakers' Antislavery Position." Master's thesis, Acadia University, 1998. https://scholar.acadiau.ca/node/2398.

Parmenter, Dorina Miller. "Material Scripture." In *The Oxford Encyclopedia of the Bible and the Arts,* vol. 2, edited by Timothy Beal, 24–35. Oxford: Oxford University Press, 2015.

Peck, Raoul, dir. *I Am Not Your Negro.* Magnolia Pictures, 2017.

Pelikan, Jaroslav. "Jefferson and His Contemporaries." In *The Jefferson Bible: The Life and Morals of Jesus of Nazareth,* 149–67. Boston: Beacon Press, 1989.

———. *The Vindication of Tradition.* New Haven: Yale University Press, 1984.

Plate, S. Brent. *A History of Religion in 5 1/2 Objects: Bringing the Spiritual to Its Senses.* Boston: Beacon, 2014.

———, ed. *Key Terms in Material Religion.* New York: Bloomsbury, 2015.

Prescod-Weinstein, Chanda. "Making Black Women Scientists Under White Empiricism: The Racialization of Epistemology in Physics." *Signs: Journal of Women in Culture and Society* 45, no. 2 (2020): 421–47.

Rahner, Karl. *Foundations of Christian Faith: An Introduction to the Idea of Christianity.* Translated by William V. Dych. London: Darton, Longman & Todd, 1979.

Rendtorff, Rolf. "The Importance of Canon for a Theology of the Old Testament." In *Canon and Theology: Overtures to an Old Testament Theology*, translated by Margaret Kohl, 46–56. Minneapolis: Augsburg Fortress, 1993.

Resnick, Brian. "The World Just Redefined the Kilogram." *Vox.com*. Updated November 16, 2018. https://www.vox.com/science-and-health/2018/11/14/18072368/kilogram-kibble-redefine-weight-science.

Roderick, Rick. *Habermas and the Foundations of Critical Theory*. New York: St. Martin's, 1986.

Rubenstein, Harry R., and Barbara Clark Smith. "History of the *Jefferson Bible*." In *The Jefferson Bible: Smithsonian Edition*, 11–36. Washington, DC: Smithsonian, 2011.

Russo, Anthony, and Joe Russo, dirs. "Pilot." *Community*. Aired September 17, 2009, on NBC.

Schlereth, Thomas, ed. *Material Culture: A Research Guide*. Lawrence: University Press of Kansas, 1985.

Schulte, Sarah. "Wheaton College Professor Suspended for Religious Post on Facebook." ABC7 Eyewitness News. December 16, 2015. https://abc7chicago.com/wheaton-college-larycia-hawkins-professor-suspended-facebook/1125581/.

Scott, James C. *Seeing like a State*. New Haven: Yale University Press, 2020.

Sechrest, Love Lazarus. *Race & Rhyme: Rereading the New Testament*. Grand Rapids: Eerdmans, 2022.

Silliman, Daniel. *Reading Evangelicals: How Christian Fiction Shaped a Culture and a Faith*. Grand Rapids: Eerdmans, 2021.

Sinfield, Alan, and Jonathan Dollimore. *Political Shakespeare: Essays in Cultural Materialism*. Manchester: Manchester University Press, 1994.

Solnit, Rebecca. *Whose Story Is This?: Old Conflicts, New Chapters*. Chicago: Haymarket Books, 2019.

Stockman, Farah. "Monticello Is Done Avoiding Jefferson's Relationship with Sally Hemings," *New York Times*, June 16, 2018, https://www.nytimes.com/2018/06/16/us/sally-hemings-exhibit-monticello.html.

Stokes, Jon. "The AR-15 Is More Than a Gun. It's a Gadget." *Wired*. February 25, 2013. https://www.wired.com/2013/02/ar-15/.

Thackaray, Lucy. "Don't Turn Notre Dame into 'Politically Correct Disneyland,' Say Renovation Critics." *The Independent*. November 30, 2021. https://www.independent.co.uk/travel/news-and-advice/notre-dame-renovation-reopening-paris-tourists-b1966780.html.

Thuesen, Peter J. *In Discordance with the Scriptures: American Protestant Battles over Translating the Bible*. New York: Oxford University Press, 1999.

Thurman, Howard. *Jesus and the Disinherited*. Cambridge, MA: Beacon Press, 1996.

Tillich, Paul. *A History of Christian Thought*. New York: Harper & Row, 1968.

Tolentino, Jia. "The Raw Devotion of Julien Baker." *The New Yorker*. October 27, 2017. https://www.newyorker.com/culture/culture-desk/the-raw-devotion-of-julien-baker.

Tractate Sanhedrin. Translated by Adin Even-Israel Steinsaltz. *Sefaria*. Accessed July 18, 2024. https://www.sefaria.org/Sanhedrin?tab=contents.

Truboff, Zachary. "Translating the Other: Franz Rosenzweig and Martin Buber on the Philosophy of Translation." July 9, 2021. YouTube video, 57:38. https://www.youtube.com/watch?v=S-zno8e_OD8.

Von Hallberg, Robert, ed. *Canons*. Chicago: University of Chicago Press, 1984.

Walker, Ken. "Between the Lines: How Fictional Characters Change Real Lives." In *Real Characters: The Psychology of Parasocial Relationships with Media Characters*, edited by Karen E. Shackleford, 277–300. Santa Barbara, CA: Fielding University Press, 2020.

Wartofsky, Marx W. *Feuerbach*. Cambridge: Cambridge University Press, 1977.

Watts, James W. *How and Why Books Matter: Essays on the Social Function of Iconic Texts*. Sheffield: Equinox, 2019.

———, ed. *Iconic Books and Texts*. Sheffield: Equinox, 2012.

———. "Mobilizing the Social Power of Iconic and Performative Texts for Justice and Reform." *Postscripts* 11, no. 2 (2020): 127–43. http://www.doi.org/10.1558/post.17903.

———. "The Three Dimensions of Scriptures." In *Iconic Books and Texts*, edited by James W. Watts, 9–32. Sheffield: Equinox, 2013.

Wenger-Trayner, Beverly, and Etienne Wenger-Trayner. "Introduction to Communities of Practice: A Brief Overview of the Concept and Its Uses." *Wenger-Trayner*. June 2015. https://wenger-trayner.com/introduction-to-communities-of-practice/.

Wexler, Jay. *Holy Hullabaloos: A Road Trip to the Battlegrounds of the Church-State Wars*. Boston: Beacon Press, 2009.

"What Tznius Is Actually About." Chabad of YouTube. November 23, 2020. YouTube video, 7:34. https://youtu.be/iJem3QQYRPU?si=yZRaLEXGHcqYjfhK.

Wigg-Stevenson, Tyler. *Brand Jesus: Christianity in a Consumerist Age*. New York: Church Publishing, 2007.

Williams, Raymond. *Culture and Materialism: Selected Essays*. London: Verso, 2020.

———. *Keywords: A Vocabulary of Culture and Society*. Oxford: Oxford University Press, 2015.

———. *Marxism and Literature*. Oxford: Oxford University Press, 1977.

———. "An Open Letter to WEA Tutors." In *Border Country. Raymond Williams and Adult Education*, edited by J. McIlroy and S. Westwood, 222–24. Leicester: NIACE, 1993.

Willsher, Kim. "Thousands of Homeless People Removed from Paris Region in Pre-Olympics 'Social Cleansing.'" *The Guardian*. June 3, 2024. https://www.theguardian.com/sport/article/2024/jun/03/homeless-people-removed-from-paris-before-olympics.

Wilson, Scott. *Cultural Materialism: Theory and Practice*. Cambridge, MA: Wiley-Blackwell, 1995.

Wittgenstein, Ludwig. *Philosophical Investigations*. Translated by G. E. M. Anscombe. 3rd ed. New York: Macmillan, 1968.

Woolman, John. "Abridgment of the Journal of John Woolman." In *Quaker Spirituality: Selected Writings*, edited by Douglas V. Steere, 159–238. New York: Paulist Press, 1984.

Yang, K. Wayne [la paperson, pseud.]. *A Third University Is Possible*. Minneapolis: University of Minnesota Press, 2017.

Žižek, Slavoj. *Violence: Six Sideways Reflections*. New York: Picador, 2008.

Acknowledgments

I credit two people in particular for the existence of this book. The first is John Kutsko, who met me for lunch one afternoon at the Fido coffee shop in Nashville. That conversation served as the seed crystal for this project, though I wager it became, in the course of its writing, something other than either of us had in mind at the time. The second is Henry Carrigan, who has been not only a dear and stalwart friend but also a real champion of my work through the years. It was Henry who suggested I speak to the folks at Yale, and who made the initial introductions that helped this project find a home there.

I am grateful to my editor, Jennifer Banks, and the entire team at Yale University Press for your patience, guidance, and care through every step of this process. When we began, I imagine we were all anticipating a very different book. Thank you for giving me the space and time to develop *The Accessorized Bible* into what it needed to be. I am grateful to the several peer reviewers who helped point out its strengths and flaws, and to Jessie Dolch for a masterful job of copy editing the manuscript. Whatever errors remain are mine, and not theirs.

I do not believe we can ever think alone, and through the years a great many friends and colleagues have shared their wisdom and challenged me with their ideas. Among these have been Jimmy Barker and Katy Attanasi, Daniel P. Horan, Fr. Bruce Cinquegrani, Heidi Schlumpf, Steven P. Millies, James Buchannan and Thea Wallace, David Dunn, Joshua Davis, Timothy Eberhart, Maria Mayo, Travis and Holly Ables, Scott Newstock, Paul Wallace, Patout Burns and Robin Jensen, Paul DeHart, Walter Brueggemann, Tyler and Natalie Wigg-Stevenson, Jacob Goodson and Brad Elliot Stone, Nicholas Adams, Kelly West Figueroa-Ray, Peter Ochs, Derek Axelson, Diana Butler Bass, Leah Payne and Brian Doak, Maia Kotrosits, Daniel White Hodge, Doug Merrill, Rick Lee James, Michael Gibson, Kelly Hughes, Barbara Mahany, Robert Wilson-Black, Jack E. Swift, Burt and Emily Fulmer, Bob McWhirter, William "Doc" Martin, Xavier Ramey, Ipsita Chatterjee, Virginia Bartlett, Joshua Braley, Aaron Simmons, George Stroup, Stan Saunders, Rav Shai Cherry, Spencer and Cindy Cox Garrard, Leonard Greenspoon, Abigail Redman, Micah Sheppard, John Thatamanil, William Franke, Alicia Ruvinsky, and Larycia Hawkins.

I benefit every day from a vibrant community of online conversation partners that includes David Dark, Kelly J. Baker, Jazz Robertson, Randall Westergaard, Adam Kotsko, Micah Carver, Joel Harris, Kyle Haden, OFM, Thomas Smith, and Eric Bowman.

I am grateful to my colleagues at *Commonweal* magazine, especially Tom Baker, Dominic Preziosi, and Griffin Oleynick, and to my colleagues and students at American Baptist College and Christian Brothers University.

I am grateful every day for Dean Peter Jones and the faculty and staff of the Institute of Pastoral Studies at Loyola University Chicago: Heidi Russell, timone davis, Deb Watson, Nat Samuel, Dan Rhodes, Mike Canaris, Bill Schmidt, Felipe Legarreta, Gosia Czelusniak, Diamond Gant, Julie Garcia, Mirta Garcia, Mariana Miller, and Kevin Pease. This book would not have made it across the finish line without their friendship and enthusiastic support. Let me also say a word in praise of my many IPS students, particularly Krysten McOsker, Anh Tranh, Claire DesHotels, Kascha Sanor, Cristin Anthony, Katie Cashman, Greer Hamilton, Sr. Sarah Simmons, and Mac Svolos. You have pushed me to think more clearly and deeply, you have expanded my imagination and my empathy, and you have helped me to understand what is really at stake for the vulnerable when we read together. Thank you.

I am especially grateful to Tim Beal, S. Brent Rodriguez-Plate, Dori Parmenter, and James W. Watts, who have supported and encouraged my work in innumerable ways, and who have offered a safe haven over the years for my eclectic ideas.

During the writing of this book, several dear friends passed away: Roger Easson, Phyllis Tickle, Michael Iafrate, Katharine MacDonald, Rahuldeep Singh Gill, David Knauert, Shane Bartlett, James Skandrick, Eugene Se'Bree, William Garland, Matthew Boice, Elizabeth Fitch, Johanna Lindemann, and my mother, Ann Dault Thomas. Their love and light have not been extinguished, despite the present darkness left by their absence. I live in hope of our meeting again.

There are also friends who along the way have become like family: Alexander Badenoch and wee Morag, Julia Sibley-Jones, Robert Pound, Madeline Faber, Jill and Doug Davis, John and Mirna Holton, Theron Welch, Matthew Reiss, Mike Traynor, and Kurt Schreiber. Thank you for all the support you have given through the years, both during and beyond this project. A special word of thanks is due to Katy Scrogin, who in addition to being a staunch creative ally these past two decades also offered invaluable help with preparation of the final manuscript for publication.

Thank you as well to Charles and Allyne Dault, Allyn and Jennifer Harris Dault, Harold and Susan Hartger, Phil Hartger,

Aurelia Bolthouse, Uncle Bob Bolthouse, Courtney Del Vecchio, and the extended Bandstra and Hartger families.

I cannot even begin to express how grateful I am for my beloved Kira, Maggie, and Beckett, and for the love and support they show to me each and every day. When I say none of this would have been possible without them, that does not even begin to tell the story.

This book is dedicated to the memory of my first philosophy professor, Rick Roderick, whose brilliance and iconoclasm continue to inspire me. I hope that, wherever in eternity this book may find him, he enjoys it.

Index